Welcome to

Raspberry Pi

The Complete Manual

The Raspberry Pi is one of the most exciting things to happen to computers since Steve Jobs revealed the iPad. As an educational tool this credit card-sized PC has reignited interest in bare-metal computing in schools. As a platform for open-source software it has inspired almost three million people to try Linux, many for the first time. Best of all, though, is that in its role as a development platform, the Raspberry Pi has empowered people from all walks of life to code and make some truly stunning projects, many of which we'll demonstrate in this book…

Raspberry Pi
The Complete Manual

Imagine Publishing Ltd
Richmond House
33 Richmond Hill
Bournemouth
Dorset BH2 6EZ
☎ +44 (0) 1202 586200
Website: www.imagine-publishing.co.uk
Twitter: @Books_Imagine
Facebook: www.facebook.com/ImagineBookazines

Head of Publishing
Aaron Asadi

Head of Design
Ross Andrews

Editor
Russell Barnes

Senior Art Editor
Greg Whitaker

Design
Perry Wardell-Wicks

Photographer
James Sheppard

Printed by
William Gibbons, 26 Planetary Road, Willenhall, West Midlands, WV13 3XT

Distributed in the UK & Eire by
Imagine Publishing Ltd, www.imagineshop.co.uk. Tel 01202 586200

Distributed in Australia by
Gordon & Gotch, Equinox Centre, 18 Rodborough Road, Frenchs Forest, NSW 2086. Tel + 61 2 9972 8800

Distributed in the Rest of the World by
Marketforce, Blue Fin Building, 110 Southwark Street, London, SE1 0SU

ISBN 978-1909758803

Part of the LinuxUser & Developer bookazine series

IMAGINE PUBLISHING

Contents

What you can find inside the bookazine

Getting started

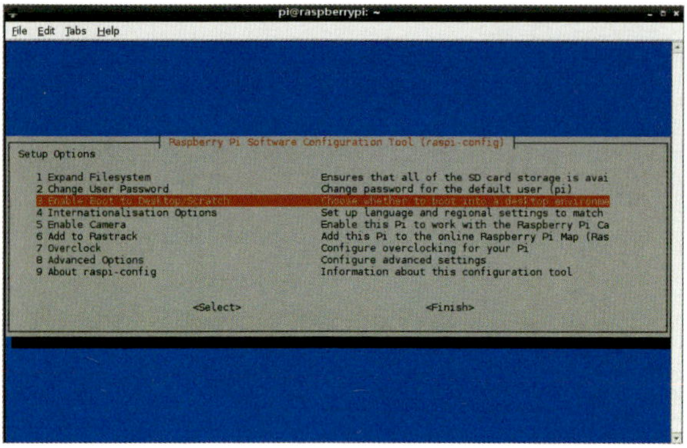

Find out how you can make a Raspberry Pi-powered car starting on page 130

The projects

Find project code at www.linuxuser.co.uk/tutorial-files

Code & create with your Pi!

Find project code at www.linuxuser.co.uk/tutorial-files

Raspberry Pi (Model A)

While more limited than Model B in terms of hardware connections, it's still a capable little machine

The main differences between the two flavours of Pi are the RAM, the number of USB 2.0 ports and the fact that the Model A doesn't have an Ethernet port (meaning a USB Wi-Fi is required to access the internet. While that results in a lower price for the Model A, it means that a user will have to buy a powered USB hub in order to get it to work for many projects. The Model A is aimed more at those creating electronics projects that require programming and control directly from the command line interface.

Both Pi models use the Broadcom BCM2835 CPU, which is an ARM11-based processor running at 700MHz. There are overclocking modes built in for users to increase the speed as long as the core doesn't get too hot, at which point it is throttled back. Also included is the Broadcom VideoCore IV GPU with support for OpenGL ES 2.0, which

SD card slot
An SD card slot is provided on the flip side of your Pi. The maximum size it can hold is 32GB

Video out
RCA composite video means you can use your Raspberry Pi to watch pictures and video

Audio out
It also features a 3.5mm jack plug for audio output

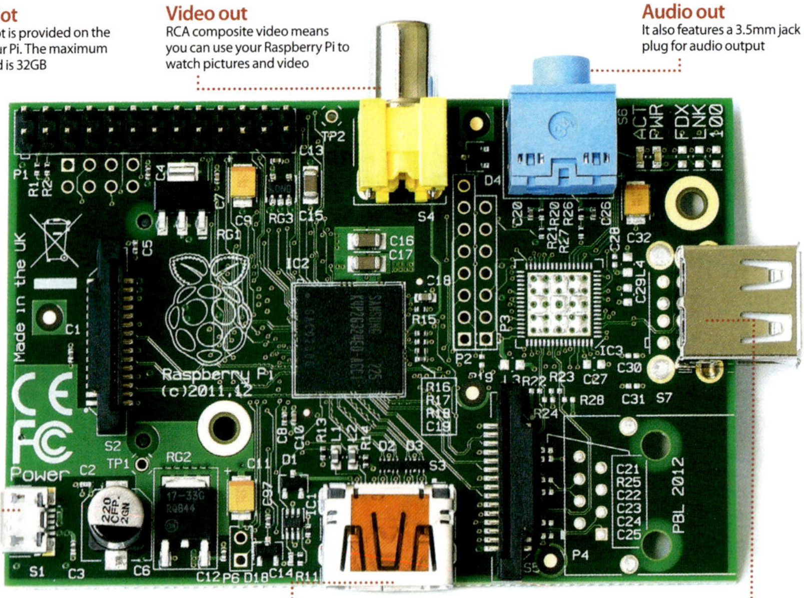

Micro USB power
The Micro USB adapter doesn't come with your Pi. It has a minimum rating of 500mA for Model A and 700mA for Model B

HDMI port
Hi-res video output with sound comes courtesy of the HDMI socket that can power TVs and monitors at 1080p

Single USB port
There is only one USB port on Model A, so the first accessory you'll probably want is a powered USB hub

Raspberry Pi (Model B)

For most users Model B is the version of choice, with its extra RAM and ethernet port

DSI display connector
You can attach an LCD panel to your Pi via the DSI display connector. It provides high-res display resulting in flawless video output

GPIO pin header
The GPIO pin header is your doorway to a world of connecting devices and electronics for direct control via the Pi

The control centre
The main chip of the Pi is a system-on-a-chip (SoC) that houses the 700MHz Broadcom CPU and the VideoCore IV GPU

CSI connection
The recently launched 5MP camera module plugs in here and provides the Pi with the ability to capture photographs and record videos

Ethernet port
Again, unlike Model A, Model B features an ethernet port, so you don't need a Wi-Fi dongle as you can connect to the internet

Dual USB port
The main advantage of Model B is that it has two USB ports (as opposed to Model A). This reduces the need for a USB hub

can perform 24 GFlops and decode and play H.264 video at 1080p resolution. Originally the Model A was due to use 128MB RAM, but this was upgraded to 256MB RAM with the Model B going from 256MB to 512MB.

The power supply to the Pi is via the 5V micro-USB socket. As the Model A has fewer powered interfaces it only requires 300mA, compared to the 700mA that the Model B needs. The standard system of connecting the Pi models is to use the HDMI port to connect to an HDMI socket on a TV or a DVI port on a monitor. Both HDMI-HDMI and HDMI-DVI cables work well, delivering 1080p video, or 1920x1080. Sound is also sent through the HDMI connection, but if using a monitor without speakers then there's the standard 3.5mm jack socket for audio. The RCA composite video connection was designed for use in countries where the level of technology is lower and more basic displays such as older TVs are used.

The starter kit

There's more to your Pi than first meets the eye. Here are some vital peripherals to get you started

In order to get the very best experience from your Raspberry Pi, you're going to have to get hold of a few extras on top of the actual Raspberry Pi board itself. For example, you're going to need a keyboard and mouse with which to enter commands and navigate. While it's possible to do projects without a keyboard and mouse attached, you'll need them for the initial setup. An SD card is also an important purchase – it's where the operating system lives. Perhaps you'll need a Wi-Fi adapter of some description, or maybe just a length of network cable. Then there's the basic electronics side of the Raspberry Pi, what would you need to start some of the beginner electronics and control experiments? Clearly, there's more to the Raspberry Pi than some might think.

When we say peripherals, we of course mean other hardware that can be attached and utilised by the Raspberry Pi. They could be something as simple as a decent HDMI or they could be the latest, greatest bespoke gadgets that enhance your project capabilities.

There is an entire world of possibilities available for the Raspberry Pi; from robot arms to remote-controlled helicopters… The only limits are the hardware available and your imagination!

Did you know…

Most online retailers sell packages complete with all the accessories you might need – even pre-installed SD cards.

Keyboard and mouse

Let's start with the most basic of components, the keyboard and mouse. Generally speaking, virtually any USB keyboard and three-button scroll mouse will work with the Raspberry Pi, and although for some projects you won't even need a keyboard and mouse, you'll need them for initial set-up.

SD card

The SD card is the storage device that contains the Raspberry Pi operating system, whichever you decide that to be. These can be bought pre-installed with the OS, or blank from a number of sources. SD cards come in a variety of sizes and speeds, but for the basics a card of 2GB or over is acceptable.

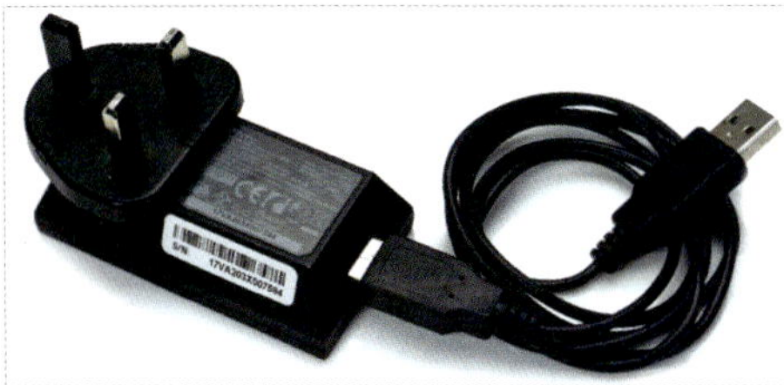

Power cable

The Raspberry Pi uses a standard micro USB connector for its power input, which should run at 5V. In most cases a micro USB to USB cable will suffice, of which one end can be plugged into a laptop or PC USB port. An Android phone charger should also work perfectly (5.25V 1500mA).

Case

Although not totally essential, placing your Raspberry Pi in a case will obviously protect it and prevent its delicate GPIO pins from being bent. Aside from accidental damage, the case can make your Raspberry Pi a more attractive or striking unit, for use as a living room media centre for example.

Video output

You'll find two video output ports, a HDMI port and an RCA Socket. HDMI is more than likely to be the primary video-output connector for most users, but if you don't have HDMI on your TV or monitor, then the RCA video-out port can be used to connect TVs, monitors or to a SCART cable.

Powered USB hub

Extra USB ports are worth considering as an early purchase with your Pi. Once you've connected a keyboard and mouse you'll realise why! Using a powered USB hub is important, to stop any power being drained from the Pi, and allow you to attach the likes of an external hard drive, for example.

Raspberry Pi camera board

This is a custom designed add-on board that attaches to one of the Raspberry Pi's on-board sockets via a flexible cable. It's extremely small, but remarkably powerful, having a native resolution of five megapixels and supporting 1080p video. It's essentially a smartphone camera for the Pi!

USB Wi-Fi adaptor

Using a USB Wi-Fi adaptor will free up the location of the Raspberry Pi. You'll no longer have to run an Ethernet cable from your router, and it could be used for more advanced projects where running a wired internet connection isn't a valid option. Just make sure it's Linux-friendly when you buy.

Set up your Raspberry Pi

Learn what goes where in your brand new Raspberry Pi with our easy-to-follow guide

While it looks daunting, setting up the Raspberry Pi for day-to-day use is actually very simple. Like a TV or a normal computer, only certain cables will fit into the specific slots, and the main job really is making sure you've got plugged in what you need at any one time. The Raspberry Pi itself doesn't label much of the board. However, most good cases will do that for you anyway – if you decide to invest in one.

Power adapter
The Raspberry Pi is powered using a microUSB cable, much like a lot of modern Android phones. It can be powered off a laptop or computer. But to make the most out of it, a proper mains adapter – like this one – is ideal

Monitor
The Raspberry Pi is capable of displaying a 1920 x 1080 output – otherwise known as 1080p. Some modern monitors allow you to plug HDMI straight into them, just like TVs do. However you may need an adapter if your TV doesn't

USB hub
There are only a limited number of USB ports on a Raspberry Pi (just one, if you have Model A). To get around this you will need a USB hub. It's important to get a powered one, as the Pi cannot supply enough juice on its own

Case and accessories
A case is not necessary to use the Pi correctly, but a decent one can keep it well protected from dust, and make it easier to move while in operation. You will need an SD card, however, of at least 4GB

Keyboard and mouse
Like any computer, you'll need a keyboard and mouse for any standard PC-style operations you do with the Raspberry Pi. The more basic the keyboard, the better; same with the mouse, as some special ones need additional software

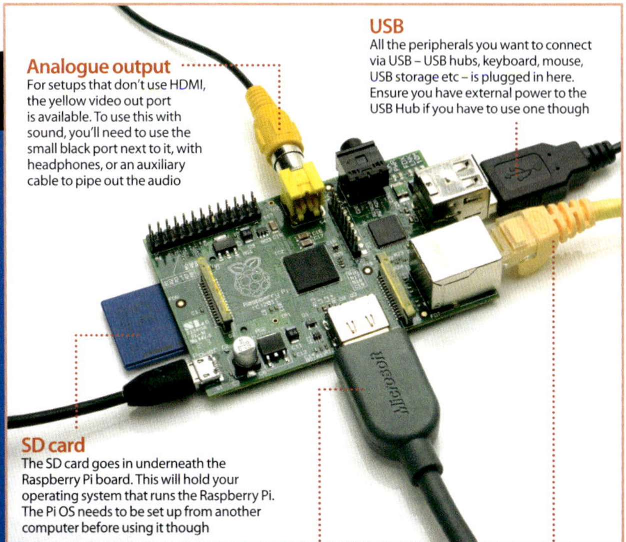

USB
All the peripherals you want to connect via USB – USB hubs, keyboard, mouse, USB storage etc – is plugged in here. Ensure you have external power to the USB Hub if you have to use one though

Analogue output
For setups that don't use HDMI, the yellow video out port is available. To use this with sound, you'll need to use the small black port next to it, with headphones, or an auxiliary cable to pipe out the audio

SD card
The SD card goes in underneath the Raspberry Pi board. This will hold your operating system that runs the Raspberry Pi. The Pi OS needs to be set up from another computer before using it though

Digital output
The HDMI port is the main video (and audio) output of the Raspberry Pi, allowing you to display videos on the desktop at a resolution of up to 1080p. TVs that support it will also pick up the audio automatically through it

Networking
The Raspberry Pi does not come with wireless internet, and while you can add a USB adapter, it's usually easier to plug in an ethernet cable. This will plug into the back of your router on the other end and give you internet and access to your home network

Cabling
Make sure you have the right selection of cables, such as an ethernet cable for networking and internet, and an HDMI or Video cable for video out. The HDMI can handle audio, but the video out will require an additional auxiliary cable

Install a distro

We take a look at some of the key aspects involved in installing a pre-built OS

What you'll need…

Raspberry Pi downloads
www.raspberrypi.org/downloads

Did you know…

The official distro for the Pi is called Raspbian. That's what we recommend, but there are other options.

With its small size and cheap price, many people might be fooled into thinking that the Raspberry Pi is only usable for basic tasks, and learning to program on. While one of the primary goals of the Pi was to increase computer literacy at a lower level rather than just learning how to create Excel spreadsheets, the Pi has many other great uses.

As the Raspberry Pi is essentially a mini PC, with an HDMI and analog TV output rather than a traditional monitor connection, it can perform many common tasks that a laptop or desktop is often used for. While it doesn't really have the processing power or RAM to run the latest version of Windows, there are other options.

There are a wealth of fully fledged operating systems, many forked from their desktop big brothers that have been optimised specifically for the Pi. One of the most popular of these is Raspbian, which is a port of Debian. Debian is a key part of the Linux ecosystem, and many other popular open source distributions are forked from the Debian source code. The original Debian was released in 1993, and it's come a long way since. Raspbian needed work to get performance levels up to standard, as the Pi uses the older ARMv6 architecture. It's now a great everyday desktop.

Card speed
It's a good idea to get a reasonably fast SD card to keep your system running smoothly. Class 4 or above is best

Card format
Before you copy your OS image, you'll need to make sure the SD card is formatted into the FAT32 file system

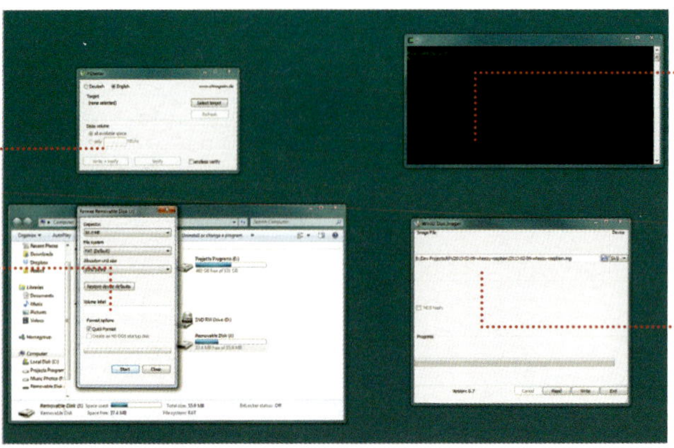

Command line
If you are using OS X or Linux, then its likely you will use the command line to install your prebuilt operating systems

Automated tools
There are a couple of graphical tools available which make installing an image onto an SD card easy

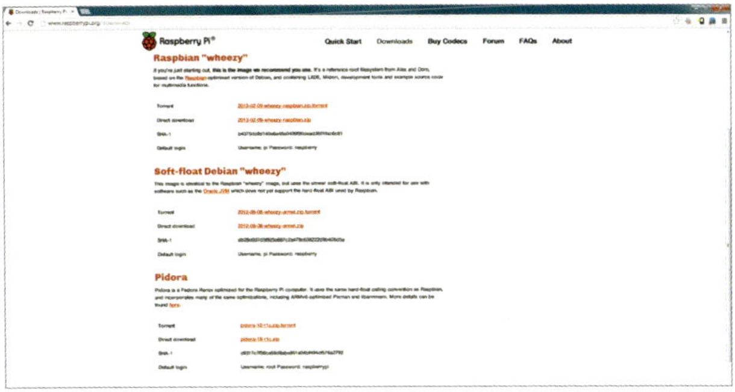

Obtaining OSs

01 One of your first questions may be "where can I find some operating systems to download?". Most of the common images can be found on the main Raspberry Pi site: **http://www.raspberrypi.org/downloads**. These are stable and well tested systems worth investigating.

Unzipping

02 When you've downloaded your image, the first thing you'll most likely need to do is unzip it. This can be done in Windows by right clicking and choosing 'extract'. In OS X, just double click to extract the files.

OS Format

03 Within the zip you'll find a file with a .img or .iso extension. These are the equivalent of a 'snapshot' of an installation CD or DVD. Simply copying the file to the SD card won't do anything; you'll need to use a program to extract it.

SD card format

04 The SD card that you'll boot from needs to be blank, so make sure there is nothing important on it first. You'll also need to format it to use the FAT32 file system. This is a common system, used by most USB sticks and cameras.

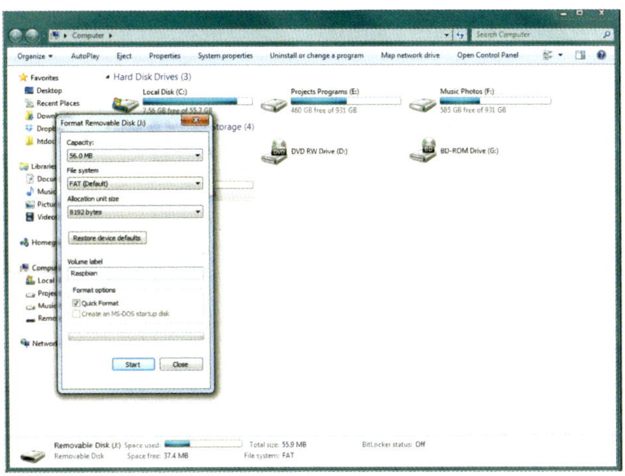

Formatting the card

05 In Windows, to format the card simply insert and wait for it to mount. Then click on 'My Computer' and then right click on the cards icon. After that choose format and then 'FAT32' from the drop-down menu.

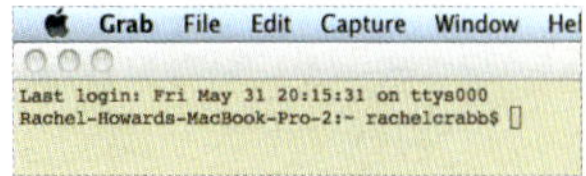

Using the terminal

06 If you are using OS X or Linux, then you'll have to use the terminal to copy the image. In OS X, the Terminal app comes installed by default, and most Linux versions come with one in some form or other. It may be referred to as the 'console' or 'command line'.

DD command

07 The command you need to use is called 'dd'. This is entered in the format of 'sudo dd bs=1m if=[img] of=/dev/[sdcard]'. An example of this can be seen below:

```
sudo dd bs=32m if=/Users/rachelcrabb/Desktop/ArchLinux/archlinux-hf-2013-02-11.img of=/dev/disk1
```

Win 32 Disk Imager

08 Windows users can use Win32 Disk Imager. Once you've downloaded the tool, simply right click on the .exe, and choose 'run as administrator' and follow the prompts. When the installation is complete you can put the SD card in your Pi. Easy!

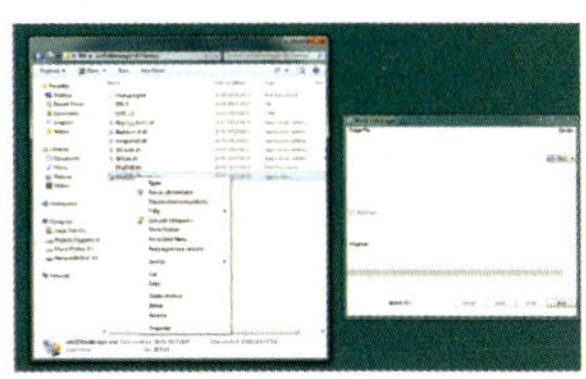

What you'll need…

Raspbian
www.raspberrypi.org

Command line basics

Learn an alternative way to control your Raspberry Pi by using the command line and your keyboard

Did you know…

The command line remembers your last commands. Simply use the Up and Down arrows to use them.

We've probably all been there with the Raspberry Pi. You've installed Raspbian or another Raspberry Pi OS to your SD card and you've rushed through the setup script or not quite done your research. You start the operating system and… you end up at a command line. The first step here is to not panic: this is perfectly normal. It may just be a bit of a foreign concept to you, only seen in films with streetwise hackers who want to bring down 'the system'.

The second step, at least in Raspbian's case, is simply to type:

```
$ start x
```

That's it. Raspbian will load up the desktop and you can start using the mouse again. Quick and painless in this case, and in that of many other operating systems as well. What you've done is use a command, specifically in this case to start the X server. The X server handles the graphical interface and can be turned off by default on some Pi systems.

Fig 1: The terminal emulator allows you to access the command line while still being in the desktop environment

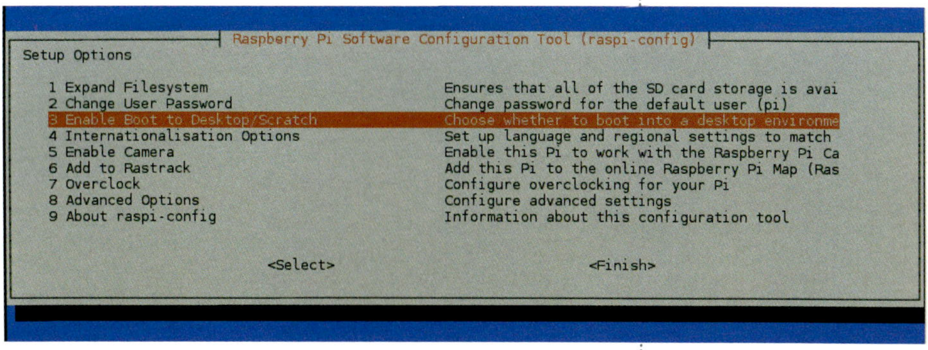

Fig 2: Access raspi-config to change settings such as boot to desktop or adding a camera module

A new world

Getting your Raspberry Pi into the desktop isn't the only thing you can do on the command line, though. There's a whole world of functionality built into the command line; in fact, most of the graphical programs you're using are just executing these commands in such a way. You don't have to leave the comfort of the desktop environment to perform these commands either, as all Raspberry Pi operating systems will come with an application known as a terminal emulator.

This creates a window where a command can be written in the same way that we launched the desktop, and use the exact same commands (Fig 1). On Raspbian, look for the app LX Terminal in the Accessories section of the menu and click on it. If you've had to use **start x** to get into the desktop, then we can now fix that before continuing. In the terminal, enter:

```
$ raspi-config
```

Here's the initial setup screen (Fig 2). From here you can enable the desktop on boot (Fig 3), and even update the firmware and add support for the official Raspberry Pi camera module. This allows you to modify Raspbian without having to reinstall again.

You won't be using those two commands very often, though, so is there practical use for delving into the command line? Very much so. For starters, Raspbian doesn't have an official package manager. This is a program that allows you to browse the available software for the operating system, similar to the Pi Store.

However, there's other software available to Raspbian that you can't get through the store. You also can't specifically update the Pi software either, and all of this can be fixed using the command line.

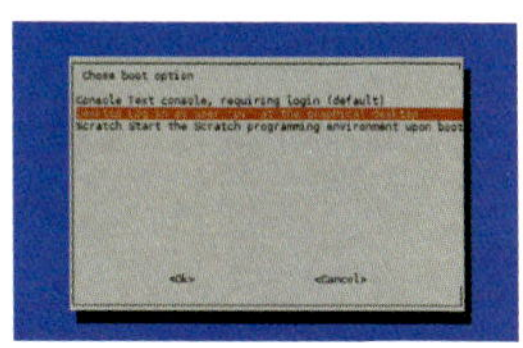

Fig 3: Change the default selection to desktop for the next time you use the Raspberry Pi

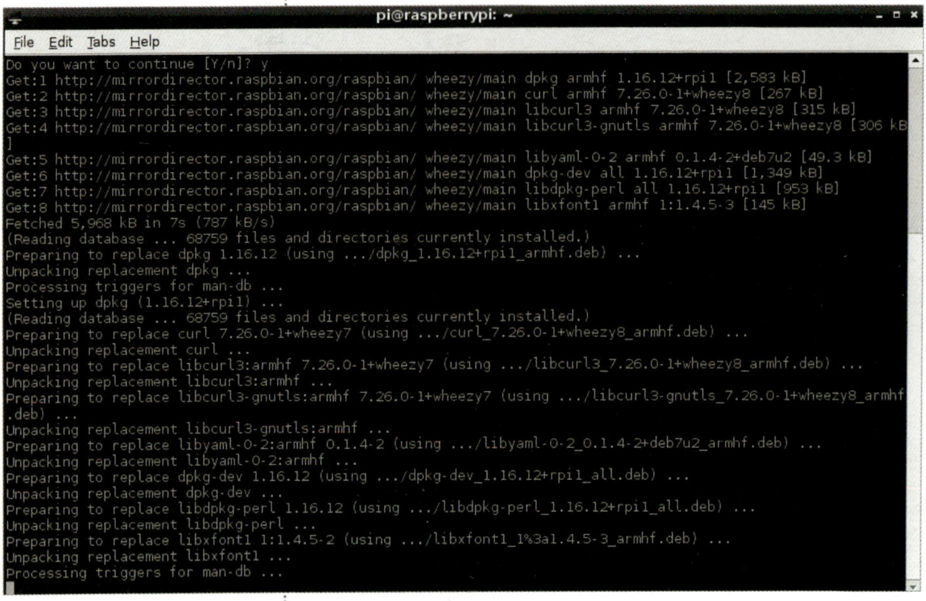

Fig 4: Upgrade your system and files, and have the latest updates and bug fixes in the process

Software for all

The first thing you'll want to do is let Raspbian know exactly what's available online. It's a very simple task; all you need to do is:

```
$ sudo apt-get update
```

This will run down a list of online repositories (or repos) that contain the software that Raspbian uses. Once it's finished, the command-line prompt will pop up again waiting for your next command. As this is the first time you've done it, you'll likely need to update the current software on your Raspberry Pi. You can do that with the command:

```
$ sudo apt-get upgrade
```

It may ask you to confirm the upgrade, in which case type 'y' and then press Enter. What we're doing both times is using the command-line package manager Aptitude (apt-get) to first check the repos, and then upgrade packages according to that (Fig 4). The first command, sudo, allows it to run the apt-get task as an administrator, and is used in a lot of other command-line operations. To install software you use **install** instead of update or upgrade, followed by the name of the package. For example, with the mathematical programming language, you can install it with:

```
$ sudo apt-get install wolfram-engine
```

Did you know…

You can use the Tab to complete commands. Just start typing and hit tab. If you like what you see hit Enter to finish!

Move and create

Installing and updating are just a couple of the many things you can do in the command line. You can also browse the entire file system, move files, create folders and delete items. All of these are very simple operations.

When you first open the terminal, it will open up in your home folder. While you can't specifically tell that it is, you can display exactly what kind of files are in the directory with (Fig 5):

```
$ ls
```

The tilde sign (~) is used to denote the home folder and can be used for navigating around the file system. To navigate, we'll be using the **cd** command, followed by the location you want to move to. This can be done like so:

```
$ cd /home/pi/Downloads
```

This will move you to the Downloads directory. As we were starting off in the home folder to begin with, we actually only needed to do this:

```
$ cd Downloads
```

It's context sensitive and knows to look in the directory it's already in. There's another trick you can use so you don't have to remember the exact name of the path – the command line or terminal will try to autocomplete the phrase if you press the Tab key while something is only partially typed. Try the cd command again, but try pressing Tab when you've only written 'Down'.

Finally, there are some quick commands you can use to manipulate files. Individual files can be copied using the command **cp**, followed by the filename and the new location like so:

```
$ cp file.txt ~/Documents/file.txt
```

You can also use this to rename files by doing:

```
$ cp file.txt otherfile.txt
```

The original file can then be deleted by using the **rm** command:

```
$ rm file.txt
```

Want to create a new folder? Use cd to move to the directory you need to add a folder to, and then use **mkdir** followed by the name you want to give the folder:

```
$ mkdir NewFolder
```

There's a lot more you can do with the command line, but these are the very basics. As you use Linux more and more, you'll be confronted with tasks that need the command line, and through this process you'll learn just how much can be accomplished when you work like a streetwise movie hacker.

Did you know…

You can always return to your Home folder in the command line by typing:
cd ~ and pressing Enter.

"The command line or terminal will try to autocomplete the phrase if you press the Tab key while something is partially typed"

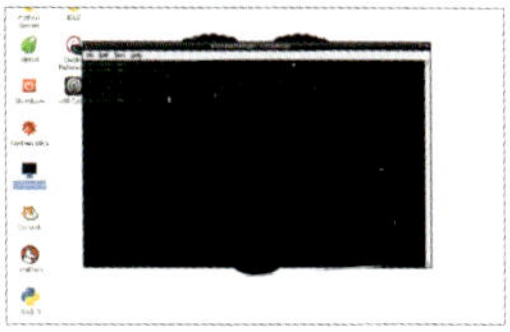

Fig 5: There are many simple command-line tools that can help you browse and use your system

The Raspbian desktop

Although the Raspberry Pi's operating system is closer to the Mac than Windows, it's the latter that the desktop most closely resembles

It might seem a little alien at first glance, but using Raspbian is hardly any different to using Windows (barring Windows 8 of course). There's a menu bar, a web browser, a file manager and no shortage of desktop shortcuts of pre-installed applications. As you'd expect, you simply double-click them to get started…

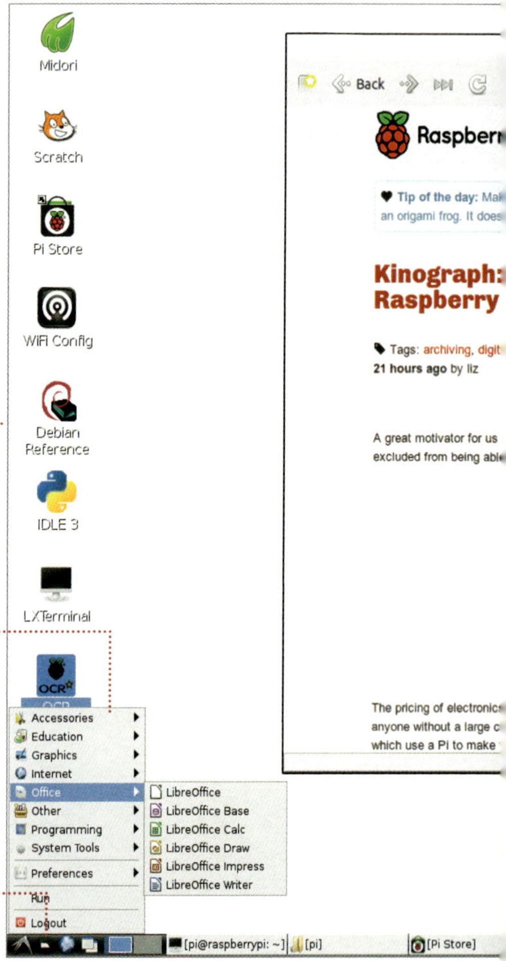

Desktop shortcuts

A number of the pre-installed apps have icons on the desktop. To run the associated app, simply double-click on the icon. The icons can be moved and dropped into other locations. Click, hold and drag to move them. There are icons for a variety of tasks – from apps such as Python and Scratch for programming, to Midori for web browsing, LXTerminal for issuing commands to the system directly, to reference materials. Icons can be renamed or even deleted if you don't want them on the desktop any more. Right-click over any icon to see the options available for it.

Menu bar

Just like Windows' Start menu, click in the corner to bring up a menu of programs and options. The main categories include accessories, apps for educational use, graphics, internet (including some alternative browsers), programming, a general assortment of apps and utilities, and the system tools. You will also find that some programs you download from the Pi Store (like LibreOffice) will appear here. There are also a set of preference options for configuring how certain elements of the system work, such as keyboard and mouse. The Run option is just like the one in Windows – it opens a command-line interpreter to run commands.

File manager

No computer would be complete without a file manager. Click here to bring it up. Files can be copied, renamed and deleted by dragging to the dustbin in the window. You can also create tabbed windows in the file browser or open further ones. Folder locations can be bookmarked for easy access and files themselves can be viewed as icons or in a detailed list. If you need to do any command-line work, the current graphical folder can also be opened in the terminal as the current folder there. Next to the file manager is a shortcut to Midori, an option to minimise all windows, and a dual desktop feature.

"It might seem a little alien at first glance, but using Raspbian is hardly any different to using Windows"

Web browser

The Pi features a number of browsers – the default one being Midori. There's a desktop icon to launch it. The window can be resized by hovering the cursor over the sides or corners. Web addresses are typed into the long address bar whereas search queries are typed into the shorter bar with the words Duck Duck Go. There are standard navigation buttons for going back and forth through webpages. Midori supports multiple tabbed windows and features private browsing and the ability to clear browsing data. Click on the Options icon at the end of the tool bar to access these functions.

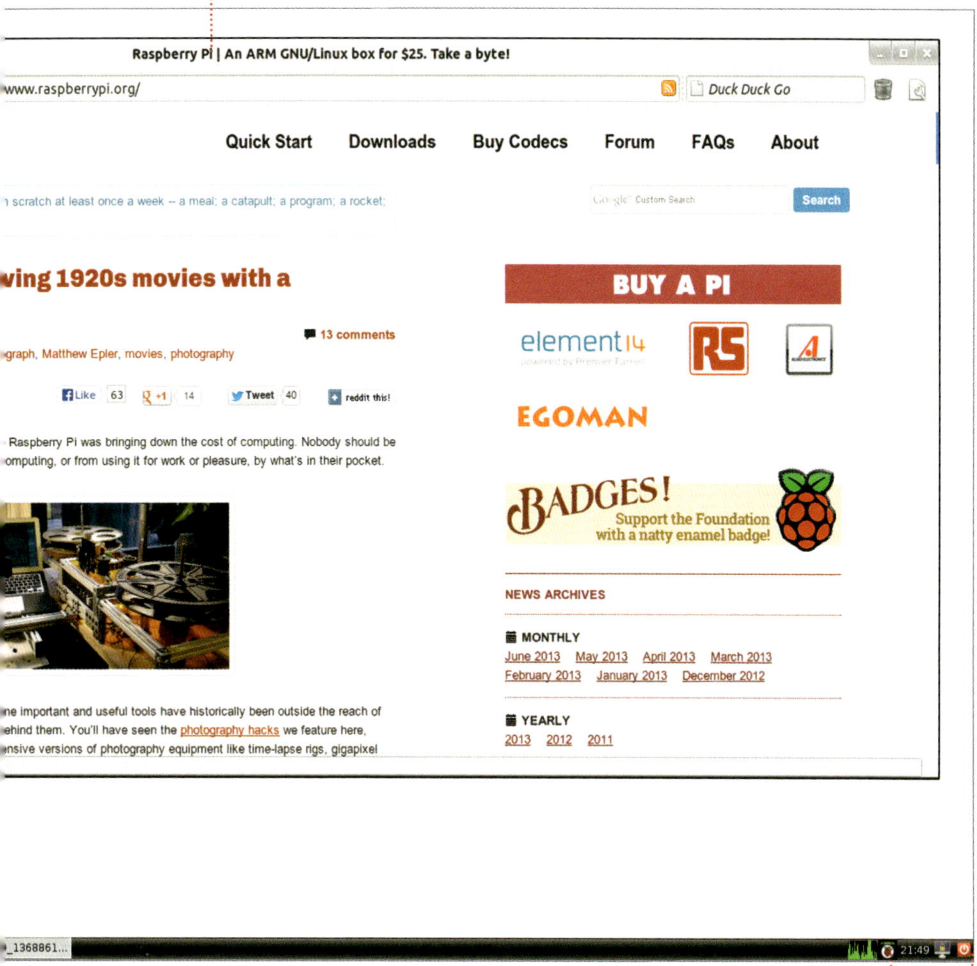

Pi Store

There's a desktop shortcut to the Pi Store and, once it's running, an icon appears here as well as a minimised window on the taskbar. You can access the Store again by clicking on it and also, messages from the Store will appear here. It works much like Steam, Google Play or the App Store. You need to sign up for an account with IndieCity, which can be done directly on the Store interface. For future visits you will need to log in. Applications downloaded and installed from the Store then appear under a tab called My Library. Some can only be run from here.

Power and time

Rather than just pulling the plug on the Pi when it is running the desktop, it is better to click here and select 'Logout of the desktop'. This closes any temporary files and leaves the desktop, dropping you back to the command line. You can then unplug the Pi. Next to the power symbol is a clock; click on this to reveal a calendar, highlighting the current date. If you right-click on the time, you get the option to go to the Digital Clock customisable settings or to remove it from the panel altogether.

What you'll need...

Rasbian:
www.raspbian.org

Did you know...

You can access the config tool anytime by typing 'sudo raspi-config' from a terminal window or the command line.

Master the Config tool

Tell your Raspberry Pi how to behave using the powerful built-in config tool

The 'RasPi Config' tool allows configuration of your system that would otherwise be trickier in the Linux environment and it's the first thing you'll see when you install Raspbian. Why? Tasks such as setting the date and time or regional settings for your keyboard are often done in a command-line interface with no dialogs, no additional help – for a new user, this is a nightmare.

There are some further specifics for the Pi and Raspbian itself, such as: the ability to easily enable overscan for your TV; change the split of memory to the computer/graphics card or even overclock your system to make it a little faster; enable remote SSH access to the system; stop the system booting into the desktop environment among other things. The Raspi Config tool takes the pain out of the process and puts real power at your fingertips.

Change password
Change the password for your default 'pi' username to make it something more personal or easier to remember for you

Expand roots
Allows you to very quickly and easily change the partition of the roots to fill the SD card completely

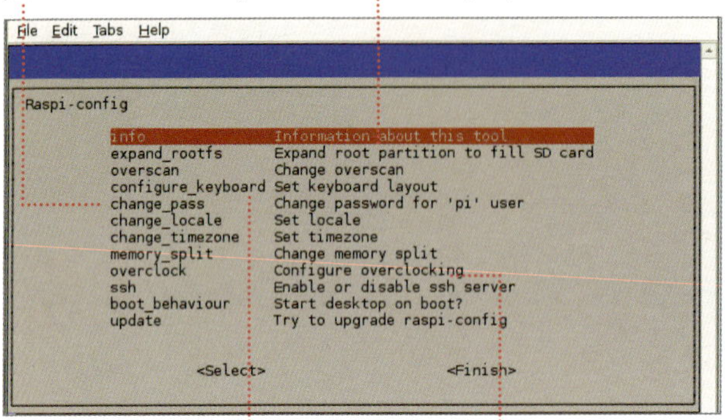

Configure your keyboard
Set the correct keyboard up – there are many different layouts. Using the wrong one can be annoying

Overclocking
Allows you to quickly and easily overclock your Pi to give you some extra speed and power with little risk

Open the raspi-config tool

01 Start by double-clicking the LXTerminal icon on your desktop. This will start the command prompt, where you'll be able to run the config tool. To do this you'll need to run a command.

```
001    sudo raspi-config
```

When asked for your password, you won't actually see it being typed.

When you've typed the password and pressed Enter to submit it, the config screen will be shown to you. There are a few settings of particular interest that we'll cover in this section, although they all have their uses in the running of your Pi. Some of the settings in this menu are important and some are irreversible, so use them with caution!

Expand the root file system

02 By default, the Raspbian root file system will be 2GB – this is done so that the image provided for it can fit on as many different SD cards as possible.

If your card is larger the 'expand_roots' option will make the OS use the entire space. Upon using this option, the command will be executed immediately. The operating can take some time. Reboot your system to see the changes.

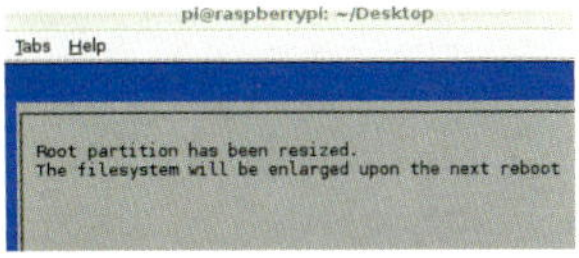

Configure your location

03 Locale is the language and regional settings that your Pi is using – while this generally has little impact on what you'll see, it is also responsible for any default currency settings, etc, so could prove to be an irritant at a later time if wrong.

Upon selecting the option, you'll be taken through a wizard. Use the arrow keys to check the built locale before building more (it takes a while). Timezone will take you to a tzdata screen where you can adjust it.

Overclock your Pi

04 You can set the clock speed and voltage of your Pi to several different presets. Setting the clock speed and voltage at higher rates than the specification may cause instability, so do so in small increments

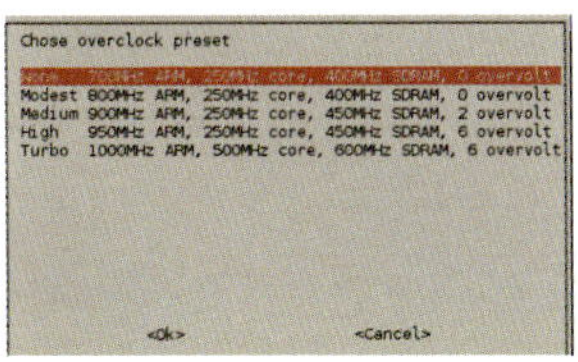

and ensure good airflow around your Pi.

If you see any noticeable instability, run this wizard again and set the clock speed back down to something slightly lower – repeat until your system is completely stable. For the scope of this tutorial, a Modest/Medium overclock is recommended – it seems to give a little extra performance with no noticeable side effects. It is also recommended to reboot your system after making this change. Hold the Shift key to temporarily disable overclocking.

Change the memory split

05 Changing the memory split of the Pi allows you to give either the system or the graphics processor a larger amount of memory.

The value you give to it must be either 16/32/64/128/256. Here are our recommendations:

32MB GPU memory for basic distro usage where video and 3D rendering aren't required.

64MB GPU memory for desktop use that requires video playback or have 3D effects enabled.

128MB GPU memory for graphical applications and games that do extensive multimedia or play 3D rendered games.

For most people, a 64MB split for graphics will suffice.

Change boot behaviour

06 By default, the Raspbian distro will boot into a command-line interface, whereby you have to first log in as 'pi'.

If you then want to run a window manager (in this case, it's called 'X'), you have to give the system a command to let it know that's what you want to do.

For a lot of people this isn't really ideal since command lines scare them. Because of this, there's an option to start X automatically, on boot. Set this option to 'Yes' to enable this behaviour by default.

You can obviously revert this at any time to return to a text-based login where you have to start manually:

```
001 startx
```

Turn overscan on and off

07 You may have noticed one of two behaviours if you're using your Pi with a modern HDTV.

There is a black border the whole way around the image output by the Pi – it just doesn't fit correctly. This is caused by underscan.

If you can't see the edges of your screen to get to them you're suffering from overscan.

If you have the former issue, you may need to either turn on overscan, or enable a 'zoom' mode or similar on your TV.

If you have the latter issue, you need to turn overscan off so that you can see the edges.

Update raspi-config

08 The raspi-config tool receives updates from time to time. This is generally to either add more features or fix small bugs, or both!

It's not a bad idea to run the updater when you use the tool – before you start changing any system settings. While it's much more likely that it'll be updated to look better or do more things, it's not impossible there could be miscellaneous bug fixes hidden within that would otherwise cause you some grief.

Remember, though, when you're trying to update your copy of the raspi-config tool, you'll need an active internet connection, either through an LAN cable or wireless dongle. Without them, it's never going to get any newer. Always try to make sure you're on the latest version.

What you'll need...

Any Raspberry Pi distro
www.raspberrypi.org/downloads

Wi-Fi dongle or Ethernet

Did you know...

If your Raspberry Pi is going to be placed near your Internet router, all you need to do is plug in an Ethernet cable.

Get online

To access a world of utilities, apps and resources you need to get online. This is how to do it...

The easiest way to get online is to buy a Raspberry Pi Model B, as it comes with an RJ45 Ethernet socket. The Model A not only lacks the Ethernet port, but is handicapped by only having one USB port. That means you will have to buy a power USB hub in order to get online. Back to the Model B though and to get online, simply plug an Ethernet cable into the socket on the Pi and connect it to a similar port on the back of your internet modem/router. Turn your Pi on and launch the desktop, then double-click on Midori and you should see the internet appear (main image). To check that it's working, look at the lights on the Pi itself. The red power light should on. Above this is the green light that flickers when accessing the SD card. Below the power light are the three Ethernet-related lights. Note that the Model A does not have these LEDs because it doesn't have the Ethernet socket. The middle light is green and comes on when it detects a Full Duplex LAN connection. This means it is able to send and receive data to the internet. The next light is green and flashes when actually accessing the internet by sending or receiving data. The last light is yellow and will come on and stay on when a 100Mb LAN connection is detected.

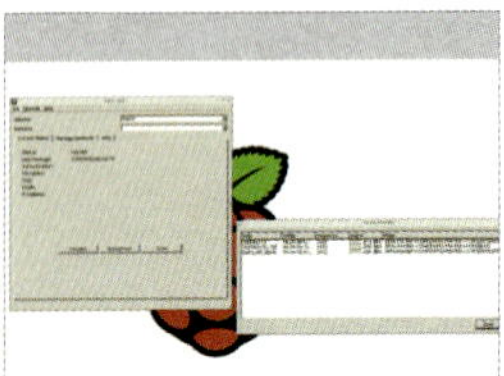

Fig 1: With a Wi-Fi dongle attached, run the utility and scan for available networks

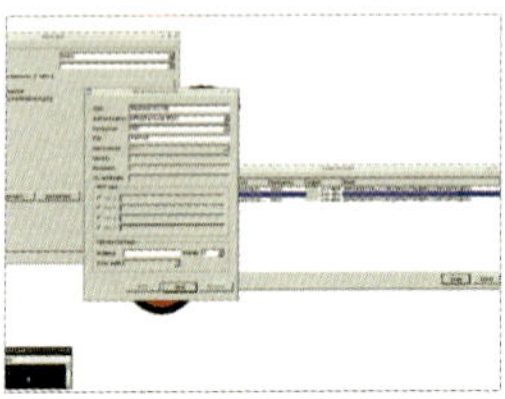

Fig 2: Enter the pre-shared key in order to connect to your home router

The Wi-Fi option

If you aren't close enough to the modem/router to be able to plug in the Ethernet connection, or you simply have a Model A, then a powered USB hub is required. This plugs into a USB port on the Pi. You can then plug a Wi-Fi dongle into this. Boot up the Pi and launch the desktop. Then double-click on the Wi-Fi Config icon. You should see a name for the dongle in the Adapter section. Click on Scan to look for networks and a list of those found should appear (Fig 1). Double-click on the one you want to connect to and the details for it will be listed. Almost all home networks use a network key, which is usually written on the modem itself. Click on PSK, which stands for pre-shared key, and type it in (Fig 2). Then click on Add. It will process this, then associate the connection and then finally, a new IP address for the Wi-Fi connection will appear. If you click on the Manage Networks tab, the network will now be listed and have an Enabled radio button active. To get on the internet, simply launch Midori and you'll be connected. The Wi-Fi utility will remain running on the bottom right of the panel. If you right-click on the Wi-Fi icon you will see options to Disconnect or Reconnect, event history and the results of the most recent scan. Click on Status to see how it's performing.

Checking the connection

To check that the Pi has a valid internet connection, double-click on LXTerminal. Enter this command:

```
ip addr
```

You should see a list of numbers, with the bottom line starting 'inet' and then the IP address of the Pi connection (Fig 3). Typically this is something like 192.168.1.11 and this shows that the connection is working because the Pi has been assigned an IP address based on the one used by your internet modem/router. If this doesn't come up then there may be a problem at the router end. The modem/router should be running a DHCP server and when the Pi connects to it, it will be given the IP address. If it isn't running then nothing else connected to it will be able to access the internet either. Use the web interface with another device to log onto 192.168.1.0 or whatever is your modem's actual IP address in order to check that the DHCP server service is turned on. Finally, in the terminal, type:

```
ping google.com
```

Sharing a connection

If you don't have a Wi-Fi dongle, a powered USB hub or a long enough Ethernet cable, but do have another computer connected to the internet, there's another way of getting access. On a Mac, connect it to the Pi via a USB or Ethernet cable. Launch System Preferences; under Internet & Wireless, click on Sharing. Click on Internet Sharing, then select Wi-Fi (or AirPort) as the connection type to share, and select how the Pi is connected to your Mac (Fig 4).

On a Windows PC, go to Windows Explorer>Networking>Networking and Sharing Center>Change Adapter Settings.

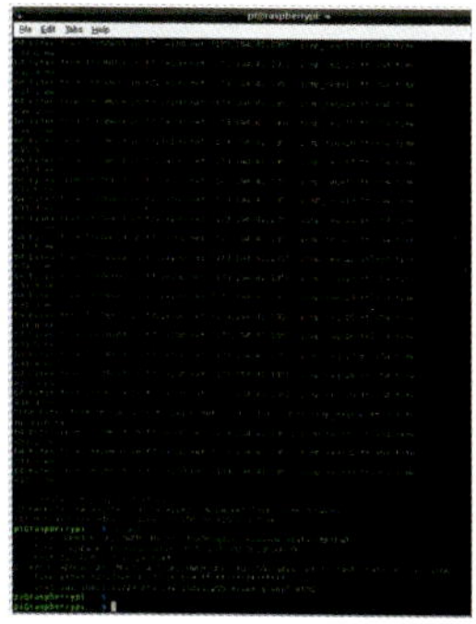

Fig 3: If it doesn't look like the connection is working, there are some easy ways of checking what's going on

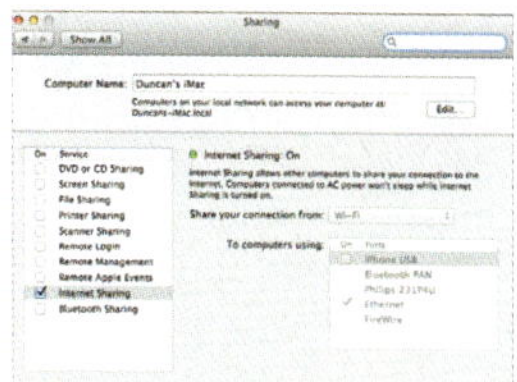

Fig 4: Both Windows and Mac computers can share their internet connections with a directly-connected Pi

The Pi Store

There's a mixture of free and paid-for games and applications in the Pi Store

What you'll need...

Raspbian
www.raspberrypi.org/downloads

Internet connection

Fig 1 The tutorial is a working piece of software to learn from along with documentation

Fig 2 This section involves a list of all the applications that you have installed. From here you can also launch installed apps or choose to delete them

Fig 3 Customise your profile with a recognisable username and a picture to be social with other users

Fig 4 Click on the Upload tab to begin editing your developer profile if you plan to upload your own creations

Launched in 2012, the Pi Store aims to provide a hub for both professional and amateur developers who want to make their software available for the Pi. The service was created by the Raspberry Pi Foundation in co-operation with companies IndieCity and Velocix.

It's possible to browse the Store and log in as a customer using a web browser or the dedicated Pi application. So far, most of the items on the Pi Store are free or low priced, and it's clear that the developers of the site hope to build a thriving community. In particular, they have emphasised that they would like to see developers of all age groups. This approach ties in with the whole strategy of using the Pi to encourage interest in software development. In addition, The Pi Store is possibly the easiest way for beginners to expand their Pi.

As well as being a platform for browsing, installing and buying applications, the Pi Store has integrated features for developers to create a profile and upload projects. Customers can also create a profile and participate in the social side of things.

Browsing the Store

The store can be browsed via the web (**http://store.raspberrypi.com**) or by using the dedicated Pi app. To install the app, type

```
sudo apt-get install pistore.
```

The Store should then be visible as a clickable icon on the backdrop.

Upon launching, you are presented with a two-pane window with tabs along the top and a main area below (main image). The first tab is Explore, and this is where you go to find new applications.

The main window itself makes use of more tabs for the content categories. The Apps and Games categories contain the meat of what people expect from a device-specific app store. Each of these items, like all store items, features customer feedback in the form of a rating out of five and a comments section. Many of the products are versions of existing programs that have been repackaged specifically for the Pi. The Dev Tools are resources and tools to help developers, such as ready-made sound and graphics packs.

The Tutorials are resource packs designed to educate you on various aspects of the Pi. The power of this feature is that these packages aren't limited to flat text files and may contain other resources. For example, one tutorial demonstrates how to build a database program using the Python programming language along with SQL, a language for accessing databases (Fig 1).

My Library

You can see what apps you have purchased and installed by clicking on the My Library tab. From here you can launch apps that you have installed, delete them from your system or reinstall them. This last feature is handy because it means that you can wipe and reinstall your Raspberry Pi without permanently losing the content you have obtained from the Store. This section also includes a running count, in icon form, of the applications that you currently have installed (Fig 2).

If you click on your username, you can edit your profile (Fig 3). You can change your username from the one that the store assigns you when you first sign up and add a link to your website and a photo. Doing this helps you to establish a presence within the community when you're giving feedback.

Uploading content

Clicking on the Upload tab allows you to create a developer profile (Fig 4). This gives you a comprehensive homepage on the site that you can customise. You can choose the colour scheme and banner image, and you can connect it to your Facebook and Twitter streams. Note that once you have created a developer page and saved it, you cannot change the name in the future.

From here, you can also add a product. When you add a product, you can specify that it will be publicly viewable or hidden and that it is finished or a work-in-progress. You can also specify the category of your project (game, application, tutorial, dev tools or media), add screenshots, box art, age rating, tags, description and prices. Once the project has gone public, you can view statistics relating to number of page views and downloads. You can also specify your preferred licence for the product. For example, you may opt to allow other people permission to remix what you have created.

The files themselves

Time to get our hands dirty! Things run smoothest if you don't directly manipulate the files themselves, but it's handy knowing where they are if something goes wrong. Files relating to your profile and configuration are not designed to be edited by hand, but they can be found in [your home directory]/indiecity. A useful file for troubleshooting is [your home directory]/indiecity/pistore/Scripts.log. This file logs all store activity and can be an invaluable source of information when troubleshooting. Right-click on this file in order to open it in Leafpad.

The files that make up the applications themselves can be stored in various locations on your SD card, but many of the biggest game and application-related files end up in /usr/local/bin/indiecity/.

What you'll need...

Apt command help page:
http://linux.die.net/man/8/apt

Apt-get help page:
http://manpages.ubuntu.com/manpages/lucid/man8/apt-get.8.html

Did you know...

If you press the Tab key the command line will attempt to auto-complete your command for you – just press Enter to finish.

Install and use packages

The Raspberry Pi is great, but it's made better with the software you install onto it

On its own, the Raspberry Pi is a near-perfect mini computer. It already contains a wealth of educational software, a few games, some programming utilities and a number of system tools. But, as with most computers, this is only the tip of the proverbial iceberg. By installing more programs, you can do much more.

These programs, known as packages, are as wide and as varied as the developers who originally designed them. In Linux, if there's a need for a particular program, then someone develops one. They then put it out to the world and make the source code freely available, hence 'open source'. Once the program has been tested, it will eventually make its way onto one of the many remote servers for that particular Linux distro.

These remote servers, called repositories, or repos, contain all the elements of the package in order for it to be downloaded and installed onto your system. The process is very quick and easy once you know how it's done...

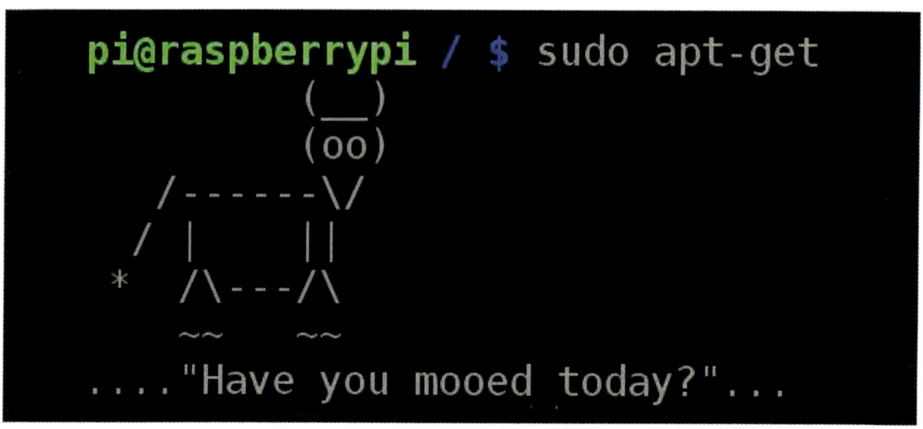

Update and upgrade

01 Getting hold of a package on the Raspberry Pi involves dropping into the command-line terminal, via the LXTerminal icon on the desktop, and entering a few commands. But before we do that, we need to make sure the system is up to date. Enter the following into the terminal:

```
sudo apt-get update
sudo apt-get upgrade
```

Or…

```
sudo apt-get update && sudo apt-get upgrade
```

Search for a package

02 The apt-get command (Advanced Package Tool) is the key to downloading and installing packages on the Raspberry Pi. In the previous instance, we updated the existing packages and system, upgraded any that needed it, and updated the current package list. Now, let's search the list of server packages for available games.

```
apt-cache search game | less
```

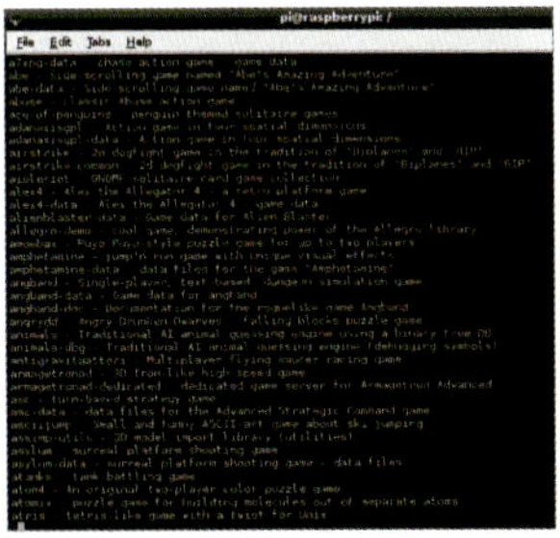

Apt searching

03 The current list you find yourself in is the name of all the packages labelled as 'games' from the available server. In the list, the part before the hyphen tells you the name of the package, which is what you will need to know to be able to install it. Use the arrow keys up/down to navigate; press 'Q' to exit.

Installing a package

04 Using the up and down arrow keys, navigate the list. If you find something you like the look of, say Angry Drunken Dwarves, remember the name of the package, in this case 'angrydd', and press 'Q' to exit the list.

To install the package, enter the following in the terminal:

```
sudo apt-get install angrydd
```

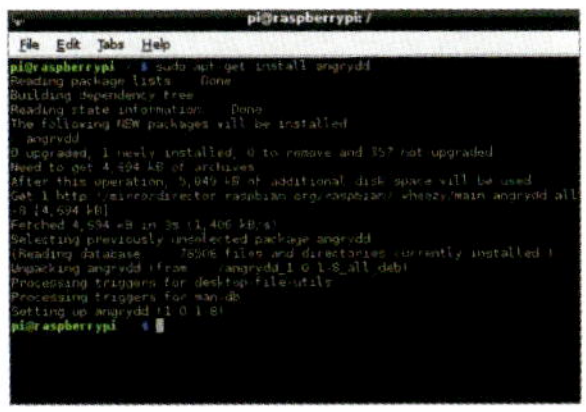

Executing the package

05 The result of the previous command should be the successful download and installation of the game, Angry Drunken Dwarves. To execute the newly installed package, you can either run it from the LXDE Menu under Games>Angry Drunken Dwarves, or by typing in the following into the terminal:

```
angrydd
```

Remove a package

06 This installing of packages is perfectly fine, and you can see just how powerful a command Apt really is. But, what if you want to remove a package?

Using the Apt command again, let's say we want to completely remove all trace of Angry Drunken Dwarves from the Raspberry Pi.

```
sudo apt-get --purge remove angrydd
```

Enter 'Y' to accept the removal.

Apt Easter eggs

07 The Apt command is a shorter, non-menu-driven variant of the Aptitude command. This command has a long history in Linux, and as a result has some rather special 'features', also known as Easter eggs. Purely for a little bit of fun, type in the following commands and see the results:

```
aptitude moo
aptitude -v moo
aptitude -vv moo
aptitude -vvv moo
aptitude -vvvv moo
aptitude -vvvvv moo
aptitude -vvvvvv moo
sudo apt-get moo
```

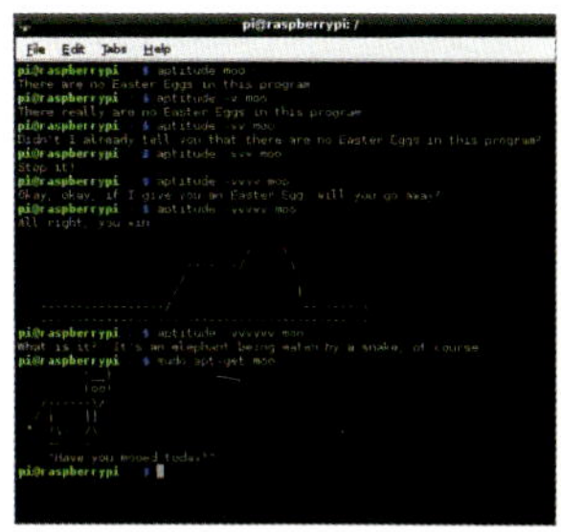

Man the Apt command

08 As you can see, there is more to the simple Apt command than what first meets the eye. There are many different sub-commands that you can run, and many different variations in which to run them.

If you want to see what else the Apt command can do, enter the following:

```
man apt
```

What you'll need…

Synaptic:
www.nongnyu.org/synaptic/

Did you know…

Synaptic has access to the same repo as via the command line as demonstrated on the previous two pages.

Use graphical installations

Would you prefer a graphical interface to install new programs? If so, then read on…

If you're new to Linux, you may find using its built-in Apt package management tool a bit intimidating and confusing. The apt-get command is used for installing applications through the internet, connecting to the remote servers – called repositories – which house the programs as packages. But it is used through the terminal command prompt, which can be daunting, so we need an alternative: a desktop environment interface method of getting hold of packages.

This is where Synaptic comes in. Synaptic is a friendly-looking graphical interface to the apt-get terminal command which allows you to manage your application installations, and removals, through the already familiar desktop environment. Think of it as a kind of online shop where you can pick and choose the programs you want and have them downloaded and installed onto your Raspberry Pi without you having to drop into the terminal.

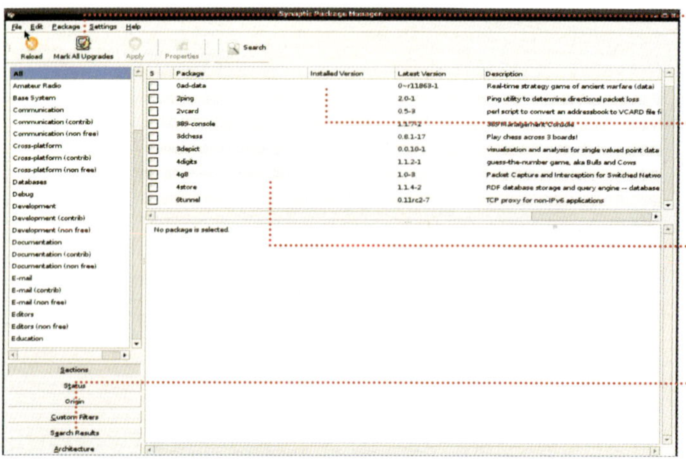

Upgrade entire systems
Synaptic has the ability to update and upgrade every program or package, and it can upgrade your entire system to the latest version

Install and more
Synaptic is a very powerful tool. With it you can install, remove, upgrade and downgrade single or multiple packages and programs

Browse all documentation
From within Synaptic, you are able to browse and read all available online documentation related to a package or program

Easily find programs
Synaptic enables you to easily locate packages and programs by name, description, version and even by who developed the program

Update the system

01 Unfortunately, if you have an aversion to dropping into the command-line terminal, then you're going to be stuck at the first step. Before we install anything, we need to make sure that the Raspberry Pi is fully updated and any existing packages are upgraded. Simply enter the following into the LXTerminal:

```
sudo apt-get update
sudo apt-get upgrade
```

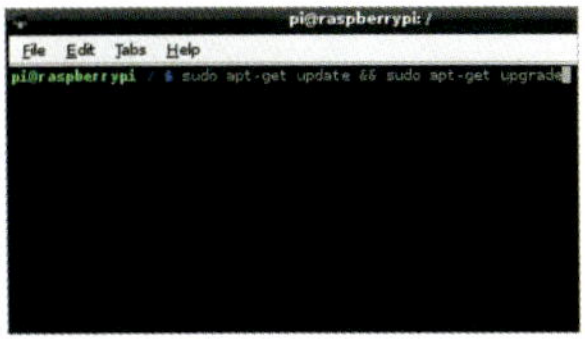

Installing Synaptic

02 To install Synaptic, you'll first need to enter the LXTerminal and run the command below – don't forget to type Y to any prompts asking you to accept the installation:

```
sudo apt-get install
synaptic
```

Running Synaptic – Part 1

03 In essence, that's all you need to do. Synaptic is now installed and ready to use. However, due to its complexity, there may be some bugs that need ironing out first, so it's best to follow these steps. To test if Synaptic is working okay, first enter the following command into the terminal:

```
gksudo synaptic
```

Running Synaptic – Part 2

04 You should be now looking at the Synaptic program window, where you can scroll through the list of available programs and click on each to download and install. Now we need to test whether it will run from the LXDE menu. Click on the icon in the bottom left, then go to Preferences>Synaptic Package Manager.

Running Synaptic – Part 3

05 Running Synaptic from the LXDE menu results in an error. Don't panic, however: all it's doing is asking for a password. . Enter the following password into the box:

```
raspberry
```

This is the default Pi password so we're assuming you haven't changed it!

Fixing Synaptic – Option 1

06 This will temporarily fix the issue, but to permanently resolve it, do one of the following. First, right-click the Synaptic icon in the menu and left-click Properties. In the Command text box, change the text to add the gksudo command. So instead of 'synaptic-pkexec', it will read:

```
gksudo synaptic-pkexec
```

Fixing Synaptic – Option 2

07 The second, and best, option is to drop back into the terminal and alter the way in which the program is executed from the menu. All that's needed is to change one line to another, so that the gksudo command is again used instead of the plain synaptic-pkexec. From the terminal, type:

```
sudo nano /usr/share/
applications/
synaptic.desktop
```

Change 'Exec=synaptic-pkexec' to…

```
Exec=gksudo synaptic-pkexec
```

Synaptic fully working

08 After you've entered those changes, exit nano via Ctrl+X, followed by Y to accept the changes, and then press Enter a couple of times to get back to the command prompt. You can now launch Synaptic from the menu, or by entering the following command when you're in the terminal:

```
gksudo synaptic
```

Top four add-on boards

Get more out of your Raspberry Pi by using these add-on boards to extend its functionality

Gertboard £30

Created by one of the original designers of the Raspberry Pi, Gert van Loo, the Gertboard is an add-on for the GPIO ports that allows the Raspberry Pi to interact with the real world. It's used for doing physical computing tasks: driving motors to open a garage door or open some curtains, sensing temperatures so you know when to turn off heating, access to LED lights and more. While it's not quite at the level of an Arduino, it's more integrated into the Raspberry Pi and a great teaching tool. It does require a little soldering to construct, although you can find Gertboards pre-assembled for very little extra if you look hard enough and don't fancy putting it together yourself – it's quite a job!

There's a great project to try out with the Gertboard over on RasPi.TV (**bit.ly/1ebauWA**) where, using a Wii Remote videogame controller, you can create a cacophony of motion and noise that shows off exactly just how much you can do with the Gertboard. From waving flags to starting fans and ringing bells, you can create your own Raspberry Pi-powered Rube Goldberg machine. All you need is a Bluetooth dongle to sync a Wii Remote up to your Raspberry Pi, and the Cwiid Python library to start messing around with it.

Gertduino £20

The big brother to the Gertboard, the Gertduino is a hybrid Arduino board that has better connectivity with the Raspberry Pi. Arduinos are open source microcontrollers that allow you to control physical objects – with a lot more control, precision and automation than what you can do with the Gertboard. The Gertduino's biggest feature is that it has the same chip as the Arduino Uno, the flagship Arduino board that a lot of folks who make hobby projects use for their electronics. It's highly configurable and all the compatible Arduino extras for the Uno work with the Gertduino.

There's also a special chip called the ATmega48 built into the Gertduino that you won't find in the Uno. Its main functions include a backup battery and a high-precision clock, both of which allow the Gertduino to be unplugged from the Pi once you've finished programming it. All of this means you can set it up to open a chicken coop at a set time each morning without the need for the Raspberry Pi to be there as well. Apparently Gert van Loo, the board's inventor, uses his Gertduino for his chickens.

The full manual for the Gertduino has some great example projects to try out with the board, and can be found on the element14 website (**bit.ly/1aFd8RD**).

PiFace £20

Physical computing is a popular addition to the Raspberry Pi, and PiFace is another series of boards that allow you to interact with the outside world on your Pi. PiFace comes with a twist, as it allows you to use a GUI to control individual parts of the PiFace boards that you can get. These include a simple LED display as well as the standard interfacing board; both of these boards have lesson plans and other educational tools available to help people learn how to program and generally use their Raspberry Pi. It's fully compatible with Scratch and can also be used with Python and C to make more complex applications.

While the PiFace doesn't actually allow you to control devices, it can detect the state of many types of digital device. You can then use this in some kind of Internet of Things, sending out tweets or manipulating network-connected devices. Some of the tutorials available from the PiFace site teach you how to create a memory game, a countdown timer/advent calendar and how to make a playable organ.

RasWIK £50

Another Arduino-based board that allows you to perform some physical computing. However, this one is for those that don't want to wrangle so much with wiring up the GPIO ports. The magic of the RasWIK is that it comes with a wireless radio chip that fits snugly onto the GPIO ports out of the box, and a custom version of Raspbian that makes the process of using the main Arduino board much quicker. It even comes with a collection of components for circuits you can build, from remote buzzers and traffic lights to light and temperature-sensing projects. Instructions on how to get going with these come with the custom Raspbian SD card, and can make the entire process easier if you don't fancy soldering together a board.

Some of these projects and more are on the Ciseco website (**bit.ly/1hTsmDD**), so you can give them a browse before finalising on getting a RasWIK. You can even use the projects without a RasWIK if you have the correct components, and it teaches you how to use Python in the process. It's an easy and hassle-free way to get into physical computing from your Pi, and the instructions are excellent for kids and novices to start with programming and controlling.

> "The magic of the RasWIK is that it comes with a wireless radio chip that fits snugly onto the GPIO ports out of the box"

Code and create with Raspberry Pi

Learn how to do much more with your credit card-sized PC

If you've been following along with the tutorials up to this point, you'll have a firm grounding with the basics of Linux and being productive with your Raspberry Pi. This is just the start of your adventure. What follows is one of the most comprehensive collections of Raspberry Pi projects you'll find anywhere in the world. Whether you want to make your Pi a media hub, learn to code, or find out how you can strap it to a remote-controlled car, we hope the following pages inspire you to create something amazing with your Raspberry Pi today…

"What follows is one of the most comprehensive collections of Raspberry Pi projects you'll find anywhere in the world"

What you'll need...

LibreOffice
Installed through tutorial using apt-get

Turn your Pi into an office suite

How to add a full, free office suite to your Raspberry Pi to turn it into the smallest home office ever

You can't get far with a computer if you don't have tools that cater for things like letter writing, spreadsheets and presentations. Thankfully this is well within the scope of the Raspberry Pi's capabilities and, although Raspbian comes bundled with a couple of text editors, sometimes you need the extra functionality a full office suite can offer. This is really easy on the Pi and the best option available is open source and thus completely free: LibreOffice.

LibreOffice is a fully featured Microsoft Office drop-in replacement and the Raspberry Pi will handle it well so long as you're not creating huge documents with hundreds of images. You'll need a working internet connection for this tutorial, so make sure your LAN cable or wireless dongle is plugged in and functional, because we'll be using the built-in package manager. Installation does take some time, though.

Presentations
A really impressive piece of kit, it allows creation of presentations in just a few simple clicks

Drawing
Not artistic drawing as you might think, but a great application for creating quick, good-looking flow-and-process diagrams

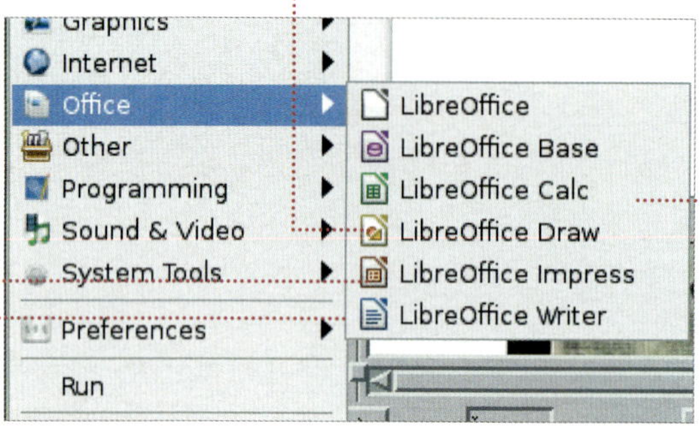

Word processing
LibreOffice comes with a great word-processing application that works brilliantly on the Pi with no hassle

Spreadsheets
Also bundled is a spreadsheet application – its ability to read any popular spreadsheet file format makes it very powerful

Install LibreOffice

01 The best thing about open-source software is the fact that you can install it any time (so long as you have an internet connection or installation medium, anyway) at your total convenience – without having to worry about handing over payment details. So, let's get right on with doing exactly that. Open your terminal – you can do this by double-clicking LXTerminal from your desktop. Install the LibreOffice office suit by using the package manager:

```
sudo apt-get install libreoffice
```

Now type in your password. Press 'Y' and Enter when prompted to install other dependency packages. Now sit back, relax or make some tea!

Explore the suite

02 When you've installed LibreOffice, you can admire your new applications by hitting the system menu. You'll see a new 'Office' category, underneath which you'll see the following applications:

LibreOffice Base – A database management application.
LibreOffice Calc – Spreadsheets.
LibreOffice Draw – To make flowchart/visualisations.
LibreOffice Impress – For creating presentations.
LibreOffice Writer – The word processor, which is very similar to Word.

Most of these applications are able to open a majority of documents created in Microsoft's Office counterparts and are almost as feature rich.

Add some style

03 We're focusing on some of the word-processing features on the Pi specifically here, so go on ahead and open up LibreOffice Writer. When you're writing documents, it's usually the formatting where people stumble. When you start writing, to the left of the font drop-down menu there's another drop-down that currently reads 'Default'. Select some text, then use this drop-down to change the current applied style. If you don't like the defaults, select 'More' from the drop-down, or press F11. This will allow you to customise the styles and more.

Add an index

04 One of the great things about using formatting is that it allows you to create a contents page for your work easily. So long as you use consistent headings for the different levels of your document, it's a quick and easy way to give a guide to what's in your document. Another advantage is that if you export the file to PDF, you'll end up with each heading in the contents hotlinking directly to the correct section within your document. To create your index, create some space at the top of your document, and then insert your index by using the menus to go to 'Insert Indexes and Tables>Indexes and Tables'. Review the selected options and click OK when you're happy. It'll insert to the section of the document that your cursor is on.

What about images?

05 There's no better way to brighten up a document than with carefully chosen imagery. This can be achieved with relative ease too.

There are a couple of solutions – the easiest of which is to drag an image in from the file manager directly into the document. Assuming the image is on your desktop, simply drag the file into LibreOffice Writer and you will see the icon change; upon letting go, your image will appear roughly where you dropped it.

Alternatively, you can use the Insert>Picture>From File option.

Export as a PDF

06 The PDF format is a very common way of exchanging documents – mainly because in its simplest form, it's an easy way of stopping accidental changes or modifications to a document. It's also easy to set passwords on PDFs and stop purposeful modifications to them.

The main advantage of PDFs, however, is that you don't really need to worry about the recipient having a specific application to view them with. Most modern operating systems have some sort of PDF viewer built in so you can be sure of a consistent experience.

With LibreOffice, this is easy. You can save your document as a PDF using the File>Export to PDF menu option. Simply choose your desired options, click Export and save it in the appropriate place.

Help yourself by using comments

07 When writing a long document you'll often think of things that you should really check up on or add to the document later. When you think of these things, you can make notes about them using 'Comments' – even more useful when there are multiple people moving through the document. Comments can be added at the current point in the document with Ctrl+Alt+C or by using the menu option Insert> Comment. If you want to get rid of the extra 'Comments' pane, you can use the View menu to toggle it.

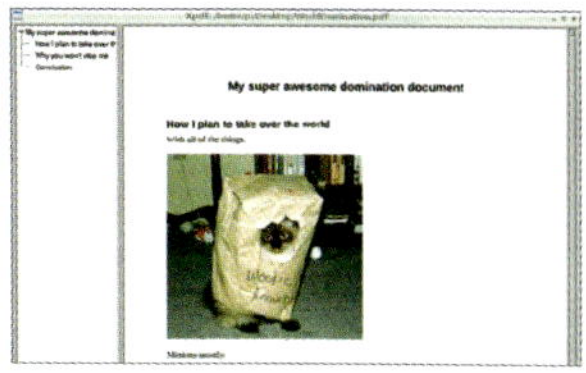

Linking out to the world

08 If you've used outside resources in a document that you want to reference, or maybe you don't directly need to include all the information – it might be handy to have a way of getting back to that document later on. You could include an Appendix of information at the end of your document that links to these other resources. You can hyperlink to these easily using the Hyperlink toolbar button or the same from the Insert>Hyperlink menu. Select your text, then click it and you'll be presented with a dialog to link to one of the appropriate places. It's important to note that direct document links use full system paths. If it's being sent to someone else, avoid using these as they'll break for the reader. Ideally use it only a personal reference guide on your own machine.

What you'll need...

Full nano manual
www.nano-editor.org/dist/v1.2/nano.1.html

Did you know...

Nano is one of the best command line editors for beginners, but there are lots of options like Kate and Vim.

Beginner's guide to nano

Learn how to edit text on the command line and in a terminal with one of Linux's best tools

If you have the itch to do more with your Pi, one of the skills you'll need to learn to pull off many projects is the ability to edit system files. The command-line text editor nano is definitely one of the best tools for the job. Text editors are very basic tools; the clue is in the name in this case. There's no formatting or colouring or anything of the sort you would get in a word processor, but that's the point. The kind of files you'll be creating or editing will generally contain code – code which doesn't require to be made bold or bulleted. Nano removes all of these distractions, but still has a few of the more handy features you'd find in a graphical text editor. We'll teach you how to make the most out of nano to make your projects run quickly and efficiently.

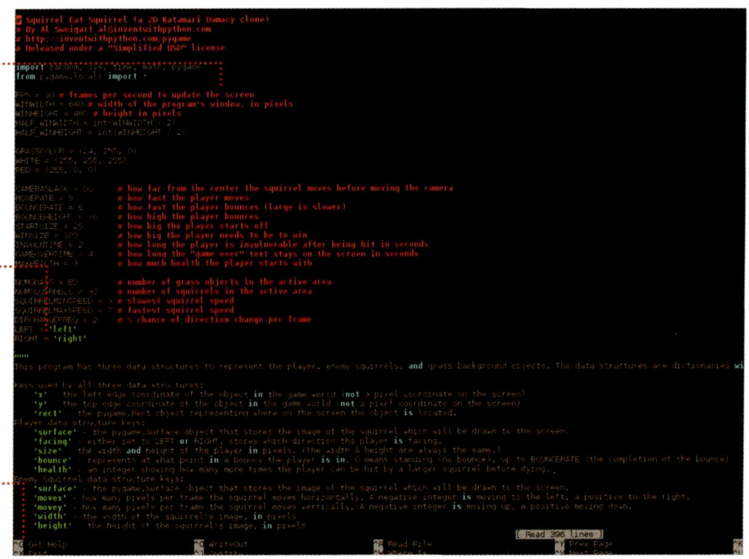

Writing
Create plain text files in the command line, even write some code for a program

Editing
Edit system files to suit your needs and projects without digging through a file manager

Advanced functions
Search, copy, paste and insert text from another file using some of the built-in nano functions

Open nano

01 Open the terminal, or enter the command line, and simply type **nano**. This will open a blank new file. From here you can create a simple text file such as a list, or create a system file, script or piece of code. How the system interprets your file depends on what you write and how you save it.

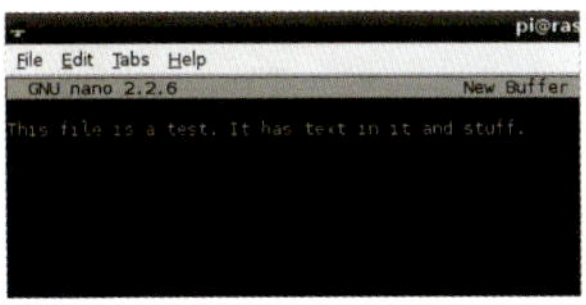

Save and continue

02 Once you've finished with nano, you can save/write out using Ctrl+O. All shortcuts and functions such as this are done using Ctrl and a letter key. It will ask you what name to save the file under. Whatever you name it, it will be saved in the directory you opened nano from unless you specify a path.

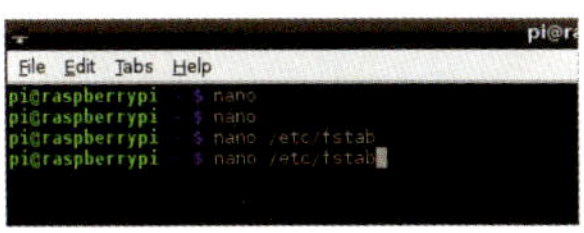

Opening files

03 To edit already existing files, you'll first need to know their location and name. To open them in nano, type the following:

```
$ nano /path/filename
```

For example, to edit fstab you would type:

```
$ nano /etc/fstab
```

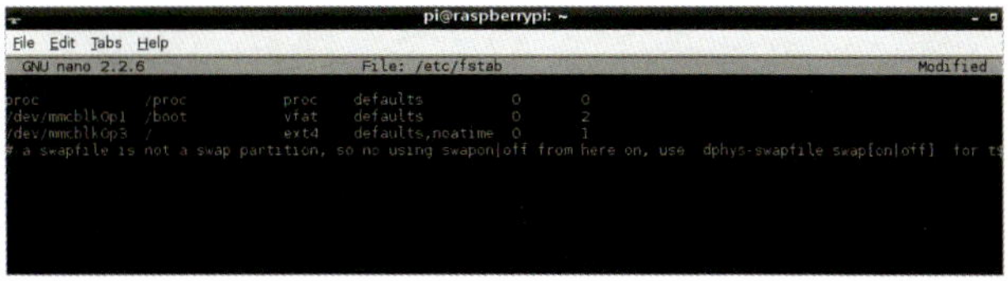

Save and exit

04 Once you've finished modifying the file and need to get on with the next task, you can press Ctrl+X to exit nano. It will ask if you want to save any modifications, which just requires a Y to confirm. If you want to exit without saving changes, you can just use N. To cancel before making a decision, use Ctrl+C.

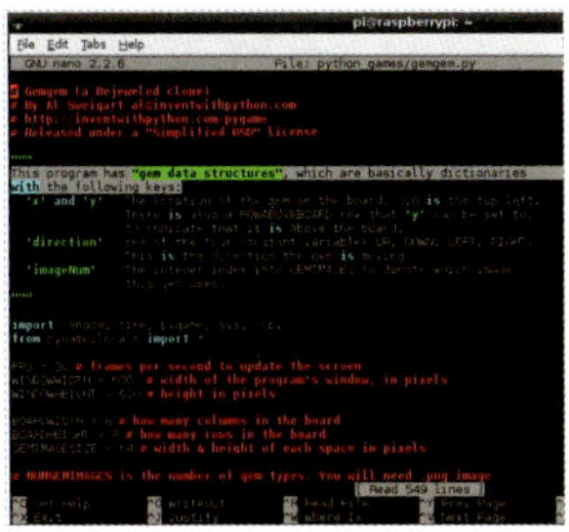

Copy and paste

05 This is more of a terminal-specific command, but it can be used just as well in nano. While you cannot use your mouse to navigate around the file in nano, you can highlight text in the same way you would in a graphical text editor. Once highlighted, pressing Ctrl+Shift+C will copy any text. Ctrl+Shift+V will paste.

Insert from file

06 If you need to directly insert the contents of another file, there's a quick way to do it without needing to use copy and paste. Typing Ctrl+R and entering the path to the file will insert it into the spot your cursor is at.

Advanced navigation

07 You've probably been using the arrow keys to move one space at a time left, right, up or down. There are other ways to move around the file, though. Using Ctrl+A will act the same way as the Home key does in a graphical editor, moving the cursor to the start of the line. Same with Ctrl+E moving you to the end like the End key. Ctrl+V is page down, and Ctrl+Y is page up.

Searching a file

08 Sometimes you'll be looking for a specific line or phrase in a large text file. Instead of using the arrow keys and tirelessly reading every line, you can use the search function via Ctrl+W. Entering the search term will begin looking through the document, and once you're finished you can press Ctrl+C to exit the search.

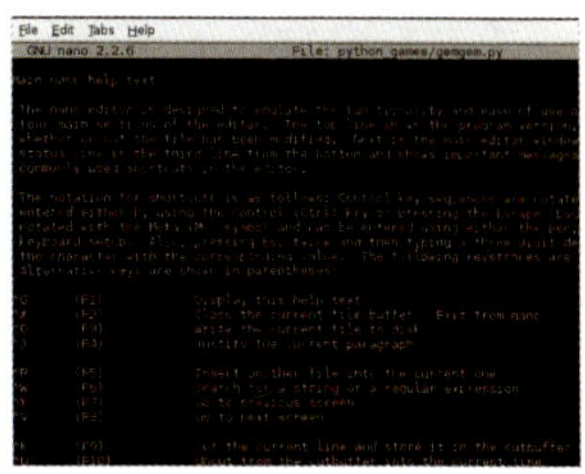

Extra help

09 There are many more functions available in nano. For a full list of commands, you can use Ctrl+G, which lists all the shortcuts and what they do. The caret symbol (^) in this list denotes the use of Ctrl on your keyboard.

What you'll need...

Geany – www.geany.org
www.geany.org/Documentation/Manual

Did you know...

Geany is just one of many great development environments available to you. Google 'Linux IDE' for more ideas.

Get started with Geany

Program better on your Pi using one of the best text editors and basic IDEs around: Geany

When you come to do some real coding on your Pi, it can be a bit confusing where you need to start. For everything Python, the superb IDLE integrated development environment (IDE) is included, and kids can get started using Scratch to make some basic games. Python isn't the only language to code in, though, and Scratch has its own way of programming that can't be used for real software. This is where the fantastic Geany comes in – a text editor and IDE.

As a very lightweight application, Geany is perfect for the Pi. One of the main features it includes for programming is syntax highlighting – where appropriate parts of the code are coloured differently. IDLE does this for Python, and some other text editors include this feature; however, Geany also allows for autocompletion of commands and can build software as well. It supports a wide variety of languages, so whatever project you're starting, you'll be able to use a familiar and comfortable environment to do it in.

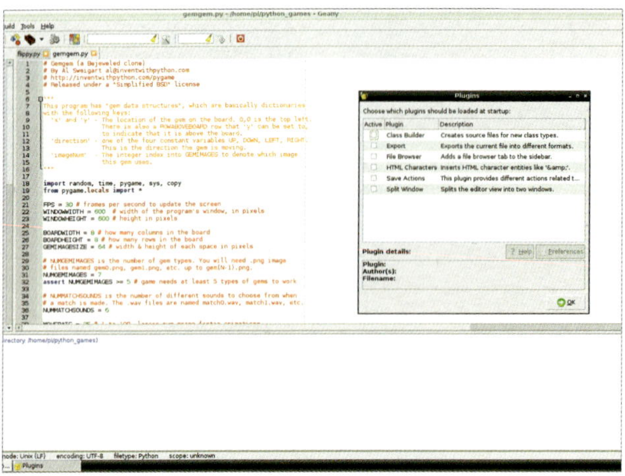

Install Geany

01 Geany should be installed by default into Raspbian. However, if it's not there, it's very simple to install otherwise. Open the LX Terminal and then type:

```
$ sudo apt-get install geany
```

This will go through the installation process; afterwards it will appear in the Programming submenu.

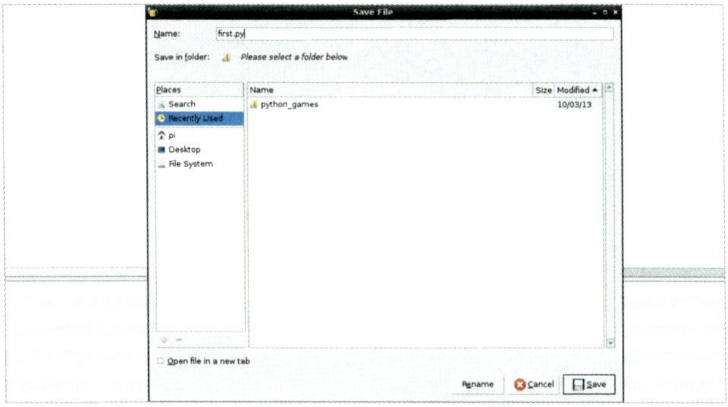

New file

02 To start a new file is as easy as pressing File followed by New, much like a word processor or text editor. It will create a blank file that you can immediately start typing into. Save it with the appropriate file type, such as .py, and Geany will recognise the code is Python and start marking it up.

Marking up

03 If you can't save it as the relevant file type, you can also force Geany to show code with a specific markup. Go to Document>Set Filetype and choose from one of the available options there. It supports at least 50 different languages.

Opening files

04 Opening a pre-existing file in Geany is easy – by clicking File followed by Open (just like in a word processor). For now, we'll test out some of Geany's features by opening one of the pre-packaged Python files from the **python_games** folder in the **pi** directory.

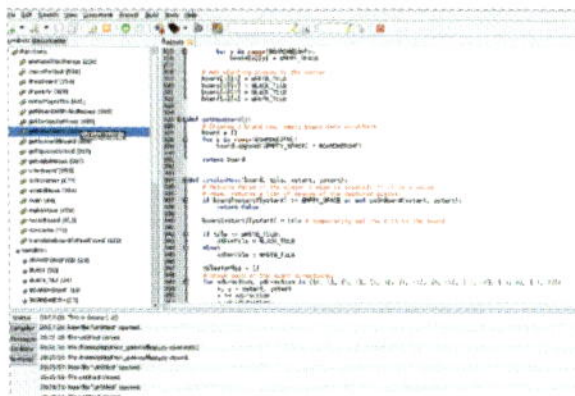

Navigating code

05 The left column of the IDE lists the line number of the important parts of your code. For Python, this includes the functions and variables that make up the program. You can also click on them individually to jump to where they first appear or are defined in the code.

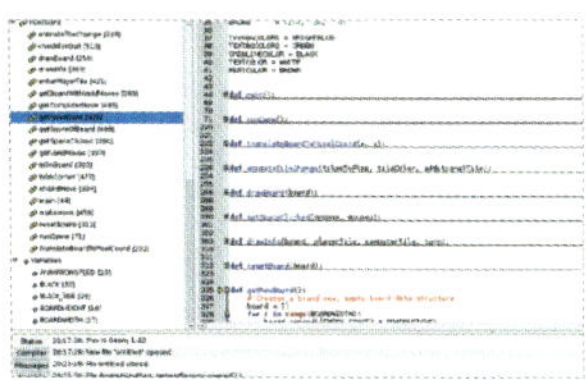

Advanced navigation

06 Your code can start looking a bit convoluted once you have multiple functions and imports dotted around. Geany is smart enough to recognise these and allows you to minimise loops, functions and a block of imports if it's not necessary while checking over your code.

Autocomplete

07 When you're writing out your program, you may notice that Geany will try to guess the function or variable you're trying to use. This can be useful if you've forgotten exactly what the variable is called, as you can use the arrow keys to move down a list of relevant commands for what you've just typed.

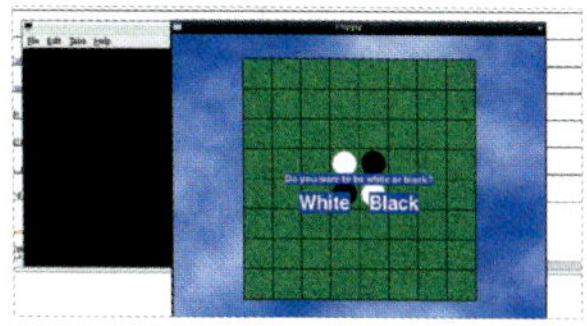

Testing your code

08 You can test your code by clicking on the gears in the top bar – these allow you to run the code. Any errors will be shown in the following window; but if everything goes to plan, it should run without any issue. Exit the windows and click on the Run button again to stop the test.

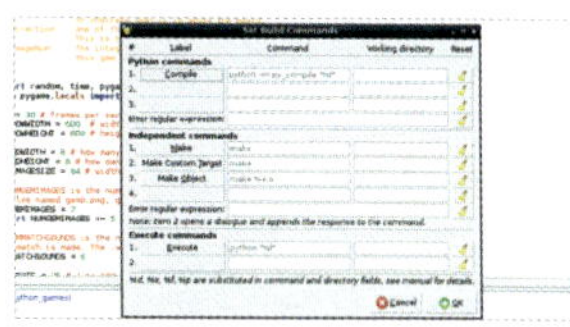

Compiling

09 Once you've finished your code, you can compile and build it using the built-in tools. Any errors that occur in the process will be documented, allowing you to sift through them one by one until you have everything working properly.

Gain remote desktop access

Learn how to get access to your Raspberry Pi desktop without it being in front of you…

VNC (Virtual Network Computing) is a graphical desktop access and sharing system that allows a user to remotely control and use the desktop of another computer from their own system.

It's handy in many ways: to give you control over a remote system; to help out another user elsewhere; to allow a computer to remain powered on, but without the need for a keyboard, mouse or even a monitor.

In our case, we aim to allow access to the Raspberry Pi desktop without it being hooked up to the aforementioned peripherals. This way, you can do everything you would normally do, but with just the power supply and network attached, thereby freeing up space and saving extra expense. In real-world terms, this means you could potentially access the Pi desktop via an Android tablet or phone!

What you'll need…

TightVNC
www.tightvnc.com/release-2.7.php

Did you know…

TightVNC Viewer is a free resource for accessing VNC servers, like the one we'll install in this tutorial.

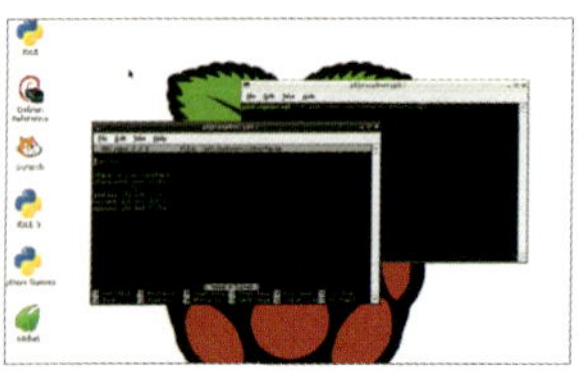

Static IP address

01 The first step for us is to make sure that the Raspberry Pi has a static IP address. Basically, an IP address is a group of numbers that your network assigns to devices in order to tell them apart. To set up a static IP address, simply double-click LXTerminal and type the following and then press Enter:

```
sudo nano /etc/network/
interfaces
```

Static IP part 2

02 This file controls the IP addressing for the Pi. You need to scroll down to the 'iface eth0' line and remove DHCP and replace it with static. Now, on the line directly below, enter the IP address that you want force your Pi to have, along with the subnet mask and the gateway:

```
address 192.168.1.93
netmask 255.255.255.0
gateway 192.168.1.254
```

Static IP part 3

03 After you've entered those details, exit nano by pressing Ctrl+X, followed by Y to accept the changes, and then press Enter a couple of times to get back to the command prompt in the terminal. You can now either reboot your Pi, or type the following into the terminal:

```
sudo /etc/init.d/networking stop
sudo /etc/init.d/networking
start
```

Installing VNC part 1

04 Now we'll install VNC and ensure that it starts automatically whenever the Pi is booted up. This used to be a bit annoying under older Raspbian versions, as configuring services often had a nasty habit of breaking the system. But no longer. Enter the following commands, pressing Enter after each one:

```
sudo apt-get update
sudo apt-get install tightvncserver
tightvncserver
```

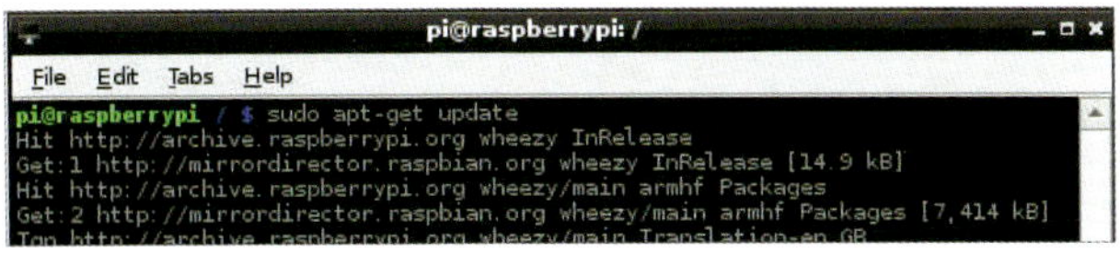

Installing VNC part 2

05 When the packages have downloaded and installed, follow the instructions on screen (see below) to set up a password and confirm it, but answer 'n' to the view only option. This really is just a security feature and since you are only accessing the Pi at home, it's not absolutely necessary – it's still good practice, though.

```
You will require a password to access your
desktops
Password:
Verify:
Would you like to enter a view-only
password (y/n)? n
New 'X' desktop is raspberrypi:1
```

Configuring VNC server

06 That's the VNC server installed, up and running. Now we need to make sure it loads up as a service every time the Raspberry Pi reboots, so you can access it even if the Pi undergoes a power cycle. To configure the Pi to do this, type the following in the terminal and press Enter.

```
sudo nano /etc/init.d/tightvncserver
```

Configuring boot service

07 We're back in nano, and we'll need to enter some lines of commands in order to allow the Raspberry Pi to activate the VNC server when it boots. In the editor, type:

```
#!/bin/sh
# /etc/init.d/tightvncserver
# Set the VNCUSER variable to the name of  the user to start
tightvncserver under
VNCUSER='pi'
case "$1" in
start)
su $VNCUSER -c '/usr/bin/tightvncserver :1'
echo "Starting TightVNC server for $VNCUSER"
;;
stop)
pkill Xtightvnc
echo "Tightvncserver stopped"
;;
*)
echo "Usage: /etc/init.d/tightvncserver {start|stop}"
exit 1
;;

esac
exit 0
```

Reboot and ready to go

08 Now press Ctrl+X, then Y to save, followed by Enter a couple of times to get you back into the Terminal. What we need to do now is edit the permissions of the script we've just created so that it's executable and active. Do this by typing the following commands into the terminal, ensuring that you press Enter after each one otherwise it will not be registered:

```
sudo chmod 755 /etc/init.d/tightvncserver
update-rc.d tightvncserver defaults
sudo reboot
```

Once you have completed these steps, the final thing that you will need to do is to unplug the Raspberry Pi and locate it somewhere that has easy access to a network cable. If you install the likes of TightVNC Viewer, or any other remote access software (as long as it uses the Tight protocol) then you should be able to point the client to the IP address 192.168.1.93:1 (or whatever the static IP address is of the network that you wish to connect the device to) and have full access to the Raspberry Pi.

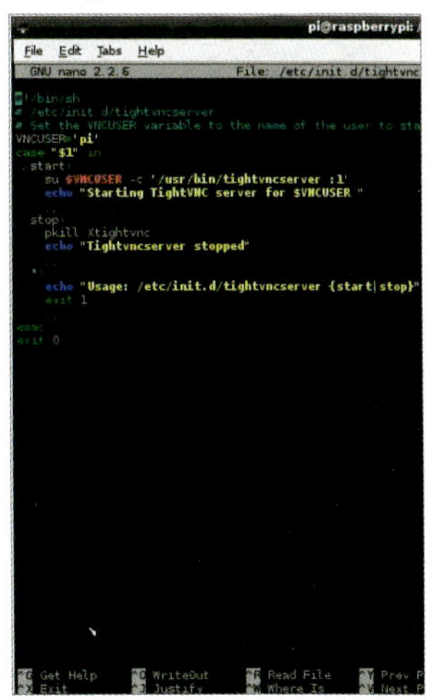

What you'll need...

Any Raspberry Pi distro
www.raspberrypi.org/downloads

Internet connection

Second computer

Access your files with SSH

Use the terminal of your home computer to gain quick and secure access to your Raspberry Pi

Did you know...

SSH is the most secure method of accessing any machine remotely. It's also quicker than VNC.

While remotely logging into the full X environment is – as we demonstrated on the previous pages – very useful, it has its disadvantages. Firstly, it's not particularly quick or convenient to do. The user experience can be slow and cumbersome too, but worst of all, it's not as secure as we'd really like.

If you want to take a more convenient and secure approach to accessing your Raspberry Pi from another computer, you'll find that all well-versed Pi enthusiasts will use SSH. SSH stands for Secure Shell and is a cryptographic network protocol which is designed to ensure secure data communication via the command line. While beginners might argue it's easier to remotely access their Raspberry Pi using the full graphical interface, as soon as you've learnt a handful of basic command-line techniques you'll quickly find 'dipping in' to your Raspberry Pi via SSH is by far the most convenient way to talk to it remotely.

You'll be pleased to hear that SSH is already well configured out of the box – there's very little you need to do to make it work, especially if your remote computer runs Linux or OS X, as we're going to demonstrate here.

SSH is easy with Linux and OS X

Assuming your Raspberry Pi is on and connected to a network either by Ethernet or a Wi-Fi dongle, the only piece of information you need is the IP address of your Pi. To discover this, all you have to do is open a terminal window on your Raspberry Pi and type the command `ifconfig` (Fig 1).

If you're connected by Ethernet cable you'll see 'eth0', then several lines of results. The IP address will be the number on the second line next to words 'inet addr'. If you're connected by Wi-Fi,

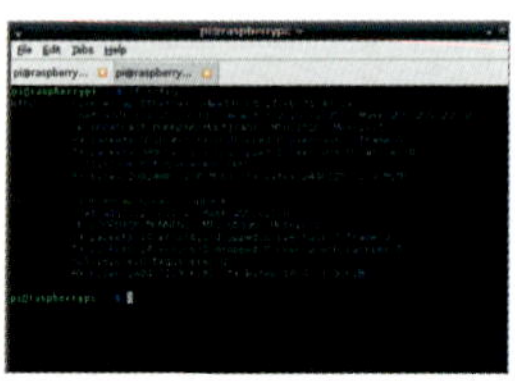

Fig 1: Use the ifconfig command in the terminal to discover the IP address of your Raspberry Pi

the result will be on the second line of 'wlan0'. The IP address itself is a group of four numbers separated by full stops. If you're on your home network, it will likely be similar to 192.168.0.15. We'll use this number for our guide, but replace it with the IP address you've seen via ifconfig.

With this information in hand, all you need to do is open a terminal window on your remote Linux PC and type:

```
ssh pi@192.168.0.15
```

This assumes your Raspberry Pi's username is still the default (which is **pi**) and you're replacing the IP address with the one you made note of just now. If you've added user accounts or changed the default, you'll need to replace the username before the '@' with whatever you've changed it to. When you press Enter, you'll be prompted to enter the password for your Raspberry Pi – again, if it's the default you can type **raspberry**, otherwise type in your Pi's password and press Return.

You'll now see that the username details on the command line have changed to reflect those of your Raspberry Pi – you're now connected remotely. Try looking through your files or using nano to open a file to edit it!

Never type another IP address

Of course, if you take your Raspberry Pi to another network, your Pi's IP address will be different. If you just want to connect to it remotely, it becomes incredibly tiresome to set up your Pi with a keyboard, mouse and monitor just to get the IP address. Wouldn't it be easier if you could just type the Raspberry Pi's name into the terminal to connect? It sounds too good to be true, but it's actually very easy to do.

All you need is a small piece of software which effectively lets you discover hosts and services on your local network by name instead of IP address (Fig 2). To set it up on your Pi all you need to do is open a terminal and type:

```
sudo apt-get install avahi-daemon
```

Once the installation is complete, all you have to do to access your Raspberry Pi via SSH is type the following into the terminal:

```
ssh pi@raspberrypi.local
```

What's more, you can use the name of your Raspberry Pi when you access it via any other form of networking, be it Samba, remote login with VNC or anything else!

SSH with Windows

As is the way with most things in the Windows world, accessing your Raspberry Pi with Microsoft's operating system isn't quite as straightforward as you'd think. Fortunately, there is a useful tool to help. Putty allows you to make your Secure Shell connection and it's easy to set up and use. You can download Putty from: **www.chiark.greenend.org.uk/~sgtatham/putty**

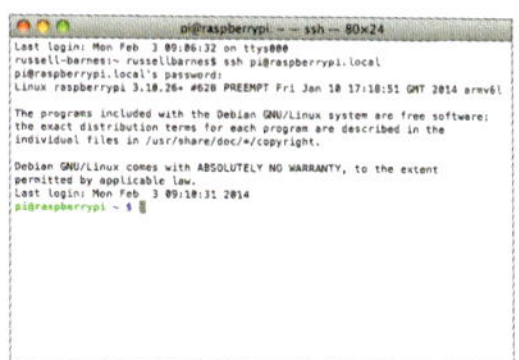

Fig 2: The Avahi tool enables you to log into your Pi via SSH by name, rather than needing to discover its IP address

What you'll need…

Raspbian
www.raspberrypi.org/downloads

Internet connection

Share your files with Samba

Configure your Pi to share the contents of the home folder over your home network

Did you know…

You can network with other Linux, Windows and Mac OS X computers with Samba – it's totally cross-platform.

Regardless of whether you plan to set your Raspberry Pi up as a media centre, gaming machine or full-on development platform, the ability to share and access the contents of your Pi from other machines is very useful.

While the Raspberry Pi is very well configured, by default it doesn't include the ability to share the contents of your home folder with your local network. As you'll see from this guide, though, it's not too difficult to accomplish thanks to Samba and can help you access your scripts, media or documents from any other machine.

```
russb78@dell:~$ sudo apt-get update && sudo apt-get install
 samba samba-common-bin
```

Update & install Samba

01 Open a terminal window and type the following into the terminal to update the Raspbian repository and then install Samba:

```
sudo apt-get update && sudo apt-get install samba samba-common-bin
```

The operation itself shouldn't take too long. Just make sure that you're connected to the internet before you start.

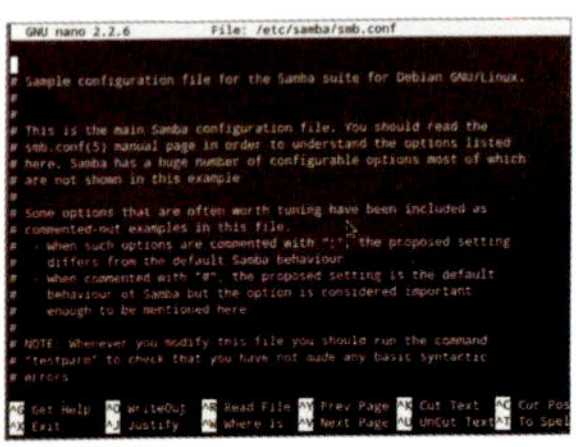

Load smb.conf

02 With the core packages installed, you now need to tell Samba how you want it to work. You do this by putting your preferred settings in Samba's configuration file. This file is called **smb.conf** and it's located in the **/etc/samba** folder.

While it's easy to locate it using the file manager, it's easiest to open and edit it from the command line. Type the following into the terminal window to open it with nano:

```
sudo nano /etc/samba/smb.conf
```

Initial setup

03 Take a look through the file. There's lots of information here and it seems a bit daunting, but there are only a handful of changes and additions to make. Firstly, you need to make sure you have assigned the correct workgroup. Unless your network has been configured differently, it will likely be called WORKGROUP.

To find the workgroup setting, press Ctrl+W and type 'workgroup' then press Enter – this will take you to the first occurrence of the word 'workgroup'. Use the arrow keys to move between lines – the mouse doesn't work in nano.

Windows support

04 If you have Windows computers in your network, you'll need to ensure WINS support is allowed. Assuming you're working from the default **samba.conf** configuration file, you'll find the flag for WINS support a few lines below the workgroup line. Edit it so it looks like this:

```
wins support = yes
```

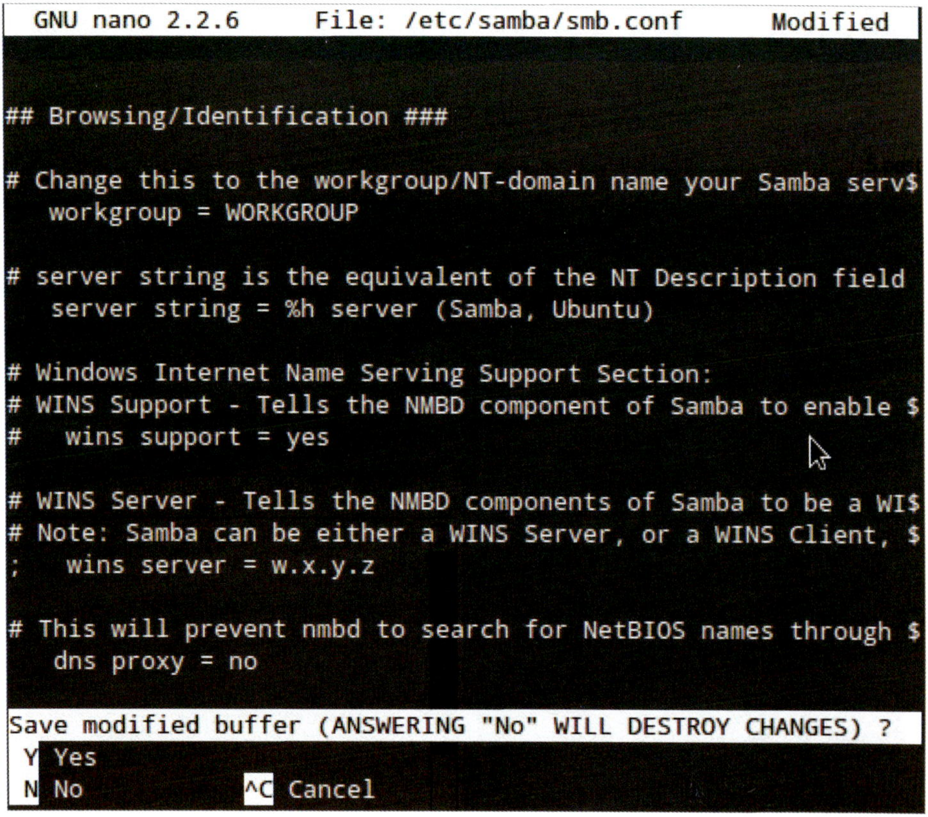

Add your share

05 Next you need to find the section of the file called Share Definitions. Again, you can use the key combination Ctrl+W to open the search function, then type 'share definitions' and press Enter to be taken directly to it – it's located right towards the end of the document.

Go to the very end of the document and add the following:

```
[pi]
path=/home/pi
only guest = no
browseable = yes
writeable = yes
create mask = 0777
director mask = 0777
public = no
```

Set up passwords

06 You have finished editing the **samba.conf** file now. So, to save and exit, press Ctrl+X, then press Y to save, and Enter to exit.

With this configuration, a layer of password security is in place, so we now need to set up a Samba password to use with it. In your terminal window, type the following command:

```
smbpasswd -a pi
```

You'll be prompted to enter and confirm a new password. This is now your username and password for accessing your files.

Restart Samba

07 The final step is simply to restart Samba for your new settings to take effect.

At the terminal, type the following command to do so:

```
sudo /etc/init.d/samba restart
```

The next time you look at your home network from another machine, you'll see your Raspberry Pi's home folder listed as a share.

What you'll need...

A second computer
External storage

Did you know...

SD cards don't last forever so always make sure you've got a backup of your files and your entire OS.

Back up your Pi

Take the initiative and back up your Raspberry Pi to make sure you never lose files again

While the Raspberry Pi is a very solid piece of kit, failure can happen, so it's best to be well prepared and keep your files safe.

The good news is that the Pi's files are all kept externally on the SD card. If your Pi breaks, everything will still be available on the SD card and accessible from elsewhere. The SD card is still susceptible to problems, though. There are a number of ways to back up a Pi. The methods can be broken down into two main categories: saving the important files and creating an exact copy of the state of the SD card. The former involves having copies of files elsewhere, while the latter has you create the same kind of image that you'd normally write to the SD card when installing Raspbian or other Pi-operating systems.

Important files

To save important files, we need to create a copy on an external source, such as external hard drive or another PC. One of the best methods to do this doesn't even involve a Pi; all you need is a PC or laptop with a card reader and you're good to go.

Turn off your Pi, unplug it and remove the SD card from the slot. Find the SD card reader on your PC and slot it in. The main file system of the SD card can be read by Linux PCs by default, and a Windows or Mac computer once you've installed a program that lets it read the ext file system, such as Ext2Fsd. On Windows, the SD card will be listed with the rest of the drives under My Computer (Fig 1). On Linux and Mac, it will be listed wherever storage is shown on the menus and file managers.

Once you've found the SD card on here, open it up and navigate to **home** and then **pi**. This is where the Documents, Downloads, Desktop and other directories can be found. All you need to do is select the files you want to copy and move them to a secure directory on your PC or a connected external hard drive.

If you want to keep the files on another computer, that's fine, but it will be prone to the exact same problems as the Pi in the long run. Keeping them on an external hard drive is a good idea, and putting them on a cloud storage service is better yet, enabling you to access them from anywhere with an internet connection (Fig 2).

Cloning

Creating a clone depends on what operating system you're using on your main computer. For Macs and Linux, you can use a simple command-line tool called **dd** to create an exact copy of the SD card (Fig 3). This is done in the terminal emulator or command line, so bring that up first. Make sure the SD card is plugged in and enter:

```
$ fdisk -l
```

This lists all connected storage devices. The SD card will have 2, 4 or 8GB of space, depending on its size. It'll likely be listed as something like **/dev/sd[x]**, where x is the letter the computer attaches to the SD card. To copy it using dd, enter the following into the terminal:

```
$ dd if=/dev/sd[x] of=backup.img bs=1M
```

You can also add a path to the image you're creating to put it in a specific folder. The process will take some time, and will produce a multi-gigabyte file which you can then write onto the SD by reversing the previous command:

```
$ dd if= backup.img of=/dev/sd[x] bs=1M
```

While this is useful as a backup, you can also use the image to mass-produce SD cards to give to friends or keep in the various places where you use your Raspberry Pi.

Windows

To create a clone on Windows, we can use the Win32 Disk Imager (Fig 4). Download it from here to install it: **bit.ly/L8JdYG**

Once installed, insert the SD card and launch the software. Choose a name for the backup file and select the SD card from the list of devices. Now press Read and it will create the backup file. Again, this might take a while; however, this time you are at least shown a progress bar.

Storing your cloned image is a little more difficult than your important files – the size of the image being in the gigabytes means it will fill up a lot of cloud-storage services. If you have the space, definitely keep it on there; however, you may need to put it on an external hard drive.

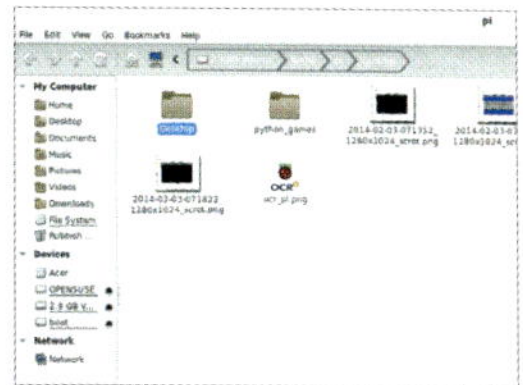

Fig 1: Accessing the SD card from another PC is an easy alternative to transferring files between machines via a USB stick

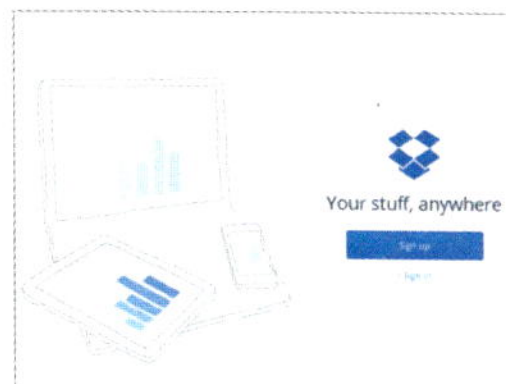

Fig 2: Cloud storage services make backing up files easy and secure, as they're a lot less prone to problems

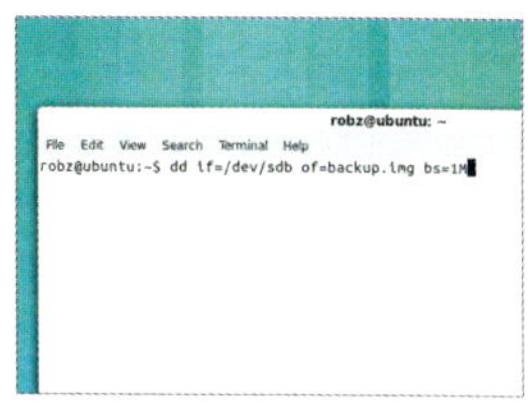

Fig 3: The dd tool is what you'll use on a Linux and Mac computer, and it's available by default in the terminal emulators

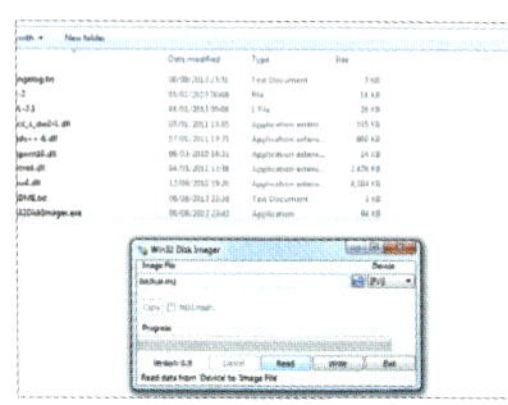

Fig 4: Win32 Disk Imager makes backing up the entire OS easy, and you can even use it to write the image back to the SD card

GPIO port explained

Learn how to harness the power of the GPIO port on your Raspberry Pi. It's easier than you think…

What you'll need…

Prototyping equipment

RPi.GPIO
https://pypi.python.org/pypi/RPi.GPIO

Above The Pi's GPIO port comprises 26 pins, used to connect it with all manner of electronic components/devices

The general-purpose input/output (GPIO) pins on your Raspberry Pi are often central to the success of the projects you'll find in this book. Without them you have no way of interfacing with the real world, be it to trigger lights, buttons or buzzers or read sensors.

GPIO pins aren't special to the Pi; they're actually a standard designed to help control input and output behaviour with all kinds of integrated circuits. Usually you'll find that any one GPIO pin has no particular use pre-defined and they tend to be turned off by default.

Raspberry Pi GPIO

The GPIO pins on the Raspberry Pi can be controlled and triggered in many ways. You can use them from the terminal directly and through Bash scripts, or you can control them using specially designed modules for popular programming languages. Since Python is the official language of the Raspberry Pi, you'll find the GPIO module for Python gives you among the best control for inputs and outputs available. The library is called RPi.GPIO and is installed by default on all Raspberry Pi, but can otherwise be installed in exactly the same way you'd install any useful Python library. The project is hosted on SourceForge and can be found at **sourceforge.net/projects/raspberry-gpio-python**. You'll also find useful links, information and examples of how to use and control the GPIO pins from within simple Python scripts. It helps to have a basic understanding of Python if you plan to use RPi.GPIO, so we'd recommend a basic introductory course like the one found at **www.codecademy.com** or by reading the official Python documentation at **www.python.org/doc**.

There are 26 GPIO pins on the Raspberry Pi and you can use the vast majority of them in any way you want. There are a few pins that have special purposes, though, so we recommend you familiarise yourself with their layout. For example, the very top row of pins are designed to offer power to external devices like buttons and lights. Since an earth line (often called 'ground') is needed to safely create a circuit, you'll also find several ground pins located in the GPIO port.

Below Become familiar with the layout of the GPIO pins and what they do – some have special purposes, such as ground pins

How to use GPIO pins

To exploit the power of the GPIO port you'll need a few essential components, the most important of which are jumper leads. Since the pins on the port are 'male', you'll need to purchase either 'female to male' or 'female to female' cables, depending on what hardware you intend to connect to your Pi. Assuming the device you're connecting to also has mail connectors, 'female to female' jumper leads will do nicely, but often you'll be using a breadboard to prototype your circuits, in which case 'female to male' connectors are preferred. Cables and breadboards can be bought very cheaply from just about any online store that sells Raspberry Pi accessories and can usually be found in the 'prototyping' section of the store.

Naming conventions

Once you're ready to connect your device, the next task is to find the right pin for the job. While it's true that all GPIO ports are multipurpose, some are more multipurpose than others! As we've already discovered, some pins are reserved for 5V, 3.3V and ground. Others also have special capabilities, but what's worse is that they can also be called different things. For example, GPIO 18 is also known as pin 12 and PCM_CLK. This particular pin (around halfway down the right side of the GPIO port) is capable of hardware pulse-width modulation (PWM), and is useful for controlling LED lights and motors among other things.

The pin-naming convention you use in your Python scripts can be set manually. This can either be set as BCM (the Broadcom pin name) or the physical pin locations (BOARD).

You'll see in any of the projects where we're using the GPIO port, the following line with either BCM or BOARD in the brackets:

```
GPIO.setmode(GPIO.BCM)
```

The easiest way to deal with the GPIO pin-naming issues is to pick a convention and stick with it!

Did you know…

The RPi.GPIO library has some really useful documentation. All you need to do is click on the 'wiki' on Sourceforge.

What you'll need...

Raspberry Pi
Raspbian:
www.raspberrypi.org/downloads

Pi Camera
Ashton's picam module:
https://github.com/ashtons/picam

Did you know...

The Camera board uses the same kind of sensor and hardware as the cameras in modern mobile phones.

Use the Camera board

Here's how to get your new Pi Camera set up on your Raspberry Pi, and how to use it...

One of the most recent Raspberry Pi accessories is the tiny Pi Camera board – a small PCB with a camera sensor mounted to it that connects via a ribbon to the Raspberry Pi. It's not exactly plug-and-play, so you'll need to do some extra set up.

The Pi Camera has multiple functions, such as for time-lapse photography, using as a webcam, or even as an optical sensor for a Pi-powered robot, like the one we're making here. Because it doesn't take up any USB slots, and draws very low power, it can be a lot more versatile than a standard webcam.

The Pi Camera itself is not a low-quality piece of kit either – with a 5MP sensor, it's also able to create up to 1080p quality video, the same as the Raspberry Pi's HDMI output.

Attach Camera

01 To attach the Camera to the Raspberry Pi, locate the slot between the Ethernet and HDMI port and gently lift up the fastener. Insert the ribbon of the Camera board, making sure to align the ribbon's connectors with those on the Pi. The blue tab on the flex should be facing the Ethernet port.

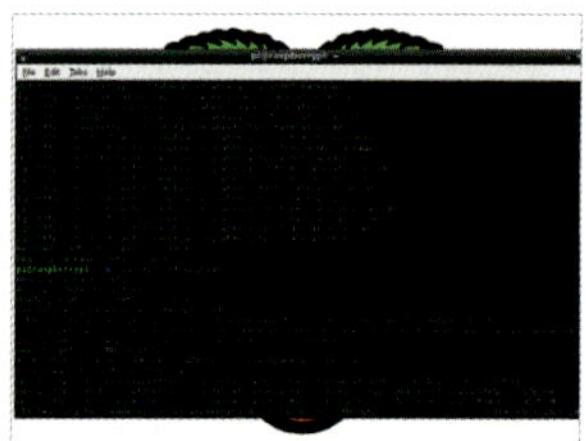

Pi preparation

02 Before we try to enable the Raspberry Pi Camera, we need to make sure our firmware and software are all up to date with a quick software upgrade. In Raspbian, we do this by opening the terminal and then using:

```
$ sudo apt-get update
```

...followed by:

```
$ sudo apt-get upgrade
```

Pi config

03 Once that's finished, run in the terminal or command line

```
$ sudo raspi-config
```

to start the standard configuration screen. Navigate down to Enable Camera, press Enter and then simply key over to enable and confirm with another press of Enter. Select Finish and then reboot.

Take pictures

04 To take pictures with the Raspberry Pi Camera, you'll simply need to enter:

```
$ raspistill -o image.png
```

This will show a five-second preview of the input of the camera and then capture the last frame of the video.

Record video

05 To record a video, we use a similar command, raspivid, like so:

```
$ raspivid -o video.h264
```

It will also take five seconds of video by default.

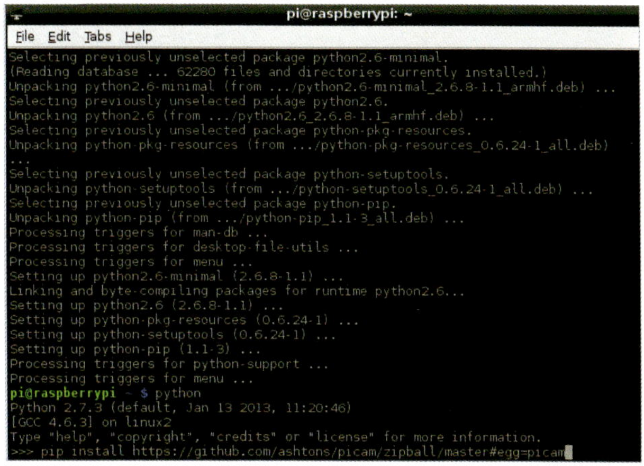

Picam

06 If you want to do a little more with the Pi Camera, there's a simple Python wrapper currently available called picam. You'll need to install it first, though, and we'll use pip for that. Install pip with:

```
$ sudo apt-get install
python-pip
```

and then enter:

```
pip install https://
github.com/ashtons/picam/
zipball/ master#egg=picam
master#egg=picam
```

Picam photos

07 With the module installed we can now use Python to construct a script to take photos with the picam module. It's not as difficult as you might think, so even if you've never used Python before it's worth a try. All you need to do is enter:

```
import picam
i = picam.takePhoto()
i.save('/home/pi/test.jpg')
```

And running it will take a photo called test.jpg.

Advanced photos

08 You can have it take photos of specific size and quality with a time-based name by editing the code to look like this:

```
import picam
import time
ii = picam.
takePhotoWithDetails(640,480,
85)
filename = "/tmp/
picam-%s.jpg" % time.
strftime("%Y%m%d-%H%M%S")
ii.save(filename)
```

Picam video and more

09 Picam also allows you to take video in a similar way to the above, with the main difference being that you'll use the recordVideo command. You can use the code to take photos or video at regular intervals for time-lapse, or have it trigger during a specified event.

> "With a 5MP sensor, it's able to create up to 1080p video, the same as the Raspberry Pi's HDMI output"

Program with Scratch

An interactive guide to coding with the Pi's graphical programming language

What you'll need...

Scratch

Internet connection

Did you know...

The website for Scratch, **http://scratch.mit.edu**, contains lots of programs and games other users have made.

Would you like to delve into the world of animation and game creation? Do you want to bring your creative ideas to life without learning a software-development language? With Scratch you can do all this, and much more.

Scratch 1.4 is already installed on the official 'wheezy' Raspbian operating system image. If your Raspberry Pi doesn't already have Scratch installed, don't worry, just hop on over to the official MIT Scratch website to find the download and install instructions.

To begin, all we need to do is open the Scratch Studio. Click on Scratch's cat icon on the desktop, or find Scratch in the LXDE desktop menu.

The Scratch Studio is a complete development environment. It's divided up into a number of separate panels. Each panel has a specific role in the app-construction process and its own specific set of features and tools.

Scratch studio projects

01 Located at the top of the Studio are three quick-access icons and the main menu (Fig 2).

The first globe-style icon sets the language for the Studio. The other two buttons provide rapid access to the project save and share features.

Under the 'File' menu there's a typical set of file-management features to open, save and import Scratch projects. There is also a 'Project Notes' option where we are able to enter feature descriptions and comments.

The 'Edit' menu contains a mixed bag of animation, image and audio-editing tools. While the 'Help' section provides access to the browser-hosted help pages.

Rather interestingly, the 'Share' menu allows us to share our projects with the whole world. Any Scratch project can be posted onto the Scratch community website via the 'Share This Project Online...' option

and the 'Upload To Scratch Server' form (Fig 3).

Let's load the 'Aquarium' example project. Select the 'Open...' option in the 'File' menu to display the Open Project dialog. From the list of large buttons on the left, click on the one called 'Examples'. Next, on the right, select the 'Animation' folder with a double click. Then select the '6 Aquarium' item. The open dialog window contents should look like the one in Fig 4.

With the Aquarium project loaded our Scratch Studio should look similar to Fig 1. We'll begin our Studio tour with the staging area.

Fig 2: Scratch Studio Menu – Scratch Studio's main menu and shortcut icons in action

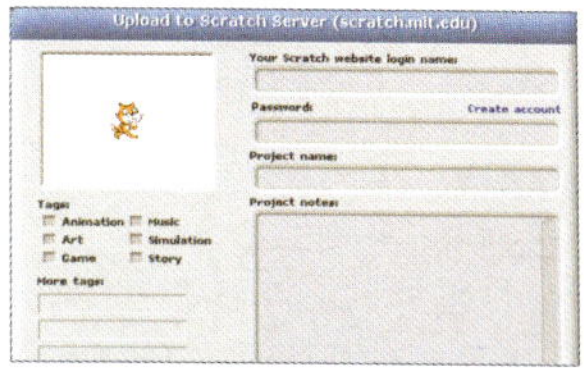

Fig 3: Project Share Dialog – We can share our projects using the Studio's Share menu

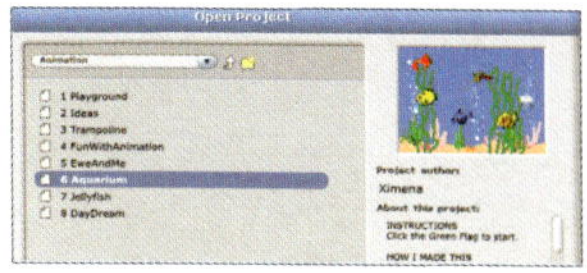

Fig 4: File Open Dialog – Use the Studio's File menu and 'Open…' to load the Aquarium project

Scratch studio stage

02 The stage is where all the action takes place and is located at the upper right of the Scratch Studio.

The stage is constructed from graphical elements called sprites. Here we have plants, bubbles, fish and other creatures. You can also add and create your own assets with scratch, but we'll come to that later.

At the top of the 'Staging Area' there's a green flag and a red circle. Click on the green flag to bring the aquarium to life. Now spend a little time studying the Aquarium animation. Note the creature's movements and rising bubbles. The red circle icon stops the action.

We can set the view mode with the three buttons located just above the green flag.

The two left-hand buttons increase or decrease the size of the Staging Area panel. A smaller Staging Area means the central area of the Studio increases in relative size compared.

The right-hand button is the Presentation Mode which displays the stage in full-screen mode (see Fig 5). Exit presentation mode with the curly arrow button at the top left, or press the 'esc' key.

Scratch studio sprites

03 Beneath the Staging Area is the collection of sprites for this project. The 'Stage' sprite is separated from the rest. It's a little different to the others and acts as the background image for the stage.

The three buttons across the top of this area offer various ways to create a new sprite. The first button opens up a blank canvas in the Paint Editor. The second button creates a new sprite based in an image file, as selected by the popup file section dialog window. The third will select a random image from the pre-installed image collection.

We can manage sprites directly from the stage using the four buttons to the right of the main menu. Here we click on a particular button and then a sprite on the stage.

Fig 5: Stage Presentation Mode – The Studio's stage presentation mode is the best way to see the project

Use Scratch blocks and tools

Getting to grips with the Scratch Studio toolbox

Situated in the centre of the Studio is the Edit Panel. The panel contents relate to the currently selected sprite.

Let's start by selecting the jelly fish sprite, called Creature1, from the Sprite Collection area.

At the top we have the sprite's image and name, plus an indication of its current stage coordinates and direction. On the left are three animation control buttons. The top button will rotate the sprite, the second switches between left and right-facing states, and the third turns animation off.

Below are three Edit Panel tabs. The script tab is where block scripts are created. Here's where we'll drag and drop our blocks, snapping them together in various combinations.

To change a sprite's visual appearance we'll use the 'Costumes' tab. Each sprite can have one or more costumes. For example, the jellyfish has two costumes (Fig 1). Each costume has buttons to edit, copy and delete. New costumes can be painted, imported or captured using the three 'New Costumes' buttons. The sound tab allows us to add audio to our project.

Fig 1: Jellyfish Sprite Costumes – The jellyfish sprite has two different costumes

Scratch Block Styles

01 The 'Blocks Palette' contains the complete collection of scripting blocks. Blocks come in three basic styles, namely hats, stacks and reporters (see Fig 3 on the opposite page).

A hat-style block will start block script execution based on a specific event. The classic hat block is the 'green flag' click event. However, there are numerous other hat blocks, including hat blocks that start script execution after a specific key press, a mouse click and even following sensor event from the some GPIO connected hardware. As you can probably tell, this offers a lot of options to Scratch programmers.

Reporter blocks allow us to specify textual, numeric and boolean values. They fit into specific shaped 'holes' in other blocks. A rectangular reporter will contain a text string. While the rounded end reporters are associated with numeric values, angle-ended reporters contain boolean true and false values.

Stack blocks are the core script building elements. They interconnect with other blocks via their top-edge notches and bottom-edge bumps. Many stack blocks contain 'holes' for reporter style blocks, which will modify their operation depending on the specified reporter block values.

The Scratch block collection is divided into groups. We select a block group using the eight buttons located at the top of the Block Palette panel, namely 'Motion', Control', 'Looks' and so on. These groups are colour coded. Apart from aiding block selection this colour coding provides a visual clue to a block's type when reading a block script in the Edit Panel.

Fig 2: Sound Recorder Tool – Scratch Studio includes a tool to record our own sounds

Scratch Block Help

02 As we've seen, there are many blocks, each with their own specific functionality and capabilities.

In one way this is great news. A large block collection means Scratch can be used in a vast range of software projects, such as games, animation, music, graphics, math, science, robotics, electronics and much more.

However, the wide selection of blocks can be quite a challenge for the novice Scratch coder. To help with this problem the Scratch Studio designers have included an informative set of block-centric help pages.

A simple right click on any block will display a pop-up help page option. The help page contains context-specific descriptions, graphical images and, where appropriate, a script example of how to use this particular block (Fig 4).

It's a terrific feature which greatly simplifies the process of deciding which blocks to use. More importantly, studying these help pages is a highly effective way to enhance our scripting skills and discover the potential contained within Scratch's feature-rich block collection.

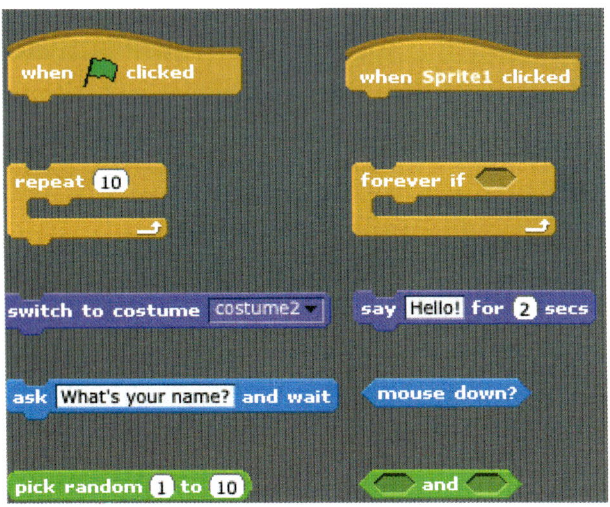

Fig 3: Block Style Examples – the Scratch blocks come in a number of different styles

> **Did you know…**
>
> There is more than one option available to start your scripts beyond the standard Green Flag block.

Block Script Walkthrough

03 Let's dig deeper into how a block script works in practice. For this, we will use a simple Aquarium project block script. From the 'Sprite Collection' panel select the Stage sprite. Then go back to the central 'Edit Panel' and select the 'Scripts' tab.

There's just a single block script. Starting at the top there's a 'green flag' hat-style block to kick off the activity. Next there's a 'forever loop'. The blocks inside this loop are actioned until the stop button is pressed. This forever loop block contains two other blocks.

The first inner script block selects the next background image. Click on the 'Backgrounds' tab to view all the stage images. The second inner block simply pauses execution for a number of seconds. Setting the value to '1' means that this script will pause for a second before then performing the action specified by the next block.

It's important that you remember these two blocks are enclosed in the forever loop block. So, the stage background images will be displayed in sequence for one second each.

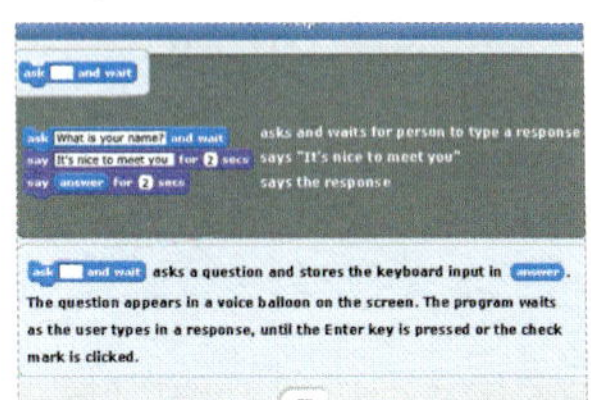

Fig 4: Block Help Window – Example of the help window associated with an 'ask and wait' block

What you'll need...

Raspbian
Scratch

Did you know...

Scratch was made by MIT Media Lab in 2003. It's ideal as a first language for children as young as five years of age.

Make a drawing app with Scratch

Here's how to add colour and pencil sizes using the built-in Pen tool

The aim of this tutorial is to use the Pen tool in Scratch to develop a more useful drawing application that you can then expand on yourself. It uses only the sprites that are bundled with the installation on the Pi, but you could easily make some custom ones to generate the colour changes.

All you have to do is move the pencil cursor over the colour sprite for it to start using that colour, then simply click and draw. Any time the colour is changed a sound is played to let you know. Pressing up or down on the keyboard arrow keys increases and decreases the size of the pencil nib, not the sprite for it. A sound plays for this as well.

As with all Scratch programs you simply click on the green flag to run the scripts, the red circle to stop.

Blocks of code
The code is split up into blocks that have specific shapes to fit into each other, representing the programming syntax visually

Sprites on call
The sprites loaded to the system appear here and will sit in the middle of the screen unless ordered otherwise

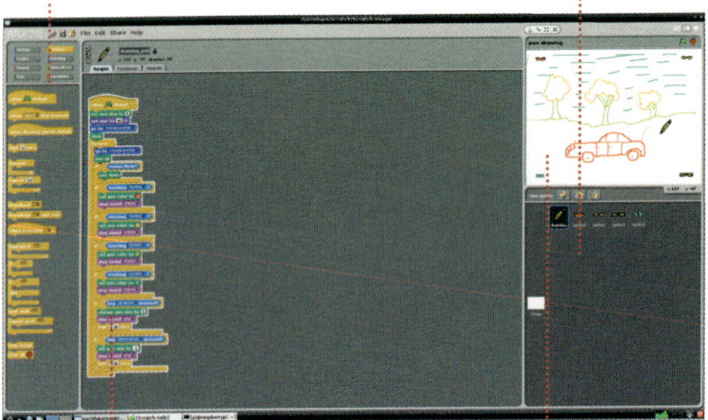

The sprite script
Each sprite has its own scripted program and can be started on a variety of conditions or actions

Customise the look
A sprite can be repainted to look completely different or it can use photos and camera grabs

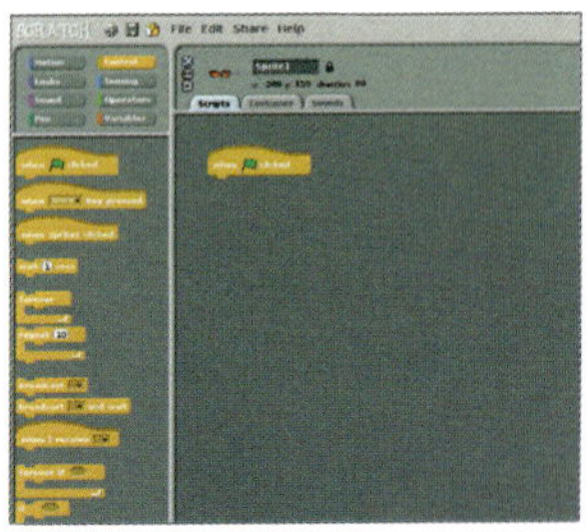

Load up sprites

01 Click in the top-right to use the Full Stage option. Then, in the sprite window, click on Load Sprite. Select the red sunglasses and load them. They will appear in the sprite window. Click on Control in the commands window. Drag the 'when clicked' header into the Script window.

Position in corner

02 Click on Motion and drag 'go to x:' into the Scripts window. Lock it to the bottom of 'when clicked'. Enter values of x=-200 and y=155. Click on Looks and drag a 'set size to' block and lock that on. Set the value to 40% by clicking and typing it in.

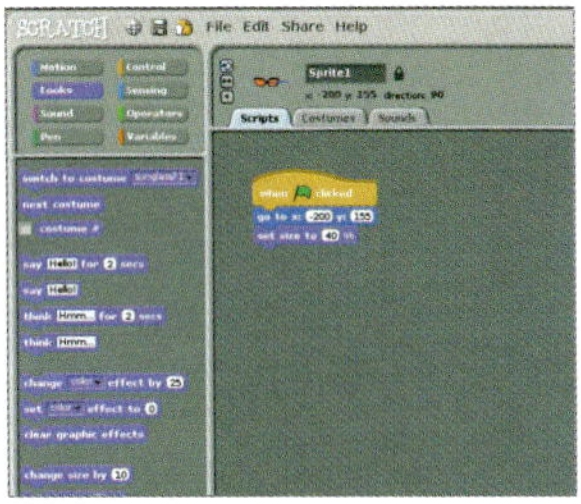

More sprites for colour

03 Repeat this process for the orange, green and blue sunglasses sprites. Create the code blocks for each, positioning them at x=200, y=155 as we did with the red. Go back to Load Sprites and load the Drawing pen. Delete the script that comes with this by right-clicking over each element and selecting Delete.

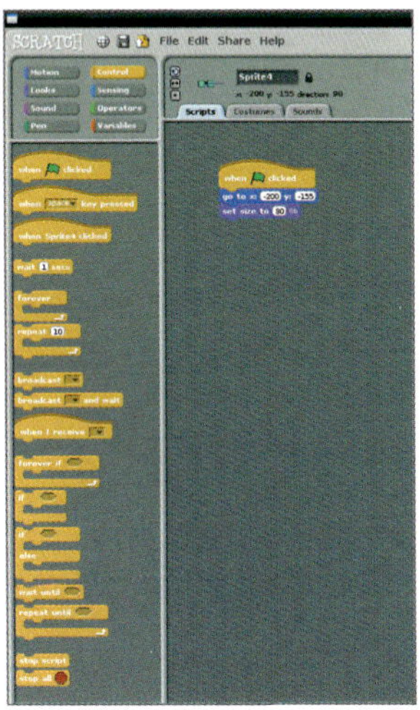

Set up the drawing

04 Under Control, drag a 'when clicked' header in. Get a 'set pen size' from under Pen. Click on the variable and enter 5. Go to Motion and get the 'go to' block. Click on the drop down arrow and select 'mouse-pointer'. From Pen group drag out 'clear'.

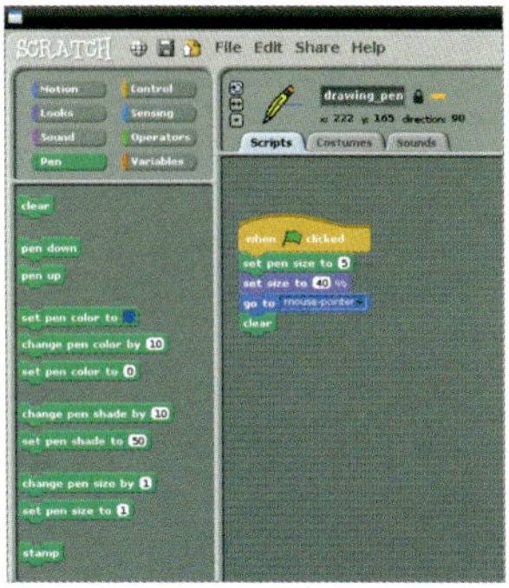

Controlling the pen draw

05 From the Control group drag out a 'forever' loop which the rest of the code goes inside. Go to Motion and drag out a 'go to'. Click on the down arrow and select 'mouse-pointer'. Go to Pen and grab a 'pen up'. Tuck this under the 'go to'.

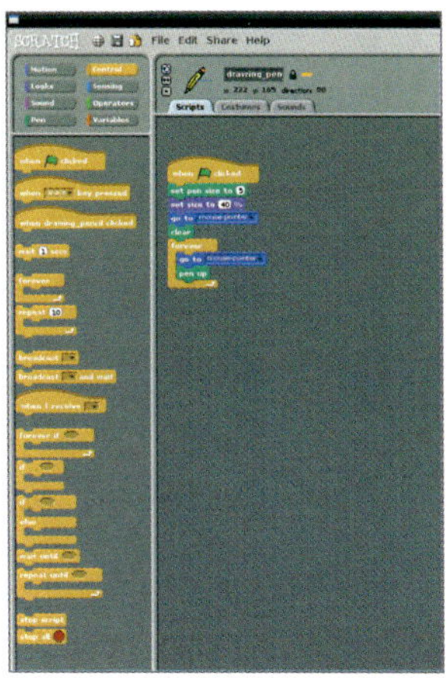

Drawing and colour control tools

06 Go to Control and grab an 'if'. Grab a 'mouse down?' from the Sensing group and place it into the 'if' operator. Get a 'pen down' from the Pen group. Put this under and inside the 'if'. The next step is repeated four times, once for each colour and sprite.

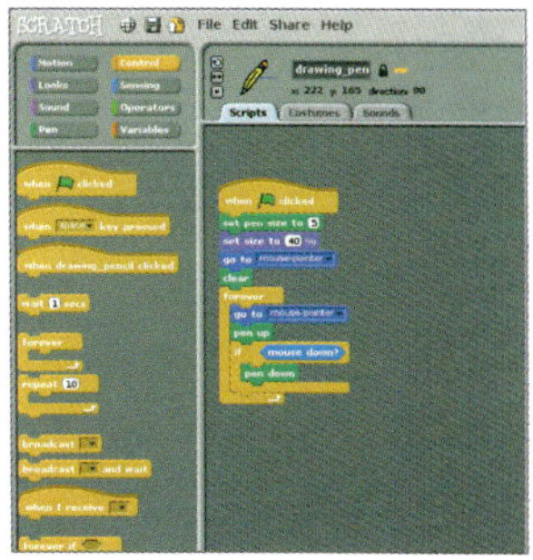

How to control the colour changes

07 From Control grab an 'if' and from Sensing put a 'touching' condition inside. Set trigger to Sprite1. From Pen get 'set pen color to', click the colour square and use the dropper to sample the sprite. From Sound get 'play sound' and select 'meow'.

Setting the pen size

08 Add another 'if' and put 'key pressed' as the subject. Select 'up arrow' as the trigger. Get 'change pen size by' and enter 1. Use a 'play sound' with 'pop' then add a 'wait' for 0.25secs. Repeat this group but with the 'down arrow' and pen size of -1.

Create a Snake clone in Scratch

Design your own version of Snake to test your new programming skills!

What you'll need...

Scratch project archives
http://http://scratch.mit.edu/explore/?date=ever

Did you know...

Snake is a very popular beginner game that started life in the arcades in the Seventies and is still popular today.

Here, we will create a version of the classic Snake game where you move the snake around the Scratch stage using the arrow keys. You control the head of the snake and must avoid a collision with either the body of the snake or the edge of the stage.

The snake body grows longer each time you eat an egg. You get points added to your score for eating good yellow eggs and lose points for eating bad black eggs. There are also bonus sprites to eat for extra points.

By following this tutorial you will learn to create your own simple sprite graphics, send and receive broadcast events, use a list variable to store data, play sound effects, generate random numbers and use sensing commands to detect when a sprite is touching something.

Egg sprite
The Egg sprite appears randomly on the screen and lets other sprites know when it has been eaten (touched by the snake tongue)

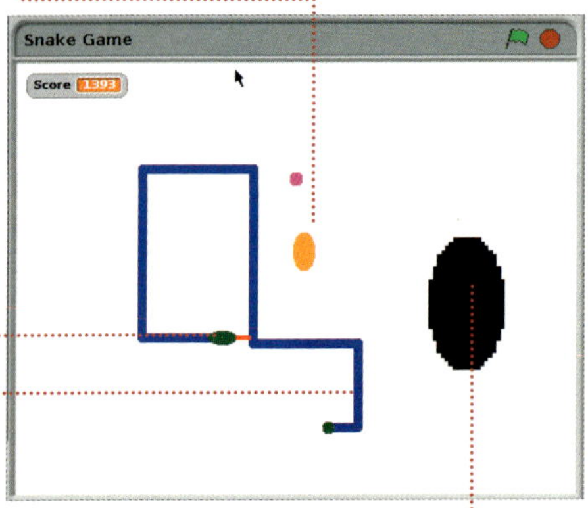

Snake sprite
The Snake sprite moves the head around the stage and draws the body behind it. It also detects collisions with the body or edge

Tail sprite
The Tail sprite follows the head, erasing the end of the body so the snake moves, and pausing when it needs to grow

Bad Egg sprite
The Bad Egg sprite also appears randomly but decreases the score when eaten. It also grows in size, getting harder to avoid

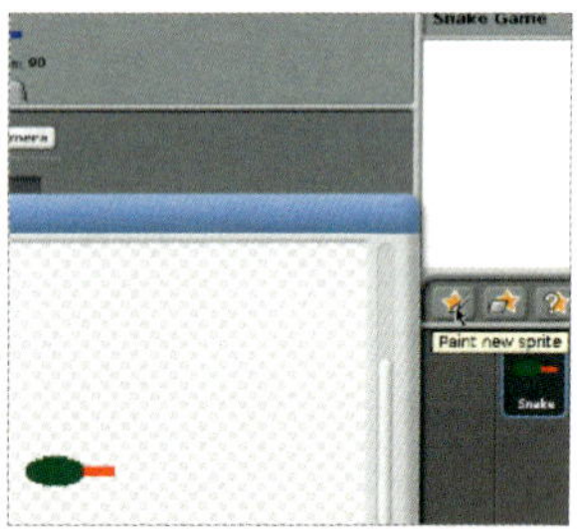

Paint the Snake sprite

01 Click the New Sprite: Paintbrush icon to paint the Snake sprite. In the Paint Editor, draw a small green ellipse for the snake head and add a red rectangle for the tongue. It's important that the tongue is a different colour to the head. Name your sprite Snake.

Add a Snake sound

02 When the Snake tongue touches the snake body or the edge of the stage, we are going to play a Game Over sound. We need to add this sound to the Snake sprite. With the Snake sprite selected, click the Sound tab and choose Import. Select the Electronic>Screech sound.

Respond to arrow keys

03 Drag four when key pressed commands from the Control palette, and four point in direction commands from the Motion palette. Configure them as shown so that the up arrow changes the direction to 0 degrees (up) and so on. Click the green flag above the stage to test this.

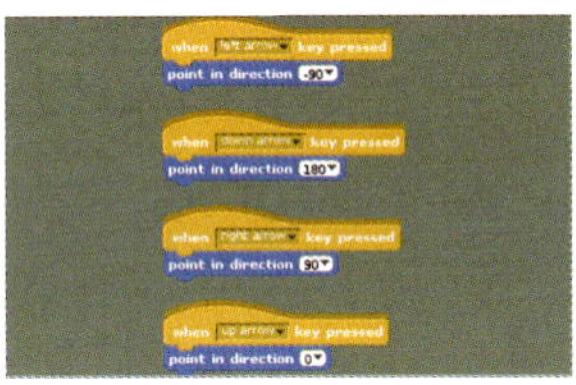

Make Snake variables

04 Click on the Variables palette. Make two variables, Score and Speed, that are visible to all sprites. Make a list called Next Direction which is visible to all sprites; it will store the sequence of directions that the head takes. Only have the Score variable checked so it appears on the stage.

Initialise Snake variables

05 Use a 'when green flag clicked' Control command and initialise the Snake variables as shown, using commands from the Variables palette. We want to start each game with an empty Next Direction list, so delete all of its entries. The Score must start at zero. The Speed sets difficulty.

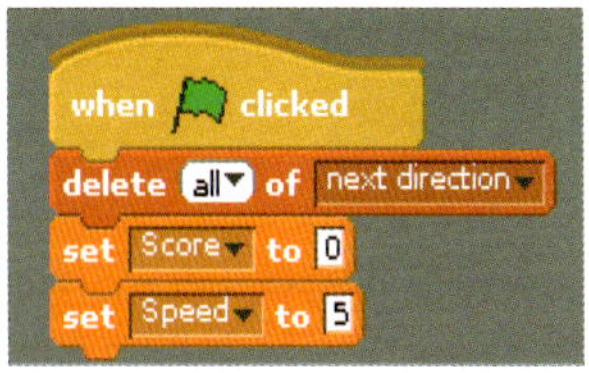

Draw Snake body

06 Use commands from the Pen palette to control the drawing of the snake body. You should also use commands from the Motion palette to move the snake to the centre of the stage and point left at the beginning of each game. The pen is up until the snake is in the starting position. In the next steps we'll use colours to check to see if the head is touching anything it shouldn't.

Add main action loop

07 Use a 'forever' command with an 'if-else' command nested inside. We have a collision if the red tongue is touching the blue body (the head is always touching the body) or the Snake sprite is touching the edge. Use the Eyedropper tool to select colours within Scratch.

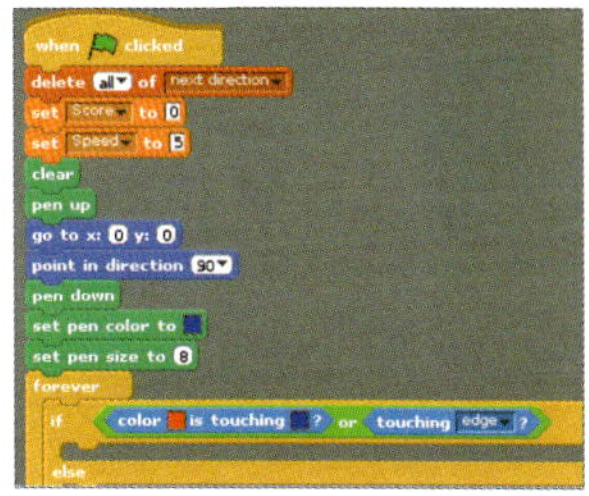

Handle Game Over

08 When a collision has been detected, broadcast a Game Over event (you'll need to create a new event) to the other sprites so they can also react. Also, play the Screech sound effect and stop all scripts so that the snake freezes in its current position at the end of the game.

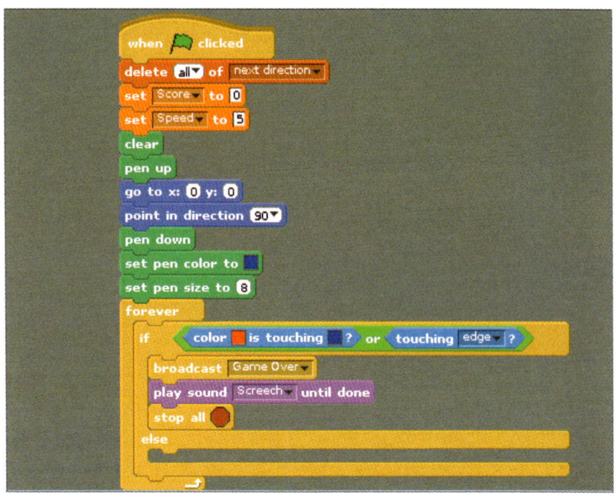

Handle movement

09 Now handle the typical case where there is no collision and the snake must move in its current direction. The pen is down so it will draw the body. The Speed variable determines how many steps to move. Add the current direction to the Next Direction list for the tail to read.

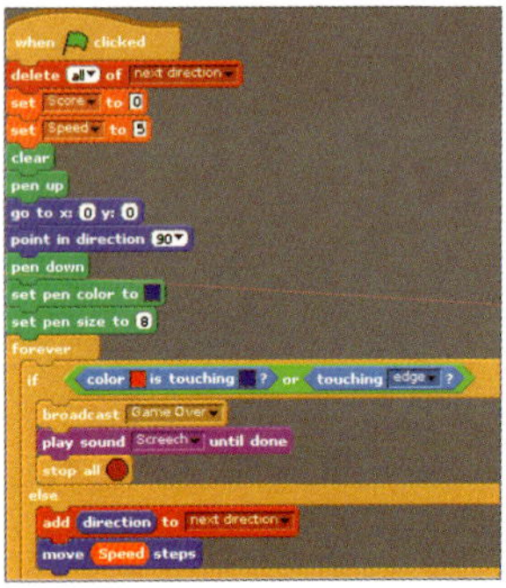

Try out the snake

10 You can now try out your Snake sprite. It will move around the screen in response to pressing the arrow keys. It will draw its body, which will just get longer and longer because we need the tail to erase it. And it will screech and end the game on detecting a collision.

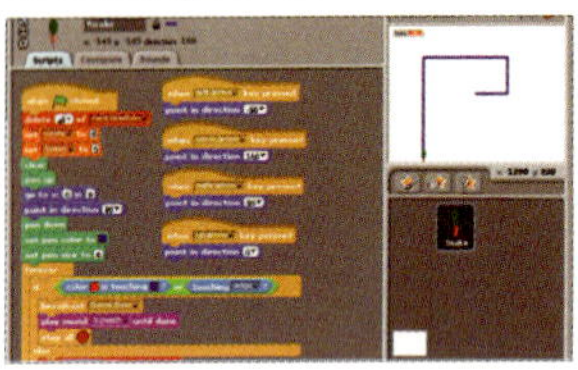

Paint the tail

11 Click the New Sprite: Paintbrush icon to paint the Tail sprite. Draw a small green circle to represent the end of the tail. Name this sprite Tail. The Tail sprite will follow the Snake and erase the end of its tail so that the snake body doesn't grow indefinitely.

Make a Grow variable

12 Make a Grow variable which is for this sprite only – no other sprites need access to it. The Grow variable is used to determine when the snake body needs to grow and the tail therefore needs to pause before following to allow the head to get further ahead.

Handle events

13 The Tail needs to listen for two new events which you create as you need them. When it receives an Egg Eaten event from one of the Egg sprites, it sets Grow=1 so that the tail can pause. And when it receives a Game Over event from the Snake, it must freeze.

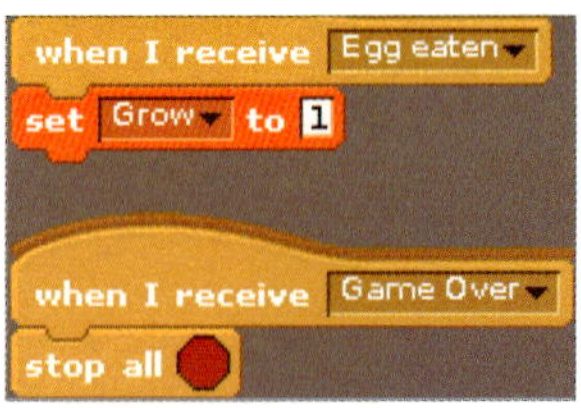

Initialise the tail

14 When the green flag is clicked to start the game, Grow is set to 1 so the snake gets a short body. Move to the centre of the stage with the pen up and configure the pen to draw a trail the same colour and size as the stage background so that it erases the body.

Grow and move

15 Use a 'forever' command to keep the tail moving. If Grow is 1 it should pause and reset Grow to 0 – this makes the body grow longer. Use the first value from Next Direction to set the direction and remove it so you get a new value next time. Move Speed steps.

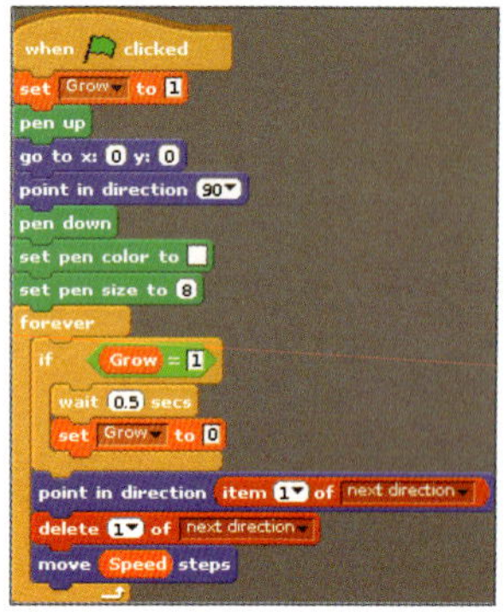

Try out the tail

16 Now you can try out the Tail sprite. The snake won't keep growing yet because it won't receive any Egg Eaten events. But the tail will follow the snake head around the stage, erasing the snake body as it goes by drawing over it with a white pen (the same colour as the background).

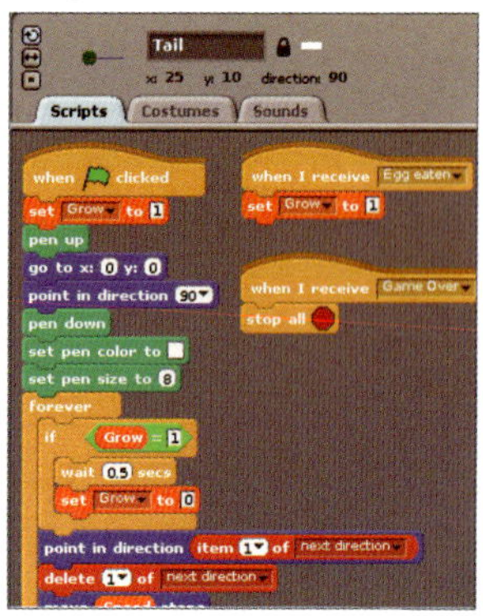

Paint the Egg sprite

17 Click the New Sprite: Paintbrush icon to paint a new sprite. In the Paint Editor, draw a small yellow ellipse. Name the sprite Egg. The Egg will appear randomly on the stage and cause the snake to grow and increase its score.

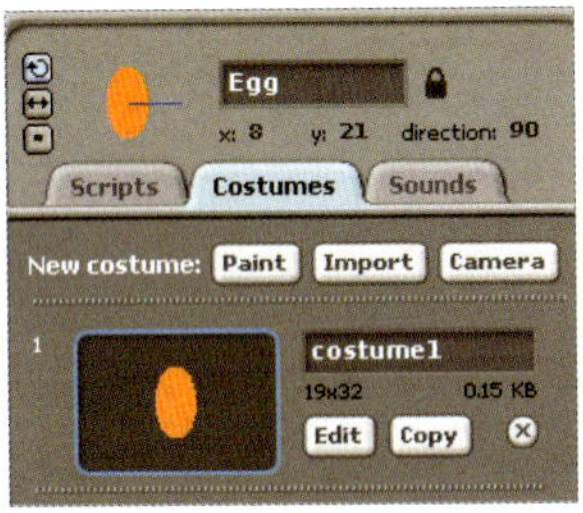

Add Egg sound

18 Go to the Sounds tab for the Egg sprite and import the Percussion>Cymbal Crash sound. Or you can choose a different sound if you like. This sound will play when the snake eats an egg.

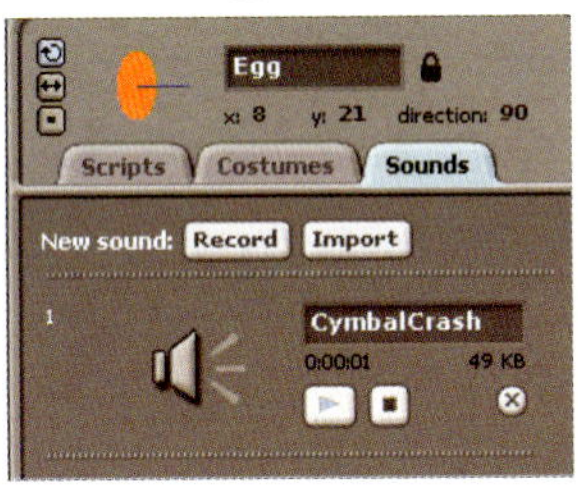

Add Egg scripts

19 Copy the Egg script so that the Egg appears randomly at the start of the game. When the Egg senses that it has been eaten, it must hide, play the Cymbal sound (or whatever you chose in step 18), update the score, broadcast the Egg Eaten event and then randomly appear again. When the Game Over event is received, it must stop.

Make Bad Egg

20 Create the black Bad Egg in the same way as the Egg but using a different graphic and the Instruments>StringPluck sound. Drag the Egg's green flag scripts onto the Bad Egg to copy them – just change the sound that's played and reduce the score instead of increasing it.

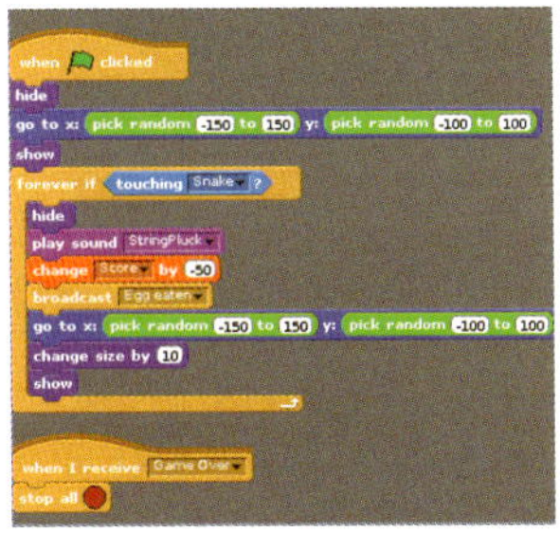

Grow Bad Egg

21 Add another 'when green flag clicked' script to the Bad Egg so it sets its size to the default 100% when a new game is started and then increases its size by 10 every 10 seconds. The Bad Egg will get bigger and bigger and harder to avoid.

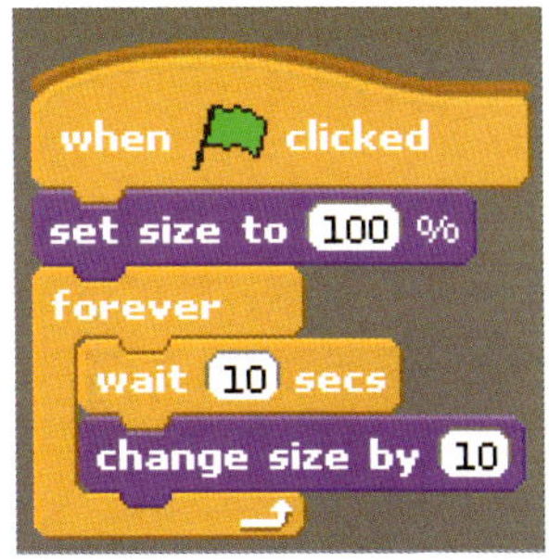

Create Bonus sprite

22 Create the Bonus sprite in a similar way. You can choose the shape and sound for the Bonus. Its scripts are similar to the Egg ones so you could drag one of those to the Bonus sprite and work from that. Make sure you change the sound and increase the score by a random bonus.

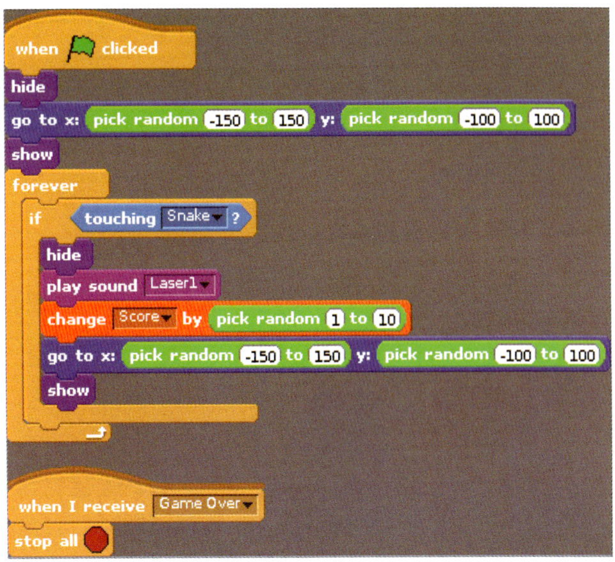

What you'll need...

Scratch

Did you know...

You can 'remix' apps made by other users by using their project as the base for your own (as long as you credit them).

Build a multiple-choice quiz

Learn how to use lists to create questions and answers for a fast-paced Scratch-based quiz

The key feature of this Scratch quiz is the ability to process text and numbers. However, Scratch is more designed for animated graphics and its weak areas – arrays, text display and variable inputs – are all required for a project like this. It centres around using lists, which are Scratch equivalents of arrays. The main drawback though is that while lists can have multiple rows, they only have one column. For this project we need columns for the questions, three different answers and a code for the right answers to match with the keyboard input. With ten questions that would require a 10x5 array variable. With Scratch, that in turn means we need five 10x1 lists. Let's get started...

Joining up words
This feature of the code is the Scratch equivalent of adding strings together, from the list, in a string variable

Questions and answers
All the text questions, answers and the right answer as a number are kept in lists, which are simple arrays

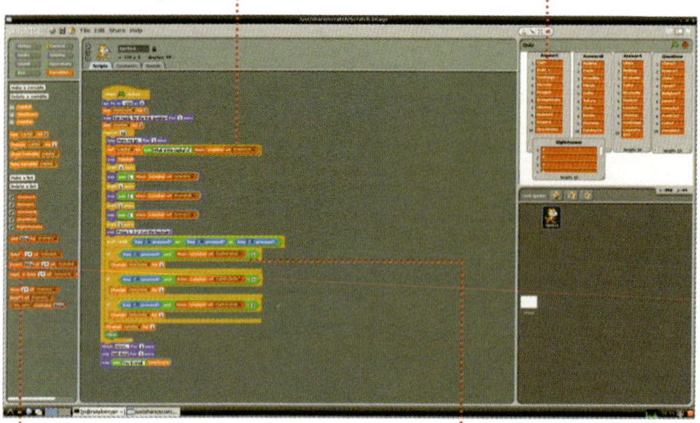

Tick boxes showing
Once all the lists have been populated you need to remove them from the screen. Untick here to do so

Got it right?
These code detects whether the correct answer has been entered by checking the answer list and incrementing the score

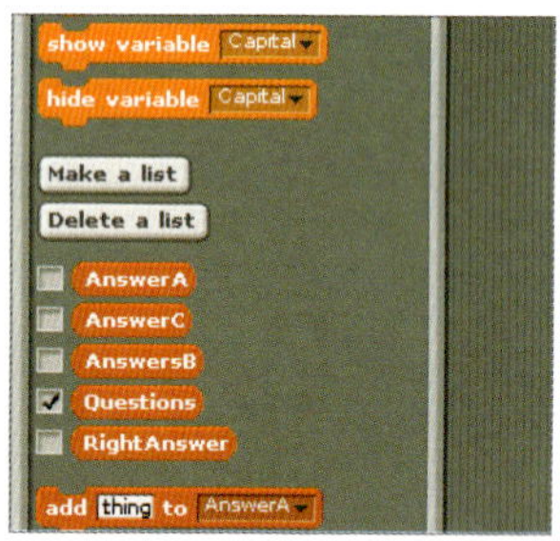

Create the lists

01 Click on Variables and make a list called Questions. As soon as you do, the list appears in the stage window ready for you to edit. Click on the Plus sign to start adding elements. Type in all the country names until you have a list of 10. Click on the x gadget of the 11th if needed.

Fill out the answers

02 Repeat this process for three new lists, each with an answer. It pays to arrange them side by side while doing this so you can ensure you get a right answer in each one. Create a final list that has a number one to three. This identifies which number list has the right answer.

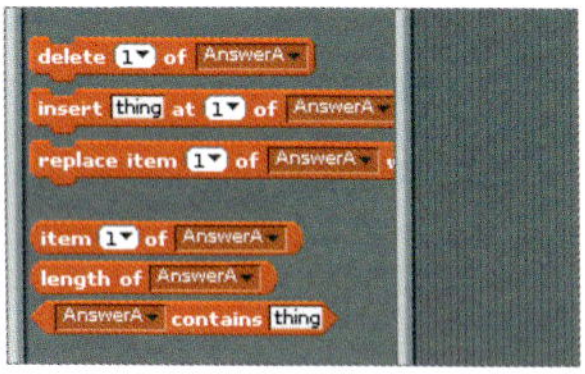

Set it up

03 Now create three new variables called, 'Capital', 'YourScore' and 'counter'. Untick all the variables in the list so they disappear from the stage. Set the 'counter' to 1 and 'YourScore' to 0. Position the sprite and warn the player to be ready.

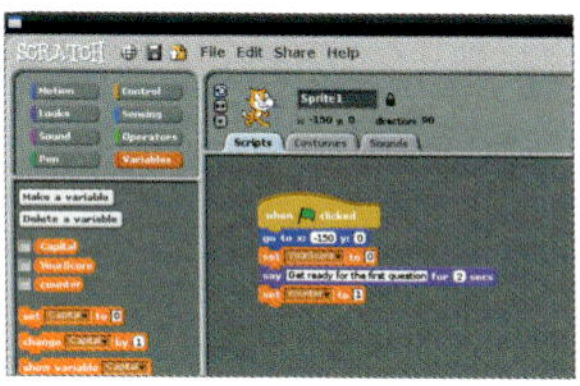

Create loop, set question

04 Drag a 'Repeat' loop from Control and set it to 10 for the number of questions. Add function 'Set Capital to ()'. Drag in an Operator called 'Join () ()'. Make the first half text. Add a variable to the other half and put 'Counter' into 'Questions'.

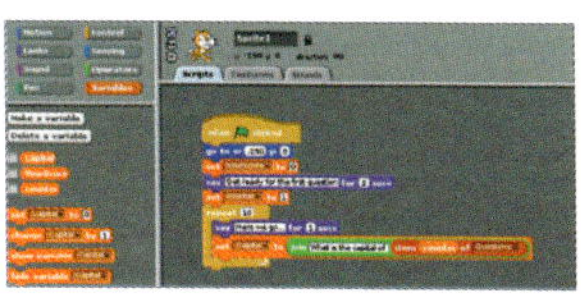

Display the answers

05 From Looks add a 'Say ()' and drop in 'Capital'. Then create the three answers by using the 'Say' command and adding a 'Join () ()'. The first entry is simply the number of the answer, the second part is the text answer from the three answer lists.

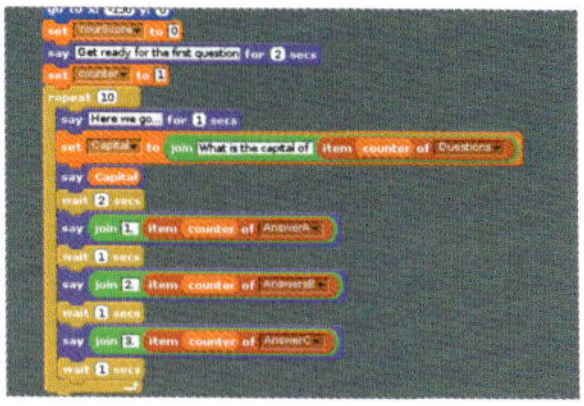

Scan for the answers

06 There are pauses between the answers being displayed. Add 'Say' to prompt to press 1, 2 or 3. Drag in a 'Wait until' Control. Go to Operators. There are only ones with two conditions so use that, then put an extra two conditions into the second box to make three.

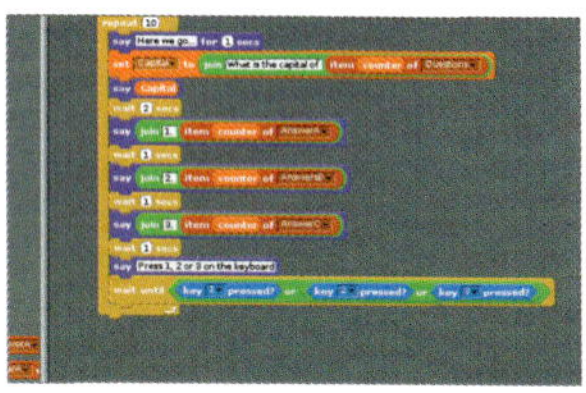

Is the answer right?

07 Drag in an 'If ()' Control. Drop a '() and ()' Operator into the space. In the first space add 'Key 1 pressed?' from Sensing. In the second add another '()=()' Operator. In the first part add 'Item () of RightAnswer' with 'Counter', and in the second type 1.

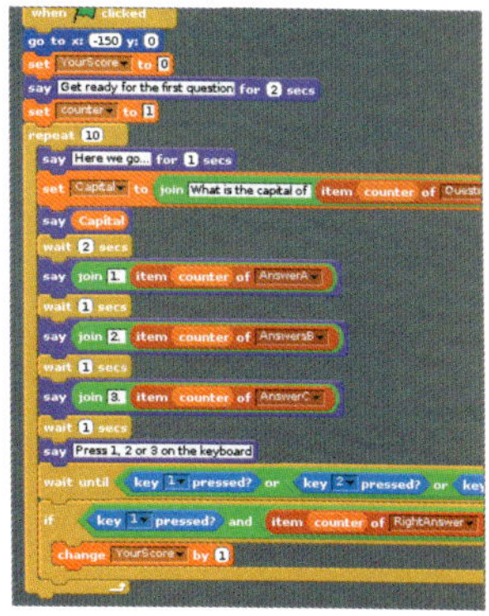

Repeat and add score

08 Add a 'Change Your Score by 1' for a correct answer. Repeat this twice for the other answers. Then increase the 'Counter' variable by 1 and clear the screen. Outside the loop add some pauses to show the quiz is over and then display the score in 'YourScore'. Well done, you've finished your first quiz game!

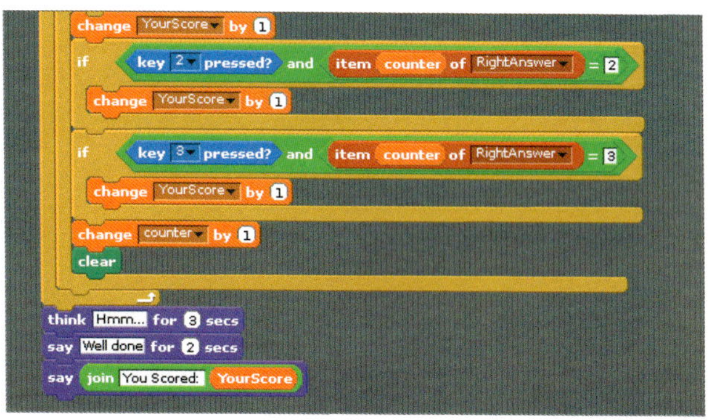

What you'll need...

Breadboard
LEDs
Buttons
Resistors
Jumper wires
ScratchGPIO3

Get interactive with Scratch

Experiment with physical computing by using Scratch to interact with buttons and lights on your Pi

Scratch is a very simple visual programming language, commonly used to teach basic programming concepts to learners of any age. In this project we'll learn how to light up an LED when a button is pressed in Scratch, and then change a character's colour when a physical button is pressed using the General Purpose Input/Output (GPIO) pins on your Raspberry Pi. With these techniques you can make all manner of fun and engaging projects, from musical keyboards to controllers for your Scratch games and animations. You'll need some components for this guide. Just search online for 'Raspberry Pi GPIO basic kit' to get you started.

Below Scratch can be used to do Internet Of Things projects with a few tweaks

"In this project we'll learn how to light up an LED when a button is pressed in Scratch using the GPIO pins"

Installing the required software packages

01 Log in to the Raspbian system with the username Pi and the password raspberry. Start the LXDE desktop environment using the command startx. Next, open up LXTerminal and then type the following commands:

```
wget http://liamfraser.co.uk/lud/install_scratchgpio3.sh
chmod +x install_scratchgpio3.sh
sudo bash install_scratchgpio3.sh
```

This will create a special version of Scratch on your desktop called ScratchGPIO3. This is a normal version of Scratch with a Python script that handles communications between Scratch and the GPIO. ScratchGPIO was created by simplesi (**cymplecy.wordpress.com**).

Connecting the breadboard

02 Power off your Pi and disconnect the power cable. Get your breadboard, an LED, a 330-ohm resistor and two GPIO cables ready. You'll want to connect the 3.3V pin (top-right pin, closest to the SD card) to one end of the 330-ohm resistor, and then connect the positive terminal of the LED (the longer leg is positive) to the other end. The resistor is used to limit the amount of current that can flow to the LED.

Then put the negative terminal of the LED into the negative rail of the breadboard. Connect one of the GROUND pins (for example, the third pin from the right on the bottom row of pins) to the negative lane. Now connect the power to your Pi. The LED should light up. If it doesn't, then it's likely that you've got it the wrong way round, so disconnect the power, swap the legs around and then try again.

Switching the LED on and off

03 At the moment, the LED is connected to a pin that constantly provides 3.3V. This isn't very useful if we want to be able to turn it on and off, so let's connect it to GPIO 17, which we can turn on and off. GPIO 17 is the sixth pin from the right, on the top row of pins. Power the Pi back on. We can turn the LED on by exporting the GPIO pin, setting it to an output pin and then setting its value to 1. Setting the value to 0 turns the LED back off:

```
echo 17 > /sys/class/gpio/export
echo out > /sys/class/gpio/gpio17/direction
echo 1 > /sys/class/gpio/gpio17/value
echo 0 > /sys/class/gpio/gpio17/value
```

Controlling the LED from Scratch

04 Start the LXDE desktop environment and open ScratchGPIO3. Go to the control section and create a simple script that broadcasts pin11on when Sprite1 is clicked. Then click the sprite. The LED should light up. Then add to the script to wait 1 second and then broadcast pin11off. If you click the sprite again, the LED will come on for a second and then go off. ScratchGPIO3

Wiring up our push button

05 Power off the Pi again. This circuit is a little bit more complicated than the LED one we created previously. The first thing we need to do is connect 3.3V (the top-right pin we used to test our LED) to the positive rail of the breadboard. Then we need to connect a 10Kohm resistor to the positive rail, and the other end to an empty track on the breadboard. Then on the same track, add a wire that has one end connected to GPIO 4. This is two pins to the right of GPIO 17. Then, on the same track again, connect one pin of the push button. Finally, connect the other pin of the push button to ground by adding a wire that is connected to the same negative rails that ground is connected to.

When the button is not pressed, GPIO 4 will be receiving 3.3V. However, when the button is pressed, the circuit to ground will be completed and GPIO 4 will be receiving 0V (and have a value of 0), because there is much less resistance on the path to ground.

We can see this in action by watching the pin's value and then pressing the button to make it change:

```
echo 4 > /sys/class/gpio/export
echo in > /sys/class/gpio/gpio4/direction
watch -n 0.5 cat /sys/class/gpio/gpio4/value
```

Let there be light!

06 Boot up the Pi and start ScratchGPIO3. Go to the control section and add when green flag clicked, then attach a forever loop, and inside that an if else statement. From the operators section and add an if [] = [] operator to the if statement. Then go to the sensing section and add a value sensor to the left side of the equality statement, and set it to pin7. Enter 0 on the right. Broadcast pin11on if the sensor value is 0, and broadcast pin11off otherwise. Click the green flag. If you push the button, the LED will light up!

What you'll need…

- Internet connection
- External hard drive
- VESA mount
- HDMI cable

Did you know…

One of the most popular uses for the Raspberry Pi is turning it into a media centre. It's fast, silent and easy to hide.

Create a complete media centre

Turn your Raspberry Pi into the perfect media centre with some simple software and tweaks

There are a few ways to use the Raspberry Pi as an HTPC, with some of the best being XBMC-powered distros. OpenELEC is a great, lightweight way to use the Pi for that sole purpose, but we're going to cover the more customisable Raspbmc, based on Debian.

Perfect for Pi
The Raspberry Pi makes the perfect media centre, and there's software to take advantage of it

Plenty of options
Choose between different HTPC solutions with different advantages and disadvantages

Use multiple shares
Watch local and network videos at full 1080p resolution, along with music and pictures

Use web apps
Get popular streaming apps for web-based video to run directly from your Raspberry Pi

Install Raspbmc

01 Raspbmc has a downloadable installer that always gets the latest image for your Pi. Create a new directory and then download it with:

```
$ wget http://svn.stmlabs.com/svn/raspbmc/release/installers/python/install.py
```

Make it executable with:

```
$ chmod +x install.py
```

And then run it with:

```
$ sudo python install.py
```

Follow the on-screen instructions and it will then install onto your Pi.

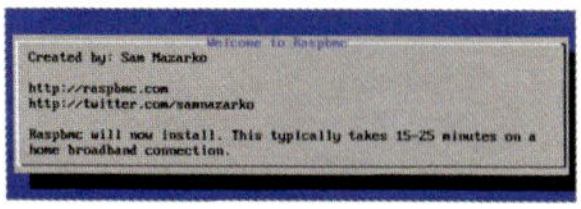

Setup

02 By installing Raspbmc this way, the distro will then download the latest image and updates to run on your Pi on first boot. This will take a while, and involve a couple of restarts, but will only happen the first time. Select your language in XBMC and you're done.

Network sharing

03 You can add file sources to XBMC by first of all going to Video, then Add Source. Go to Browse and you can add local or networked files. For network shares, choose either UPnP or SMB shares to see what's visible on the network, or 'Add network location' if you know the direct path. This works the same for Music and Pictures.

Scrape your media

04 After selecting a source, you can choose what service to scrape information from. This gives you more info on the files you're watching, such as episode summaries and proper names. Make sure your films have the year appended to them, and that your TV shows do too.

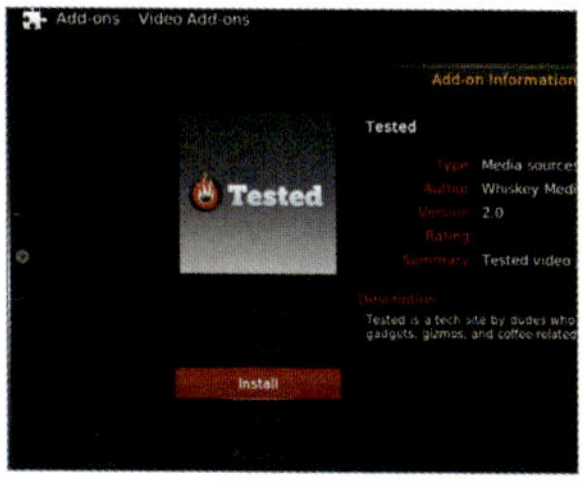

Get some apps

05 On any content tab, go to Add-Ons. It will display the apps you already have, which is none by default. By selecting Get More, the full list of available apps will be shown and you can install them with one button click from there.

Web remote

06 In Settings, go to Services and then Webserver. Enable it and you will now be able to control your Raspberry Pi using a web browser. To access the web browser remote, enter the IP address – found in System Info under the home screen's Settings tab – into your browser, followed by ':80'.

Android Remote

07 There's an official Android Remote app on the Google Play Store that can control XBMC once the web server is enabled. Download it to your phone and launch it. Go to the Settings, add new host, and enter the IP address and port (80 by default) like in the previous step.

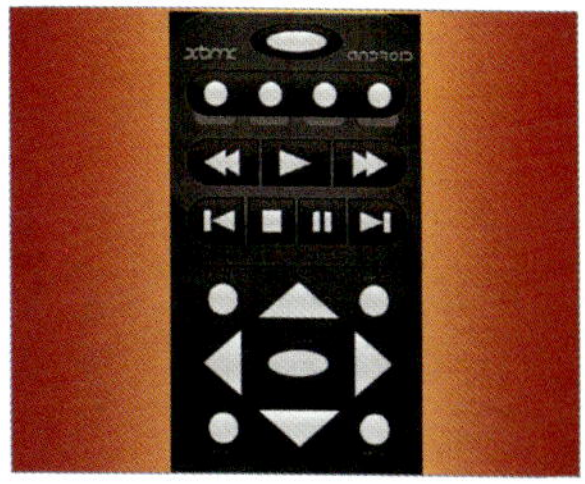

Using CEC

08 If your TV supports it, CEC can be used over HDMI to control your XBMC-powered Pi. CEC should be enabled by default, so you can control your setup with one remote control. Refer to the XBMC wiki to see if your TV supports CEC, and how you can take advantage of it: **bit.ly/18kdVHf**

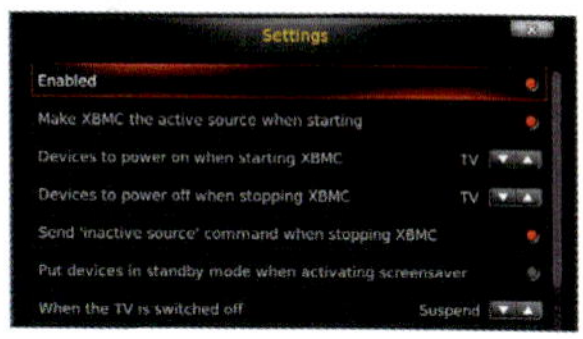

Traditional remotes

09 XBMC supports a large number of universal remotes that include, or support, USB IR receivers. One of the best devices for this is the FLIRC, a fully programmable USB IR receiver that allows you to use any remote with the Pi.

What you'll need…

RetroPie
blog.petrockblock.com/download/retropie-project-image/

Make your own retro games console

Get your retro gaming fix with RetroPie, a distro for getting the games of yesteryear onto your Pi

Did you know…

Emulation is something of a legal minefield. You must own the original games to emulate them on your Pi.

There's a growing trend for people to create their own arcade cabinet or hack together their own retro console, and the Raspberry Pi's size and power makes it perfect for this. Follow our tutorial to turn your Pi into a fully functional emulating powerhouse.

Install RetroPie

01 Download the latest RetroPie image from the website and unzip it. Like installing other Raspberry Pi distros, you simply need to write the image to the SD card with:

```
$ sudo dd bs=4M if=[path to image] of=/dev/[path to sd card]
```

Initial setup

02 On the first boot, you'll be asked to configure a controller, which can be done with a keyboard, a standard USB controller or a PS3 controller. The initial setup on RetroPie is for very limited controls, and you'll need to launch a separate tool for better config.

Calibrating controllers

03 Press the menu button you set up, and go to exit. You'll get to a command line. Connect a USB controller and enter the following:

```
$ cd RetroPie/emulators/RetroArch/tools
```

…and then:

```
$ ./retroarch-joyconfig >> ~/RetroPie/configs/all/retroarch.cfg
```

Follow on the on-screen instructions to properly configure your controller.

Using an Xbox 360 pad

04 To use a wired or PC-compatible Xbox 360 controller, you'll first need to install the correct drivers:

```
$ sudo apt-get install xboxdrv
```

Then edit `/etc/rc.local` by adding:

```
xboxdrv --trigger-as-button --wid 0 --led 2 --deadzone 4000 --silent &
sleep 1
```

…before exit 0. Change --wid to --id if it's a wired controller. Reboot.

Recognising the 360 controller

05 Add the 360 pad to your configuration file by first going to tools with:

```
$ cd ~/RetroPie/emulators/RetroArch/tools
```

Then type in the following:

```
$ ./retroarch-joyconfig -o p1.cfg -p 1 -j 0
```

And finally add the files to RetroArch with:

```
$ sudo cat p*.cfg >> ~/RetroPie/configs/all/retroarch.cfg
```

Save and reboot.

Add some games

06 Adding games to your Raspberry Pi is fairly simple. Grab the SD card from the Pi and put it in your PC. Move any ROMs or compatible PC files to the relevant folders in:

`[path to SD card]/home/pi/RetroPie/roms/`

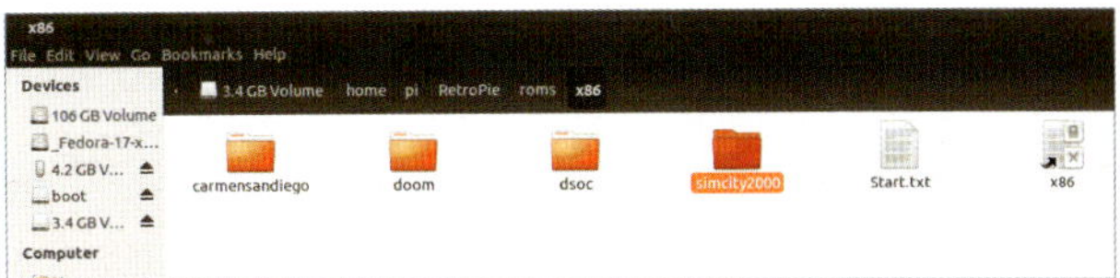

Navigate RetroPie

07 RetroPie will automatically know if there are games for a specific emulator and allow you to access it. Pressing left or right will move between the emulators, which then have options to load the games on the SD card.

Two players

08 For multiplayer gaming, it's best to use two controllers of the same type. Go to the bottom of `~/RetroPie/configs/all/retroarch.cfg` and copy and paste the code from `input_player1_joypad_index = "0"` to the bottom. Change each instance of player1 to player 2, and a second controller will now work.

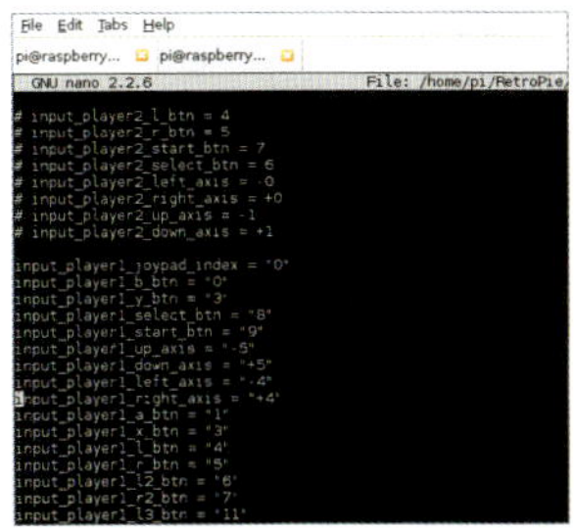

Safe restart

09 Some of the emulators can't be quit out of, meaning you'll need to physically reboot your Pi by unplugging it each time. We can add a hotkey to exit the emulators by again going to `retroarch.cfg` and adding to the end:

```
input_enable_hotkey_btn = "X"
```

```
input_exit_emulator_btn = "Y"
```

…with X and Y being the corresponding numbers of buttons on your controller.

What you'll need...

Portable speakers or headphones

Sonic Pi
www.cl.cam.ac.uk/projects/raspberrypi/sonicpi/teaching.html

Did you know...

Sonic Pi is installed by default on the latest versions of the Raspbian operating system. If it's missing, follow step one!

Make music

Program your own melodies using Sonic Pi and create musical cues or robot beeps

One of the major features of Scratch is its ability to teach the fundamentals of coding to kids and people with no computing background. For kids, it's especially appealing due to the way it allows them to create videogames to interact with as part of their learning. In this kind of vein then, Sonic Pi teaches people to code using music. With a simple language that utilises basic logic steps but in a more advanced way than Scratch, it can either be used as a next step for avid coders, or as a way to create music for an Internet of Things or a robot.

"We can start making more complex melodies by using more of Sonic Pi's functions"

Below Sonic Pi is a great way to learn basic coding principles and have fun

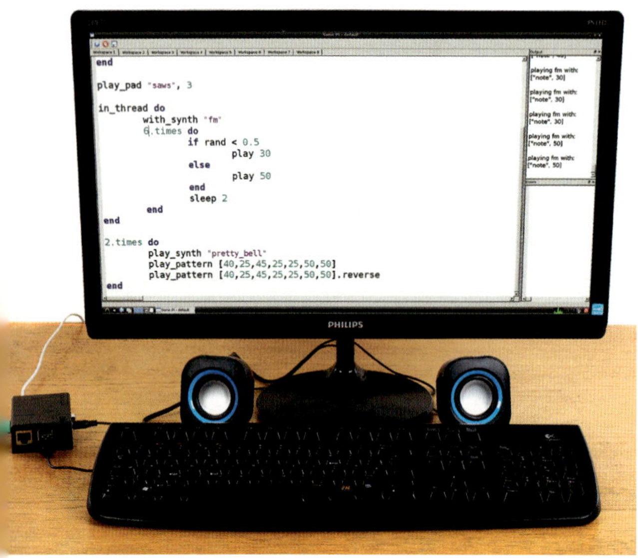

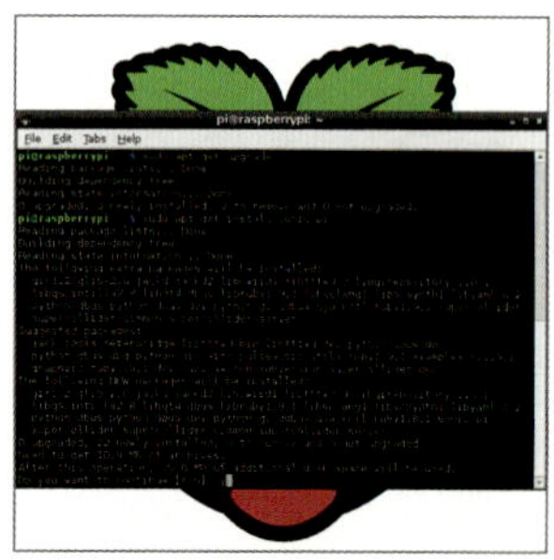

Getting Sonic Pi

01 If you've installed the latest version of Raspbian, Sonic Pi will be included by default. If you're still using a slightly older version, then you'll need to install it via the repos. Do this with:

```
$ sudo apt-get install sonic-pi
```

Starting with Sonic Pi

02 Sonic Pi is located in the Education category in the menus. Open it up and you'll be presented with something that looks like an IDE. The pane on the left allows you to enter the code for your project, with proper syntax highlighting for its own style of language. When running, an info pane details exactly what's being played via Sonic Pi – and any errors are listed in their own pane as well, for reference.

Your first note

03 Our first thing to try on Sonic Pi is simply being able to play a note. Sonic Pi has a few defaults preset, so we can get started with:

```
play 50
```

Press the Play button and the output window will show you what's being played. The pretty_bell sound is the default tone for Sonic Pi's output, and 50 determines the pitch and tone of the sound.

Full code listing

```
with_tempo 200
play_pattern [40,25,45,25,25,50,50]
2.times do
    with_synth "beep"
    play_pattern [40,25,45,25,25,50,50]
    play_pattern [40,25,45,25,25,50,50].reverse
end
play_pad "saws", 3
in_thread do
    with_synth "fm"
    6.times do
          if rand < 0.5
                    play 30
          else
                    play 50
          end
          sleep 2
    end
end

2.times do
    play_synth "pretty_bell"
    play_pattern [40,25,45,25,25,50,50]
    play_pattern [40,25,45,25,25,50,50].reverse
end
```

Set the beat

04 For any piece of music, you'll want to set the tempo. We can start by putting:

```
with_tempo 200
```

...at the start of our code. We can test it out by creating a string of midi notes using play_pattern:

```
play_pattern
[40,25,45,25,25,50,50]
```

This will play pretty_bell notes at these tones at the tempo we've set. You can create longer and shorter strings, and also change the way they play.

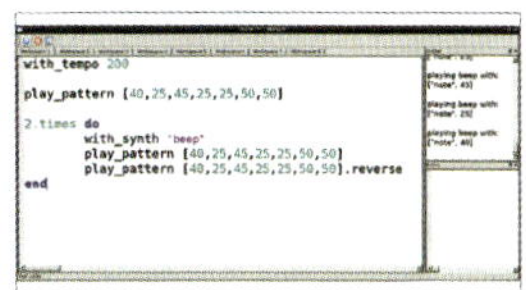

Advance your melody

05 We can start making more complex melodies by using more of Sonic Pi's functions. You can change the note type by using with_synth, reverse a pattern, and even create a finite loop with the x.times function; do and end signify the start and end of the loop. Everything is played in sequence before repeating, much like an if or while loop in normal code.

Playing a concert

06 Using the in_thread function, we are able to create another thread for the Sonic Pi instance, and have several lines of musical code play at once instead of in sequence. We have made it create a series of notes in a random sequence, and have them play alongside extra notes created by the position and velocity of the mouse using the play_pad function.

What you'll need...

Breadboard:
www.proto-pic.co.uk/half-size-breadboard

3mm LED light:
www.ultraleds.co.uk/led-product-catalogue/basic-leds-3-5-8-10mm.html

Wires:
www.picomake.com/product/breadboard-wires

270-ohm resistor:
http://goo.gl/ox4FTp5ntj0091

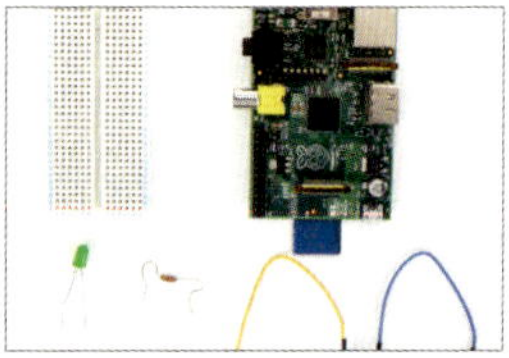

Fig 1: All the items you will need to get going adjusting an LED using PWM. The wires should have a male and female ends

Fig 2: Place the female end onto the Pi, noting pin number 1 being identified by the small 'P1'. The blue wire is ground

Fig 3: Once everything is connected up, plug in your USB power cable

Fig 4: Switch the power on. The LED will light up. If it's dim, use a lower-rated resistor

Control an LED using GPIO

An introduction into using an external output, such as an LED, on the Pi

After you have fired up your Pi, maybe installed XBMC and had a play around with streaming, you might be ready for your next challenge. One route to go down is to find interesting uses for one of the many desktop OSs available for the little computer, perhaps using it as a web server, an NAS or retro arcade console. This is all great fun, but an often-overlooked feature of the Pi is its hardware pinouts. If you've never done any electronics before, then the Pi is a great place to start. Or maybe you have used a programmable microcontroller such as Arduino in the past; the Pi, with its increased CPU and RAM over the Arduino, opens up many more possibilities for fun projects.

The Raspberry Pi features a single PWM (pulse width modulation) output pin, along with a series of GPIO (General Purpose Input/Output) pins. These enable electronic hardware such as buzzers, lights and switches to be controlled via the Pi. For people who are used to either just 'using' a computer, or only programming software that only acts on the machine itself, controlling a real physical item such as a light can be a revelation.

This tutorial will assume no prior knowledge of electronics or programming, and will take you through the steps needed to control an LED using the Raspberry Pi, from setting it up to coding a simple application.

"We'll take you through the steps needed to control an LED using the Pi, from setting it up to coding"

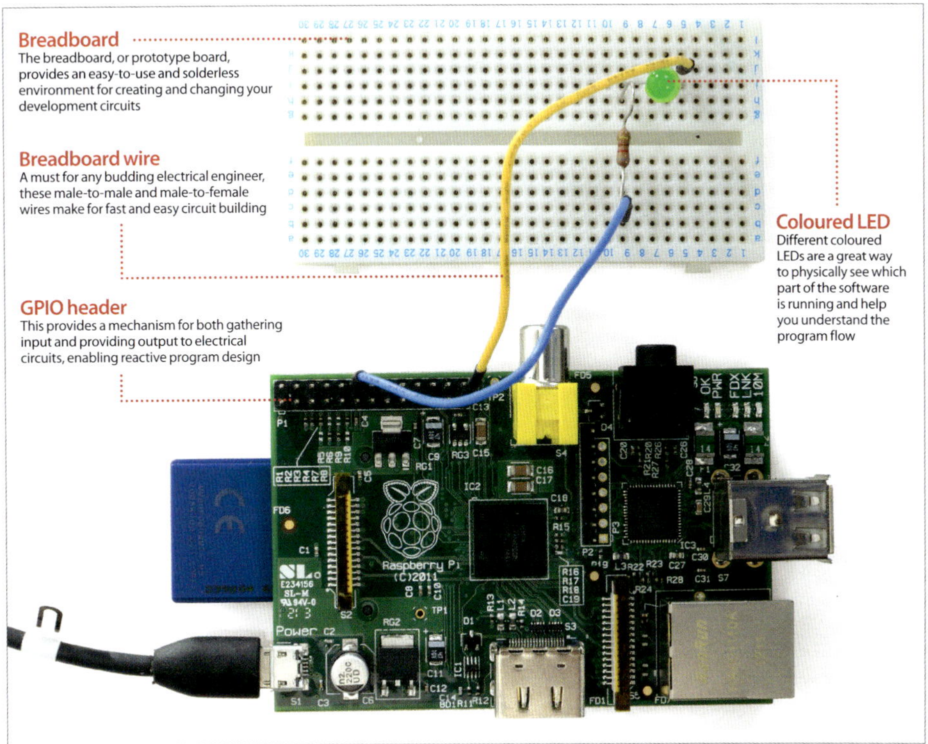

The Pi's pins

01 Before we dive into writing code, let's take a look at the layout of the pins on the Pi. If you have your Pi in a case, take it out and place it in front of you with the USB ports on the right. Over the next few steps we'll look at some of the issues you'll encounter when using the GPIO port.

Pi revision 1 or 2?

02 Depending on when you purchased your Pi, you may have a 'revision 1' or 'revision 2' model. The GPIO layout is slightly different for each, although they do have the same functionality. Here we have a revision 1; revision 2s became available towards the end of 2012.

Pin numbers

03 If you take a look at the top left of the board you will see a small white label, 'P1'. This is pin 1 and above it is pin 2. To the right of pin 1 is pin 3, and above 3 is 4. This pattern continues until you get to pin 26 at the end. As you'll see in the next step, some pins have important uses.

Pin uses

04 Pin 1 is 3V3, or 3.3 volts. This is the main pin we will be using in this guide to provide power to our LED. Pins 2 and 4 are 5V. Pin 6 is the other pin we will use here, which is ground. Other ground pins are 9, 14, 20 and 25. You should always ensure your project is properly grounded.

GPIO pins

05 The other pins on the board are GPIO (General Purpose Input/Output). These are used for other tasks that you need to do as your projects become more complex and challenging. Be aware that the USB power supply doesn't offer much scope for powering large items.

Basic LED lighting

06 Okay, so let's get down to business and start making something. Firstly, get your breadboard, two wires, a 270Ω resistor and an LED. Note the slightly bent leg on one side of the LED; this is important for later on. Make sure your Pi is unplugged from the mains supply.

Wiring the board

07 Plug one wire into the number 1 pin, and the other end into the breadboard. Note that it doesn't matter where on the breadboard you plug it in, but make sure there are enough empty slots around it to add the LED and resistor to. Now get another wire ready.

Adding another wire

08 Place the female end of the wire into pin number 6 (ground) and the other end into the breadboard, making sure to leave room for the resistor, depending on how large it is. Next, get your resistor ready. You can use a little higher or lower than 270 ohms, but not using a resistor at all will likely blow the LED.

Add the resistor

09 Next we need to add our resistor. Place one end next to the ground wire on the breadboard, and the other one slot below the 3V3 wire connection. This will sit next to the LED when we add it in a second. Note that there is no correct or incorrect way to add a resistor.

Add the LED

10 Grab your LED and place the 'bent' leg end next to the 3V3 wire in the breadboard. Place the other leg next to the resistor leg opposite the ground wire. This now completes the circuit and we are ready to test out our little task.

Power it up

11 Now get your micro-USB socket and either plug the mains end into the wall, or plug it into a computer or laptop port (and powered on!). You should see the LED light up. If not, then check your connections on the breadboard or Pi, or try a different LED.

Setting up programming environment

12 Now, we need to be able to do a little bit more than just turn a light on – we want to be able to control it via code. Set up a new Raspbian installation (a guide to this is found on page 28). You don't need a GUI for this – it can all be done via the terminal if you so wish. Before starting, it's best to check everything is up to date with:

```
sudo apt-get dist-upgrade
```

Open up terminal

13 Assuming we want to use the GUI, rather than SSH into the Pi, open up a new terminal window by double-clicking on the LXTerminal icon. We need root access to control the LEDs, so either enter su now, or remember to prefix any commands with sudo.

```
su
```

followed by password or add

```
sudo
```

to the start of each command.

Downloading GPIO library

14 There is a handy GPIO Python library that makes manipulating the GPIO pins a breeze. From within your terminal window, use wget to download the tarball file, then extract it using tar. This will give us all the files in a new directory.

```
wget https://pypi.python.org/packages
source/R/RPi.GPIO/RPi.GPIO-0.5.2a.tar.gz
tar zxf Rpi.GPIO-0.5.2a.tar.gz
cd Rpi.GPIO-0.5.2a
```

Install the library

15 Now we need to install the library. This is simply a case of using Python's install method; so we need the dev version of Python. Make sure you are in the directory of the library before running this command.

```
sudo apt-get install python-dev
sudo python setup.py install
```

Importing the library in a script

16 Create a new Python script. Next import the main GPIO library and we'll put it in a try-except block. Save the file using Ctrl+X and choosing 'yes'.

```
cd /
cd Desktop
sudo nano gpio.py
try:
        import RPi.GPIO as GPIO
except RuntimeError:
        print("Error importing GPIO lib")
```

Did you know…

The official Python docs are a great resource for beginners and professionals alike. **http://python.org/doc.**

Test the script

17 Now to make sure that the script imported okay, we just need to run the python command and then tell it the name of the script that we just created. If all goes well, you shouldn't see any error messages. Don't worry if you do, though. Just go back through the previous steps to check everything is as it should be.

```
sudo python gpio.py
```

Set GPIO mode

18 Reload the script in nano again. We will then set the GPIO mode to BOARD. This method is the safest for a beginner and will work whichever revision of the Pi you are using. It's best to pick a GPIO convention and stick to it – it saves confusion later on.

```
sudo nano gpio.py
GPIO.setmode(GPIO.BOARD)
```

Set pin mode

19 A pin has to be defined as either an input or an output before it can work. This is simplified in the GPIO library by calling the GPIO.setup method. You then pass in the pin number, and then GPIO.OUT or GPIO.IN. As we want to use an LED, it's an output. You'll be using these conventions frequently, so learn them as best you can so they soak in!

```
GPIO.setup(12, GPIO.OUT)
```

Using PWM

20 The next step is to tell the pin to output and then set a way of escaping our program. Here we call the GPIO class again and then the PWM method, passing in the pin number; the second value is the frequency in hertz – in this case, 0.5.

```
p = GPIO.PWM(12, 0.5)
p.start(1)
input('Press return to stop:')
p.stop()
GPIO.cleanup()
```

Adjusting PWM

21 To add a timer to the LED so it fades out, we first need to import the time library and then set the 12 pin to have 50Hz frequency to start off with.

```
import time
import RPi.GPIO as GPIO
GPIO.setmode(GPIO.BOARD)
GPIO.setup(12, GPIO.OUT)
p = GPIO.PWM(12, 50)  # channel=12 frequency=50Hz
p.start(0)
```

Add the fade

22 Then we add in another try-except block, this time checking what power the LED is at – and once it reaches a certain level, we reverse the process. To run this code, simply save it from nano and then sudo python gpio.py.

```
while 1:
        for dc in range(0, 101, 5):
                p.ChangeDutyCycle(dc)
                time.sleep(0.1)
        for dc in range(100, -1, -5):
                p.ChangeDutyCycle(dc)
                time.sleep(0.1)
        except KeyboardInterrupt:
                pass
p.stop()
GPIO.cleanup()
```

"We'll set the GPIO mode to BOARD. This will work whichever revision of the Pi you are using"

What you'll need…

- Portable USB speakers
- python-espeak module
- eSpeak
- Raspbian (latest image)

Did you know…

Using eSpeak you can control the way the words are spoken to add emphasis or make the voice sound different

Voice synthesizer

Add the power of speech to your Raspberry Pi projects with the versatile eSpeak Python library

We've shown how the Raspberry Pi can be used to power all kinds of projects, but as a tiny computer it can also be the centre of an Internet of Things in your house too. For these reasons and more, using the Raspberry Pi for text-to-voice commands could be just what you're looking for. Due to the Debian base of Raspbian, the powerful eSpeak library is easily available for anyone looking to make use of it. There's also a module that allows you to use eSpeak in Python, going beyond the standard command-line prompts so you can perform automation tasks.

Everything you'll need

01 We'll install everything we plan to use in this tutorial at once. This includes the eSpeak library and the Python modules we need to show it off. Open the terminal and install with:

```
$ sudo apt-get install espeak
python-espeak python-tk
```

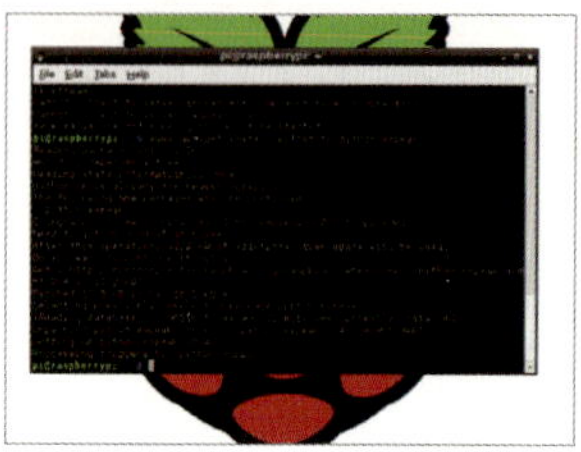

Pi's first words

02 The eSpeak library is pretty simple to use – to get it to just say something, type in the terminal:

```
$ espeak "[message]"
```

This will use the library's defaults to read whatever is written in the message, with decent clarity. Though this simple command is fun, there's much more you can do…

Say some more

03 You can change the way eSpeak will read text with a number of different options, such as gender, read speed and even the way it pronounces syllables. For example, writing the command like so:

```
$ espeak -ven+f3 -k5 -s150
"[message]"
```

…will turn the voice female, emphasise capital letters and make the reading slower.

Taking command with Python

04 The most basic way to use eSpeak in Python is to use subprocess. Import it, then use:

```
subprocess.call(["espeak", "[options 1]", "[option 2]",..."[option n]", "[your message here]")
```

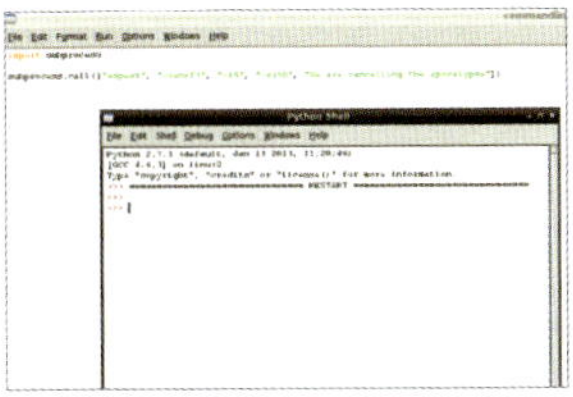

The native tongue

05 The Python eSpeak module is quite simple to use to just convert some text to speech. Try this sample code:

```
from espeak import espeak
espeak.synth("[message]")
```

You can then incorporate this into Python, like you would any other module, for automation.

A voice synthesiser

06 Using the code listing, we're creating a simple interface with Tkinter with some predetermined voice buttons and a custom entry method. We're showing how the eSpeak module can be manipulated to change its output. This can be used for reading tweets or automated messages. Have fun!

Full code listing

Import the necessary eSspeak and GUI modules, as well as the module to find out the time

```
from espeak import espeak
from Tkinter import *
from datetime import datetime
```

Define the different functions that the interface will use, including a simple fixed message, telling the time, and a custom message

```
def hello_world():
    espeak.synth("Hello World")

def time_now():
    t = datetime.now().strftime("%k %M")
    espeak.synth("The time is %s"%t)

def read_text():
    text_to_read = input_text.get()
    espeak.synth(text_to_read)
```

Create the basic window with Tkinter for your interface, as well as creating the variable for text entry

```
root = Tk()
root.title("Voice box")
input_text = StringVar()
box = Frame(root, height = 200, width = 500)
box.pack_propagate(0)
box.pack(padx = 5, pady = 5)
```

The text entry appends to the variable we created, and each button calls a specific function that we defined above in the code

```
Label(box, text="Enter text").pack()
entry_text = Entry(box, exportselection = 0, textvariable = input_text)
entry_text.pack()
entry_ready = Button(box, text = "Read this", command = read_text)
entry_ready.pack()

hello_button = Button(box, text = "Hello World", command = hello_world)
hello_button.pack()
time_button = Button(box, text = "What's the time?", command = time_now)
time_button.pack()

root.mainloop()
```

"There's even a module that allows you to use eSpeak in Python, so you can perform automated tasks"

What you'll need…

Internet connectivity

Web browser

Google Coder
googlecreativelab.github.io/coder/raspberrypi/sonicpi/teaching.html

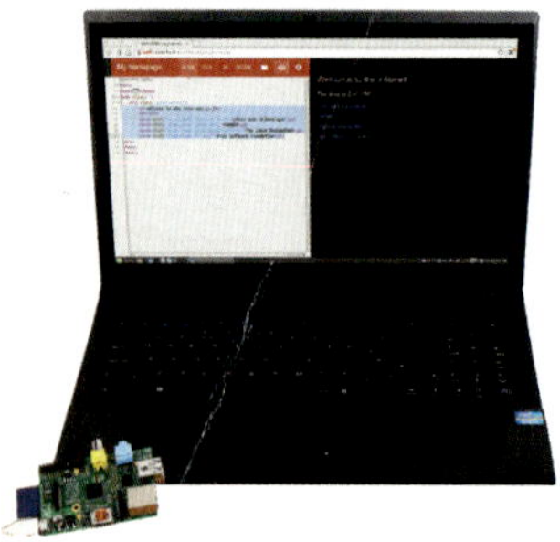

Build your first web server

Use Google Coder to turn your Raspberry Pi into a tiny, low-powered web server and web host!

We're teaching you how to code in many different ways on the Raspberry Pi in this book, so it only seems fitting that we look at web development too.

There's a new way to use the web on the Raspberry Pi as well: internet giant Google has recently released Coder specifically for the tiny computer. It's a Raspbian-based image that turns your Pi into a web server and web development kit. Accessible easily over a local network and with support for jQuery out of the box, it's an easy and great way to further your web development skills.

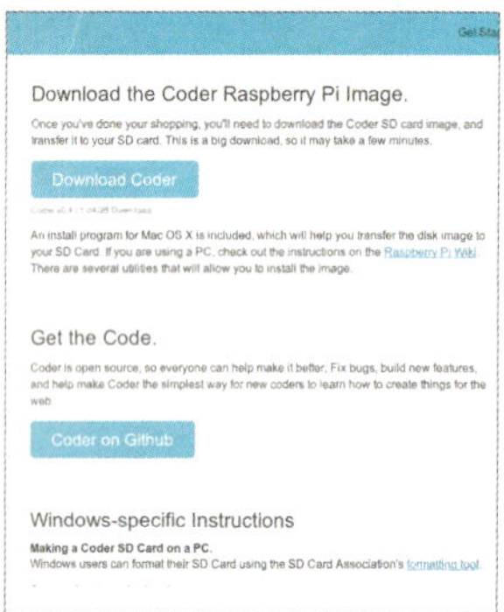

Get Google Coder

01 Head to the Google Coder website, and download the compressed version of the image. Unpack it wherever you wish, and install it using dd, like any other Raspberry Pi image:

```
$ dd if=[path to]/raspi.img
of=/dev/[path to SD card] bs=1M
```

Plug in your Pi

02 For this tutorial, you'll only need to connect a network cable into the Pi. Pop in your newly written SD card, plug in the power and wait a few moments. If you've got a display plugged in anyway, you'll notice a Raspbian startup sequence leading to the command-line login screen.

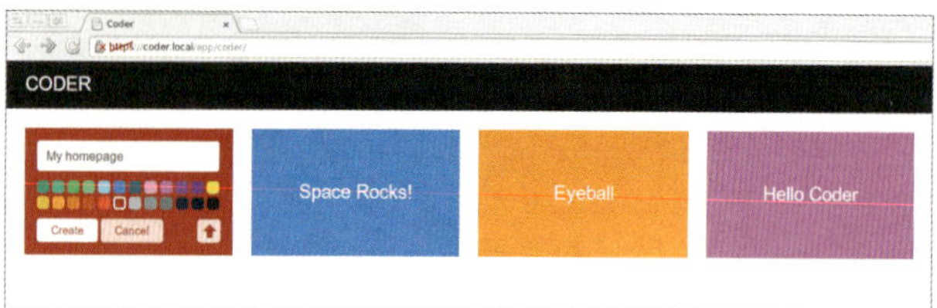

Connect to Coder

03 Open up the browser on your main system, and go to **http://coder.local**. You may have to manually accept the licence. It will ask you to set up your password, and then you'll be in and ready to code.

Language of the web

04 Now it's time to create your own app or website. Click on the '+' box next to the examples, give your app a name and then click Create. You'll be taken to the HTML section of the app. Change the Hello World lines to:

```
<h1>This is a HTML header</h1>
<p>This is a new block of default text</p>
```

Styled to impress

05 Click on the CSS tab. This changes the look and style of the webpage without having to make the changes each time in the main code. You can change the background colour and font with:

```
body {
        background-color: #000000;
        color: #ffffff;
 }
```

Querying your Java

06 The third tab allows you to edit the jQuery, making the site more interactive. We can make it create a message on click with:

```
$(document).click(function() {
        alert('You clicked the website!');
        }
 );
```

Full code listing

HTML

Some simple HTML code that can point us to some important websites. The h2 tag is used to display the time thanks to Java

```
<h1>Welcome to the internet...</h1>
<h2></h2>
<p><a href="http://www.linuxuser.co.uk">Linux User & Developer</p>
<p><a href="http://www.reddit.com/">Reddit</p>
<p><a href="http://www.linuxfoundation.org/">The Linux Foundation</p>
<p><a href="http://www.fsf.org/">Free Software Foundation</p>
```

Java

We're calling the current time using jQuery in the JS tab so that we can ultimately display it on the webpage

We're going to display the time as a 12-hour clock in the first if statement, and use AM and PM to differentiate the time

We make the minutes readable by adding a 0 if it's below 10, then concatenate all the variables and assign to the tag h2

```
var d = new Date;
    var hours = d.getHours();
    var mins = d.getMinutes();
    if (hours > 12) {
        var hour = (hours - 12);
        var ampm = "PM";
    }
    else {
        var hour = hours;
        var ampm = "AM";
    }
    if (hours == 12) {
        var ampm = "PM";
    }
    if (mins > 9){
        var min = mins;
    }
    else {
        var min = "0" + mins;
    }
    var time = "The time is " + hour + ":" + min + " " + ampm;
    $("h2").html(time);
```

> "Coder is a Raspbian-based image that turns your Raspberry Pi into a web server and web development kit. It's an easy and great way to further your skills"

How to play Minecraft-Pi

Play one of the greatest games ever made on your Raspberry Pi!

What you'll need...

Keyboard & mouse

Internet connection

Did you know...

stuffaboutcode.com is a great resource for fun and functional games and projects to do with Minecraft-Pi.

Mojang's *Minecraft* is probably the biggest game on the planet right now. The exploits of its main protagonist, a simple block character called Steve, fill hundreds of thousands (if not millions) of hours of YouTube video, and modifying and reskinning the game has become a cottage industry all of its own. The game is available on just about any format you can imagine, from PCs to gaming consoles to mobile phones. It should probably come as no surprise that it's also available on the Raspberry Pi. While at first glance Minecraft-Pi is a simplified version of the Pocket Edition (designed for tablets and smartphones), the Raspberry Pi edition is very special since it's the only version of *Minecraft* that you're allowed (and even encouraged) to hack yourself.

We're going to demonstrate how you can create your own fun Minecraft-Pi mini-games by exploiting the Python API in the next project over the page. In this article, however, we will explain how to install and play the game, and prepare your environment for easy hacking.

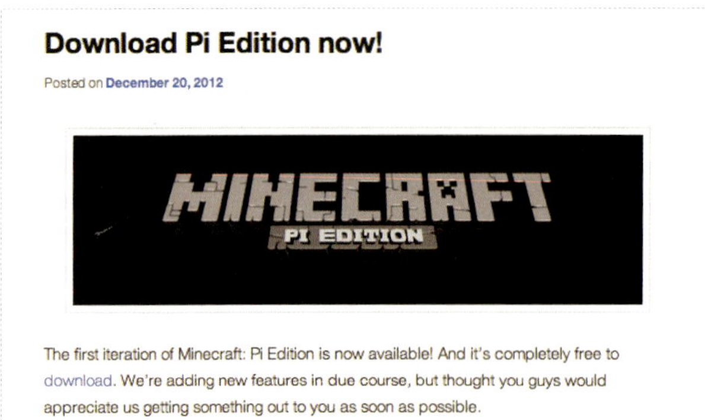

Requirements

01 Minecraft-Pi requires you to be running Raspbian on your Pi, so if you're not, go to **raspberrypi.org** and set it up. You can find our guide to doing just that on pages 14-15 of this book. With the current version of Minecraft-Pi you need to have X Window loaded too. So, assuming your Raspberry Pi doesn't boot into the graphical interface by default, once you've entered your username and password, at the command prompt you just need to type `startx`.

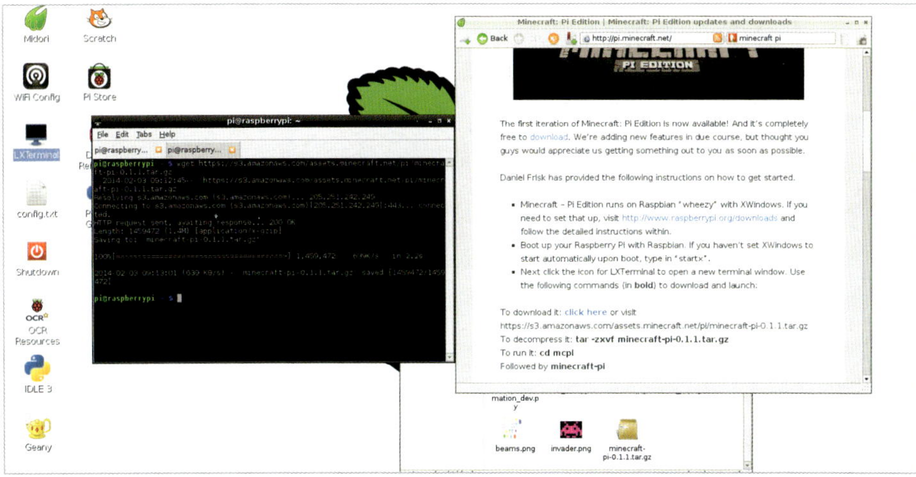

Installation

02 There's no official package for Minecraft-Pi in the Raspbian repositories, so unlike most of the extra programs you'll install from the projects in this book, we can't use 'sudo apt-get install'. Instead we'll first download the compressed package for the game from the official source, decompress it with the **tar** command and then learn how to manually start the game.

Make sure you're already in your home folder (by typing `cd ~` in the terminal) and download the Minecraft-Pi package with the following command:

```
wget https://s3.amazonaws.com/assets.minecraft.net/pi/minecraft-pi-0.1.1.tar.gz
```

Once it has finished downloading, we'll need to decompress it to use it. Copy the following command into the terminal window:

```
tar -zxvf minecraft-pi-0.1.1.tar.gz
```

Next, we need to move into the newly decompressed Minecraft-Pi directory and try running the game for the first time. In the terminal window, type the commands:

```
cd mcpi
./minecraft-pi
```

Assuming you've followed all the commands correctly, the game will load up into a window. While, like us, your first instinct might be to expand the window to the full width and height of your screen, due to a mouse pointer bug in this early version of Minecraft-Pi you'll lose control of part of the screen. If you plan to hack the game with Python, you'll need the game to be running in a relatively small window anyway, so you can 'tab out' of the game and into your Python script.

Minecraft-Pi controls

03 Firstly, have a good look around the game. If you're not familiar with *Minecraft* already, you control movement with the mouse and the WASD keys. Numbers 1-8 select items in your quickbar, the space bar makes you jump, and Shift makes you walk slowly (so you don't fall off edges). 'E' will open your inventory and double-tapping the space bar will also toggle your ability to fly.

Minecraft-Pi limitations

04 The Raspberry Pi edition of the game is very similar to the Pocket Edition of *Minecraft* designed for tablets and smartphones. You can only play in Creative Mode, however, and fans of the latest version of *Minecraft* might be a little disappointed to find that none of the more recent additions to the game are present – cats, horses, new flowers and the like. It's also currently not possible to sprint or use the bow that's included in the inventory screen.

"If you're not familiar with Minecraft already, you control movement with the mouse and the WASD keys"

What you'll need…

Raspbian (latest release)
www.raspberrypi.org/downloads

Minecraft-Pi tarball
http:// http://pi.minecraft.net/

Keyboard & mouse

Internet connection

Program Minecraft-Pi

Learn to program while playing one of the most popular games in the world today…

Now you've got the hang of *Minecraft* for the Raspberry PI it's time to try your first project. Over the next four pages we'll show you how you can use Python to program Minecraft-Pi to make fun games and projects. We'll implement a version of Hide & Seek created by Martin O'Hanlon that challenges you to find a block of diamond hidden somewhere within 50 blocks of your current position. The game uses a simple algorithm to test to see how far you are away from the block and it will tell you if you're getting warmer or colder! Don't worry if you've never programmed in Python before. You can copy our code and follow the instructions to take it for a test run. Once you've got the hang of it, you can try changing the settings to create your own version of the game.

Did you know…

Minecraft-Pi is based on a very old build of the Pocket Edition of *Minecraft*. We hope there will be a new version soon!

Below Unlike all other versions of *Minecraft*, the Pi version encourages you to hack it

What is Minecraft: Pi Edition?

Posted on December 17, 2012

Minecraft: Pi Edition is a version of Minecraft that's designed to work on the Raspberry Pi: a cheap, credit card-sized computer that can help you learn to program.

Configure the API

01 To take control of Minecraft-Pi with the Python API, you next need to have convenient access to the Python API folder from within the /mcpi folder. This contains all the secret sauce you need to hack your own little games and projects together. The easiest way to do this (and keep the original folder clean in case of problems) is to create a new copy of the folder and its contents into a new folder. To do this open the terminal and type the following:

```
cp -r ~/mcpi/api/python/↵
mcpi ~/ minecraft
```

Once this is complete we can create a 'boilerplate' Python document that connects the API to the game. You can use it as a template for all your projects. Write the following into the terminal to enter your folder and get started:

```
cd ~/minecraft
nano minecraft.py
```

With nano open, copy the following and then save and exit with Ctrl+X, pressing Y (for yes), then Enter to return to the command prompt:

```
from mcpi.minecraft import ↵
Minecraft
from mcpi import block
from mcpi.vec3 import Vec3
mc = Minecraft.create()
mc.postToChat("Minecraft ↵
API connected")
```

Test your script

02 The short script you created contains everything you need to get started with hacking Minecraft-Pi in the Python language. For it to work, you need to have the game already running (and be playing). To grab control of the mouse while in-game, you can press Tab. Open a fresh terminal window, navigate into your minecraft folder and start it:

```
cd ~/minecraft
python minecraft.py
```

You'll see a message appear on screen to let you know the API connected properly. Now we know it works, let's get coding…

Hide & Seek

03 As you'll see from the code on the next two pages, we've created a game of Hide & Seek adapted from Martin O'Hanlon's original creation (which you can find on **www.stuffaboutcode.com**). When you launch the script, you'll be challenged to find a hidden diamond in the fastest time possible. We've used it to demonstrate some of the more accessible methods available in the API. Follow along with the next few steps in the guide to get an idea of how they work and how you can use them in your future projects. Hacking *Minecraft* is serious fun!

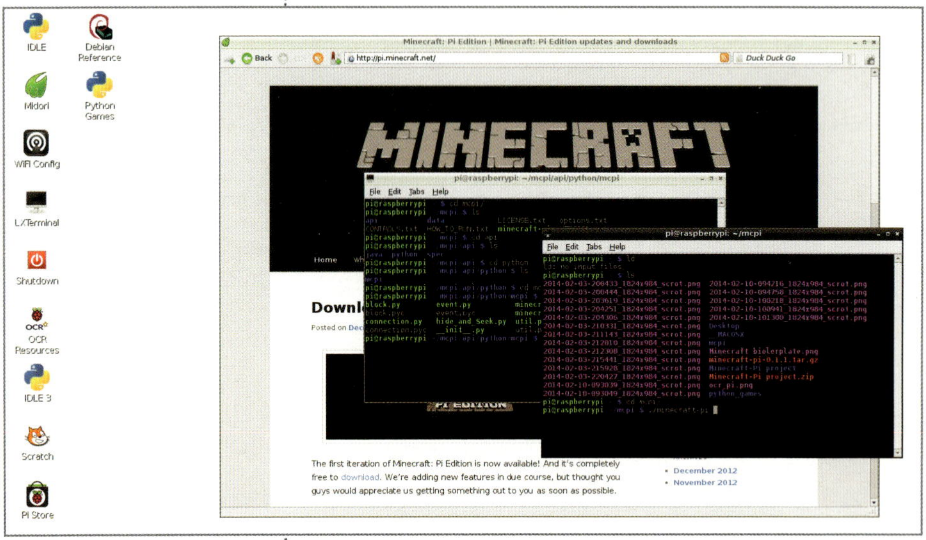

Creating the game

04 If you look at the start of our full code listing to the right you'll see that our boilerplate imports have grown somewhat to include things like `sleep` and `time`. All the imports listed beyond `Vec3` are all part of Python's standard library so will work straight away without having to install any more packages. One of the less clear things about the early code is probably the function `distanceBetweenPoints`. It's probably one of the most important parts of the game and it's what calculates exactly how far away you are from the target block in 3D space. The answer is returned as a square root of the constituent parts. You don't need to understand how this function works, but it's great to keep it in mind for future projects as it's sure to come in very handy indeed. The next function uses the `random` library to place the diamond.

Full code listing

```
# !/usr/bin/env python

from mcpi.minecraft import Minecraft
from mcpi import block
from mcpi.vec3 import Vec3
from time import sleep, time
import random, math

mc = Minecraft.create() # make a connection to the game
playerPos = mc.player.getPos()

# function to round players float position to integer
position
def roundVec3(vec3):
    return Vec3(int(vec3.x), int(vec3.y), int(vec3.z))

# function to quickly calc distance between points
def distanceBetweenPoints(point1, point2):
    xd = point2.x - point1.x
    yd = point2.y - point1.y
    zd = point2.z - point1.z
    return math.sqrt((xd*xd) + (yd*yd) + (zd*zd))

def random_block(): # create a block in a random position
    randomBlockPos = roundVec3(playerPos)
    randomBlockPos.x = random.randrange(randomBlockPos.x - 50, randomBlockPos.x + 50)
    randomBlockPos.y = random.randrange(randomBlockPos.y - 5, randomBlockPos.y + 5)
    randomBlockPos.z = random.randrange(randomBlockPos.z - 50, randomBlockPos.z + 50)
```

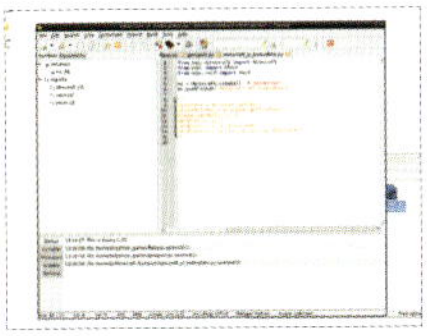

"Once you've got the hang of it, try changing the settings to create your own version of the game"

```
    return randomBlockPos

def main(): # the main function of Hide & Seek
    global lastPlayerPos, playerPos
    seeking = True
    lastPlayerPos = playerPos

    randomBlockPos = random_block()
    mc.setBlock(randomBlockPos, block.DIAMOND_BLOCK)
    mc.postToChat("A diamond has been hidden somewhere ↵
nearby!")

    lastDistanceFromBlock = distanceBetweenPoints(
randomBloc kPos, lastPlayerPos)
    timeStarted = time()

        # This is the main loop of the game
    while seeking:
        # Get players position
        playerPos = mc.player.getPos()
        # Has the player moved
        if lastPlayerPos != playerPos:
            distanceFromBlock = distanceBetweenPoints(
randomBlockPos, playerPos)

            if distanceFromBlock < 2:
                #found it!
                seeking = False
            else:
                if distanceFromBlock < ↵
 lastDistanceFromBlock:
                    mc.postToChat("Warmer " + ↵
str(int(distanceFromBlock)) + " blocks away")
                if distanceFromBlock > ↵
lastDistanceFromBlock:
                    mc.postToChat("Colder " + ↵
str(int(distanceFromBlock)) + " blocks away")

            lastDistanceFromBlock = distanceFromBlock

        sleep(2)

    timeTaken = time() - timeStarted
    mc.postToChat("Well done - " + str(int(timeTaken)) + ↵
"seconds to find the diamond")
if __name__ == "__main__":
    main()
```

The 'main' function explained

05 Next we have the main() function. As the name suggests, this is where the meat of the program resides. We will create a new random block for the player to find, and post to the chat window to let the player know the game has begun. We then make use of the **time** library to help us keep reporting how far the player currently is from the secret block of diamond. We then check to see if the 'seeking' variable is set to True. If so, we keep checking the player's location and then report back to say whether the player has got closer or further away from the secret block. We will then overwrite the last distance with the new distance.

Finding diamonds

06 How do we see if the player has found the diamond? We keep repeating the block of code inside 'while true' until the player's position is less than two blocks in distance away from the diamond. If the player is next to the diamond, it's fair to assume they've spotted it, so we can stop the clock and let them know they've succeeded and tell them exactly how long it took them to find it. It's a very quick and simple game, but it really shows off the API's tools. Have fun making your own projects!

Code your own Twitter bot

Create your very own Twitter bot that can retweet chunks of wisdom from others

Twitter is a useful way of sharing information with the world and it's our favourite method of giving our views quickly and conveniently. Many millions of people use the microblogging platform from their computers, mobile devices and possibly even have it on their televisions.

You don't need to keep pressing that retweet button, though. With a sprinkling of Python, you can have your Raspberry Pi do it for you. Here's how to create your own Twitter bot…

What you'll need…

Internet connectivity

Latest version of Raspbian
www.raspberrypi.org/ downloads

Installing the required software

01 Log into the Raspbian system with the username Pi and the password raspberry. Get the latest package lists using the command sudo apt-get update. Then install the Python Package installer using sudo apt-get install python-pip. Once you've done that, run sudo pip install twython to install the Twitter library we'll be using.

Registering your 'app' with Twitter

02 We need to authenticate with Twitter using OAuth. Before this, you need to go to **https://dev.twitter.com/apps** and sign in with the account you'd like your Pi to tweet from. Click the 'Create a new application' button. We called our application 'LUD Pi Bot' and set the website to **www.linuxuser.co.uk**.

Full code listing

```
#!/usr/bin/env python2

# A Twitter Bot for the Raspberry Pi that retweets any
content from

import sys
import time
from datetime import datetime
from twython import Twython

class bot:
    def __init__(self, c_key, c_secret, a_token, a_token_ ↵
secret):
        # Create a Twython API instance
        self.api = Twython(c_key, c_secret, a_token, ↵
a_token_secret)

        # Make sure we are authenticated correctly
        try:
            self.api.verify_credentials()
        except:
            sys.exit("Authentication Failed")

        self.last_ran = datetime.now()

    @staticmethod
```

Creating an access token

03 Go to the Settings tab and change the Access type from 'Read only' to 'Read and Write'. Then click the 'Update this Twitter application's settings' button. Next we create an access token. Click the 'Create my access token' button. If you refresh the details page, you should have a consumer key, a consumer secret and access token, plus an access token secret. This is everything we need to authenticate with Twitter.

Authenticating with Twitter

04 We're going to create our bot as a class, where we authenticate with Twitter in the constructor. We take the tokens from the previous steps as parameters and use them to create an instance of the Twython API. We also have a variable, last_ran, which is set to the current time. This is used to check if there are new tweets later on.

Retweeting a user

05 The first thing we need to do is get a list of the user's latest tweets. We then loop through each tweet and get its creation time as a string, which is then converted to a datetime object. We then check that the tweet's time is newer than the time the function was last called – and if so, retweet the tweet.

The main section

06 The main section is straightforward. We create an instance of the bot class using our tokens, and then go into an infinite loop. In this loop, we check for any new retweets from the users we are monitoring (we could run the retweet task with different users), then update the time everything was last run, and sleep for five minutes.

```
    def timestr_to_datetime(timestr):
        # Convert a string like Sat Nov 09 09:29:55 +0000
        # 2013 to a datetime object. Get rid of the timezone
        # and make the year the current one
        timestr = "{0} {1}".format(timestr[:19], datetime. ↵
now().year)

        # We now have Sat Nov 09 09:29:55 2013
        return datetime.strptime(timestr, '%a %b %d %H:%M: ↵
%S %Y')

    def retweet_task(self, screen_name):
        # Retweets any tweets we've not seen
        # from a user
        print "Checking for new tweets from ↵
@{0}".format(screen_name)

        # Get a list of the users latest tweets
        timeline = self.api.get_user_timeline ↵
(screen_name = screen_name)

        # Loop through each tweet and check if it was
        # posted since we were last called
        for t in timeline:
            tweet_time = bot.timestr_to_datetime ↵
(t['created_at'])
            if tweet_time > self.last_ran:
                print "Retweeting {0}".format(t['id'])
                self.api.retweet(id = t['id'])

if __name__ == "__main__":
    # The consumer keys can be found on your application's
    # Details page located at https://dev.twitter.com/
    # apps(under "OAuth settings")
    c_key=""
    c_secret=""

    # The access tokens can be found on your applications's
    # Details page located at https://dev.twitter.com/apps
    # (located under "Your access token")
    a_token=""
    a_token_secret=""

    # Create an instance of the bot class
    twitter = bot(c_key, c_secret, a_token, a_token_secret)

    # Retweet anything new by @LinuxUserMag every 5 minutes
    while True:
        # Update the time after each retweet_task so we're
        # only retweeting new stuff
        twitter.retweet_task("LinuxUserMag")
        twitter.last_ran = datetime.now()
        time.sleep(5 * 60)
```

What you'll need...

Arduino Uno

Internet connectivity

Nanpy
https://github.com/nanpy

Code Arduino with Python

Enjoy all the features and benefits of the Arduino microcontroller in your Raspberry Pi projects

You might be wondering why you would want to attach an Arduino to your Raspberry Pi. While there are lots of reasons, probably the most poignant is the extra six PWM-capable pins and another six analogue pins that a standard Arduino Uno offers.

While the Raspberry Pi has an excellent array of pins and capabilities, it can't do analogue and it can't do real-time processing out of the box. With an Arduino, additions like servos, potentiometers and a whole array of analog sensors are trivially easy to trigger and control. With this guide you can control it from your Raspberry Pi and you don't even have to program in C++!

Did you know...

The Arduino is better than the Raspberry Pi at controlling lights and motors, but the Pi is more powerful elsewhere.

Grab an Arduino

01 Before you can do anything, you need an Arduino. We recommend the Uno, since it's the default choice with the best balance of features, convenience and affordability. Since you'll want to put it to use straight away, we recommend investing in a 'starter kit' that includes LEDs, servos and all that fun stuff. Just Google 'Arduino Starter Kit' and you'll be inundated with results.

Satisfying dependencies

02 We're assuming you're using Raspbian, so open your terminal. At the terminal, type:

```
wget https://bitbucket.org/pypa/setuptools/raw/bootstrap/ez_setup.py
python ez_setup.py user
```

Once this is complete, you'll be able to use the easy_install command to install pyserial...

Final preparations

03 Since the communication between the Arduino and Raspberry Pi will happen over the USB serial connection, we need to get the Python-serial library. Open a terminal and type:

```
easy_install pyserial
```

We also need to install the Arduino software so the Pi knows how to deal with the device when it's plugged in. Next, in the terminal, type:

```
sudo apt-get update
sudo apt-get install arduino
```

Install Nanpy

04 There are only two steps remaining in the configuration. First, we need to get the Nanpy package downloaded and installed on the Pi. Our preferred way is to clone it with Git. Navigate to your home folder in the terminal (cd ~) and do the following in the terminal, one after the other:

```
easy_install nanpy
sudo apt-get install git
git clone https://github.com/nanpy/nanpy.git
```

Configure your Arduino Uno

05 Why have we cloned the original Git repository? Nanpy relies on an update to the Arduino firmware to function correctly, so you'll need to access the firmware folder from the nanpy project directory to do it. Before typing the following into the terminal, plug your Arduino Uno into a spare port on the Raspberry Pi. Beware: the following takes some time!

```
cd nanpy/firmware
export BOARD=uno
make
make upload
```

Testing Arduino

06 With the installation finally complete, we can test the setup to make sure it works properly. Before we do a proper 'Hello World' application in the code segment to the right, let's first ensure Nanpy is properly installed and the connection between Pi and Arduino is working. From your home folder (cd ~), type the following into the terminal:

```
nano nanpy_test.py
```

In the nano editor, simply write:

```
from nanpy imort Arduino
```

Now press Ctrl+X, Y, then Enter to save your new file.

Finally, in the terminal, type:

```
Python nanpy_test.py
```

If you don't see an error, then everything should be working fine. Now you can play with the code across the page to start learning your way around Nanpy.

Full code listing

```
# Like all good hardware-based 'Hello, World' applications,
we'll start
# by making the light on the Arduino board flicker off and on.
from nanpy import Arduino
from time import sleep
Arduino.pinMode(13, Arduino.OUTPUT)
for i in range(10):
Arduino.digitalWrite(13, Arduino.HIGH)
sleep(2)
Arduino.digitalWrite(13, Arduino.LOW)
sleep(2)

# This will make the light controlled by pin 13 on the Arduino
# turn on and off every two seconds ten times.
light = 13
Arduino.pinMode(light, Arduino.OUTPUT)

# You can also assign multiple pins at the same time:
red_pin = 3
green_pin = 5
blue_pin = 9
for pins in (red_pin, green_pin, blue_pin):
    Arduino.pinMode(pins, Arduino.OUTPUT)

# if you've got an LED screen for your RasPi you'll probably
# find it works out of the box with Nanpy. Just make sure you
# assign the right pin numbers for your screen:

from nanpy import (Arduino, Lcd)
screen = Lcd([7, 8, 9, 10, 11, 12], [16, 2])
screen.printString("Hello, World!")

# If you're using potentiometers, buttons or analog sensors,
# you'll need to assign them as inputs
knob = 0
Arduino.pinMode(knob, Arduino.INPUT)
value = Arduino.analogRead(knob)
for i in range(10):
    print "The value of the knob is:", knob
    sleep(1)

# Sometimes you want to delay what the arduino does.
# This can help you get consistent, solid readings

def get_value():
    value = Arduino.analogRead(knob)
    Arduino.delay(100)
    return value

for i in range(100):
    print "The value is:", get_value()
```

Create a three-colour lamp

Use the power of Arduino to do otherwise impossible projects with just a Raspberry Pi alone

What you'll need...

Arduino Uno
Breadboard
Set of prototyping cables
RGB LED (cathode)
3x potentiometers
3x 330 Ohm resisters

In the previous project we showed you how you can use an Arduino microcontroller to help the Raspberry Pi become proficient in new skills that can drastically increase the reach of your projects. With the aid of the extra 12 pins capable of PWM and analogue input, you could easily add multiple servos, analogue sensors and even add input devices like joysticks.

In this project we're going to demonstrate this by creating a three-colour lamp that employs three potentiometers (twisty knobs) to control each of the three colours in an RGB LED light. With it you can make most of the colours of the rainbow.

Program with Arduino

01 Assuming you've followed the steps from the previous two pages your Raspberry Pi and Arduino Uno are ready to go. You'll also need the components from the list above. The resistors should be 330-ohm ideally, but can be of a higher resistance if needed. A quick visit to **www.cpc.co.uk** should fill any holes with missing components.

Populate the breadboard

02 The circuit for this project might look a little complicated at first glance, but actually there's very little going on. As you'd expect, we want to control the LED light using PWM-enabled pins (to have fine-grained control of the brightness) and the potentiometers (pots) are being read by the analogue pins.

Full code listing

```
#!/usr/bin/env python

from nanpy import Arduino
from time import sleep

# set LED pins - these go to the Digital pins of your Arduino
redPin = 3
greenPin = 6
bluePin = 9
# set pot pin numbers - these go to the
# (A)nalog pins of your Arduino
pot_r_Pin = 0
pot_g_Pin = 3
pot_b_Pin = 5

#set three coloured pins as outputs
for pins in (redPin, greenPin, bluePin):
        Arduino.pinMode(pins, Arduino.OUTPUT)
# set pot pins as inputs
for pins in (pot_r_Pin, pot_g_Pin, pot_b_Pin):
        Arduino.pinMode(pins, Arduino.INPUT)

debug = False
```

```
def get_pots():
        """
        Grab a reading from each of the pot pins and
        send it to a tuple to be read by the colour mixer
        """
        r = Arduino.analogRead(pot_r_Pin) / 4
        Arduino.delay(1)
        g = Arduino.analogRead(pot_g_Pin) / 4
        Arduino.delay(1)
        b = Arduino.analogRead(pot_b_Pin) / 4
        Arduino.delay(1)
        return r, g, b

def colour_mixing():
        """
        Call get_pots() and set
        the colour pins accordingly
        """
        r, g, b = get_pots()
        Arduino.analogWrite(redPin, r)
        Arduino.analogWrite(greenPin, g)
        Arduino.analogWrite(bluePin, b)
        Arduino.delay(1)

def close_pins():
        """
        Close pins to quit cleanly (doesn't work with a 'for
        loop' despite the pins happily initialising that way!)
        """
        Arduino.digitalWrite(redPin,Arduino.LOW)
        Arduino.digitalWrite(greenPin,Arduino.LOW)
        Arduino.digitalWrite(bluePin,Arduino.LOW)

def main():
        """
        Mix the colours using three pots.
        Ctrl+C cleans up the pins and exits.
        """
        try:
                print "Adjust the pots to change the colours"
                while True:
                        colour_mixing()
                        sleep(0.2)
                        if debug:
                                print "Red: {:d} | Green: ↵
{:d} | Blue: {:d}".format(r, g, b)

        except KeyboardInterrupt:
                close_pins()
                print "\nPins closed"

if __name__ == '__main__':
        main()
```

Connect the Arduino and Raspberry Pi

03 Assuming you don't plan to write up the code immediately yourself, you can grab it from the website and drop it in your home folder. With the USB cable from the Arduino plugged into the Raspberry Pi, run the code with the following:

```
python RGB_Mixer.py
```

Adjust the pots for the corresponding colour of the LED and the colours should change. If the pots are adjusting the wrong colours, just swap the wires over.

Setting up the pins

04 As we demonstrated in the last project, it's easy to name and set the Arduino pins with Nanpy – in our code we've used two simple for loops. The debug value below simple prints the values of each pot to the terminal – very useful for debugging or getting a better handle on the code.

Functional operation

05 There are only really three main functions to worry about. get_pots() reads in the analogue pin value associated with each pot-pin and returns a tuple of the value for red, green and blue respectively. This is used by colour_mixing() to assign values to each of the associated PWM pins to change the colours of the LED.

Keeping things running

06 The main() function is where the other functions are set to work. Inside the function, we're asking Python to mix the colours forever, except if we press Ctrl+C – initiating the keyboard interrupt. Since we want to clean up after, this action with trigger close_pins() turning off the pins attached to the LED.

What you'll need...

ADXL accelerometer
shop.pimoroni.com

Latest Raspbian Image
www.raspberrypi.org/downloads

Breadboard
shop.pimoroni.com

Male-to-female prototyping cables
shop.pimoroni.com

30W soldering iron
shop.pimoroni.com

Use an accelerometer

Adding tilt technology to your next Raspberry Pi project is easier than you might think

In this project we'll be using an ADXL345 accelerometer kit to create a prototype controller for a Space Invaders-style game we're working on. The kit is only £20, but does require about 15 minutes of basic soldering. Beyond that, the physical setup is really quite simple. We'll be placing the ADXL345 on our breadboard 'controller' and using just four wires to communicate with the Raspberry Pi's GPIO pins using I2C. You'll have a full set-up guide available from the retailer.

Let's start by making sure your Pi is up to date. Open a terminal window and type: `sudo apt-get update && sudo apt-get upgrade`

Install i2c-tools

01 In a terminal, type: `sudo apt-get install i2c-tools` followed by `sudo nano /etc/modprobe.d/raspi-blacklist.conf`. This will open a file in nano – locate the line 'blacklist i2c-bcm2708' and comment it out so it looks like this:

```
#blacklist i2c-bcm2708
```

Save with Ctrl+X, then press Y and Enter to exit. Finally, edit the /etc/modules file with nano, adding the line `i2c-bcm2708 i2c-dev` to ensure it loads every time you boot. Reboot to finish the operation.

Connect the hardware

02 We'll also need to install the smbus Python library. Type `sudo apt-get install python-smbus` in the terminal. Then wire up the accelerometer to the Pi with male-to-female prototyping cables. The correct pins are marked on the ADXL345, but check our pictures for where to plug things into the Pi.

Full code listing

```
import pygame
from adxl345 import ADXL345

adxl345 = ADXL345() # Initialise the accelerometer
pygame.init() # Initialise Pygame

# Create a screen of 800x600 resolution
screen = pygame.display.set_mode([800, 600])

# Name the game window
# Set the mouse visibility and start an FPS clock
pygame.display.set_caption('ADXL345 Space Test - Press ESC ↵
to quit')
pygame.mouse.set_visible(False)
clock = pygame.time.Clock()

# Load the images we're using from:
# http://opengameart.org/users/rawdanitsu
background_image = pygame.image.load("Space-Background-4_0.↵
jpg").convert()
player_image = pygame.image.load("ship0.png").convert()

# We can use colour key method to remove the
# background from the ship
player_image.set_colorkey([0, 0, 0])

player_position = [450, 350] # Initial ship tarting point
game_over = False # decide if the game should end
```

"We'll be placing the ADXL345 on our breadboard 'controller' using I2C"

```
def update_pos():
    """ Poll the adxl345 and update player pos based on ↵
readings"""
    move_data = adxl345.getAxes(True) # Returns a dict of ↵
axes results
    if move_data['x'] < -0.1 or move_data['x'] > 0.1:
          player_position[0] += move_data['x'] * 20
    if move_data['y'] < -0.1 or move_data['y'] > 0.1:
          player_position[1] += move_data['y'] * 20

def check_pos():
    """ Check player pos to make it
    wrap-around the game window"""
    if player_position[0] > 850:
          player_position[0] = -75
    elif player_position[0] < -75:
          player_position[0] = 850

    if player_position[1] > 650:
          player_position[1] = -75
    elif player_position[1] < -75:
          player_position[1] = 650

###### MAIN PROGRAM LOOP ######
while not game_over: # Handle control events while the ↵
game is in play
    for event in pygame.event.get():
          if event.type == pygame.QUIT:
                game_over = True # Quit if close button ↵
is pressed
          if event.type == pygame.KEYDOWN:
                if event.key == pygame.K_ESCAPE:
                      game_over = True
                      # Quit if escape key is pressed

    update_pos() # Update the player's position
    check_pos() # Check the player's position

    # Update the background then the player's position on ↵
the screen
    screen.blit(background_image, [0, 0])
    screen.blit(player_image, [player_position[0],player_ ↵
position[1]])

    pygame.display.flip() # Refresh the screen
    clock.tick(20) # Force frame-rate to desired number

pygame.quit() #Quit gracefully when 'game_over' is True
```

Final checks

03 With accelerometer attached to Pi, power it up, open a terminal window and type: sudo i2cdetect -y 1. The '1' at the end assumes you're using a Rev 2 Pi – replace it with '0' if yours is older. You should see some numbers denoting that the ADXL345 has been recognised. Finally, we'll use Git to grab the project – type the following:

```
sudo apt-get install git
```

Cloning and testing

04 From the terminal, navigate to your home folder (with cd ~) and create a project folder for the project to live in using: **mkdir adxl345_project**. Cd into the folder and from the terminal, type the following to clone the finished project from our Github.com account: **git clone https://github.com/russb78/adxl345_project.git**

How it works

05 To run the project from the **adxl345_project** folder type:

```
sudo python adxl_345_project.py
```

The Pygame window will open. Pick up your breadboard 'controller' and tilt it around. The ship should move around the screen in reaction to your movements. If it's backwards, you can adjust the orientation of the breadboard – it might just be 'upside down'!

Why it works

06 The code for this project is an excellent backbone for a Space Invaders-style game written in Python and Pygame. The code collects data from the ADXL345 accelerometer in the **update_pos()** function using the **move_data** variable. This data is piped to the **player_position** array – which is in the form of x and y co-ordinates. The move_data pushes the image of the spaceship around the screen.

What you'll need...

A router or switch

Raspbian
www.raspberrypi.org/downloads

An iOS or Android device

A Linux computer

Stream music

Remotely control a Raspberry Pi that plays your music collection and stream your music to your phone

Music Player Daemon (MPD) is a piece of software that acts as both a music player and a music server. It can output audio to any sound card connected to the system, and be controlled by an MPD client. Clients are available for almost any platform, including iOS and Android. MPD can also output audio to a stream, which can be used by most clients. This is great for people with large music libraries who can't fit it all on their device.

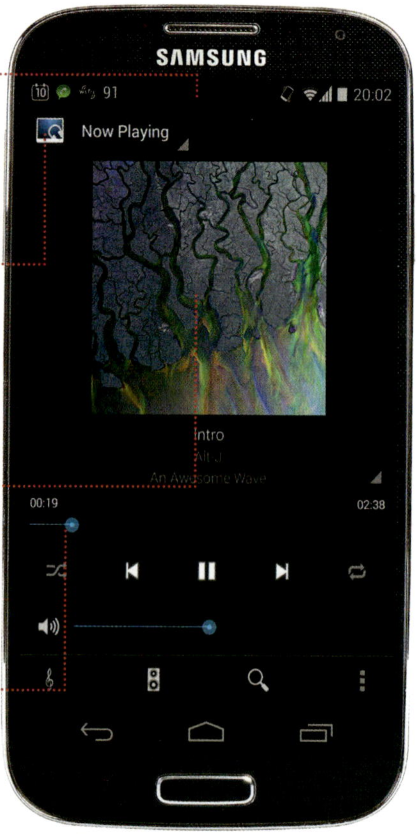

Android & iOS
While there are lots of applications suitable for this project, we recommend MPDroid for Android and MPoD for Apple's iOS devices

Music collection
Your music collection must be stored in the directory /var/lib/mpd/music on your Raspberry Pi. Once the daemon is set up, you can access it from any mobile device or computer

Server connection
Once your Android or iOS app is set up, we are able to connect to our music server using the Raspberry Pi's IP address

Streaming daemon
We can configure the Raspberry Pi Music Player Daemon to listen on all interfaces so we can access the music from all kinds of devices

Install the required software

01 Log into the Raspbian system with the username `pi` and the password `raspberry`. First, find the IP address of the Pi using `ip addr | grep inet` and note it down for use later. Get the latest package lists using the command `sudo apt-get update`. Then install MPD using `sudo apt-get install mpd`. There may be some errors, but you'll just be able to ignore those. Next we need to change some permissions...

Add music

02 The default music directory for mpd is /var/lib/mpd/music. We will first make this folder world-readable, writable and executable so that the Pi user can write to it. Do this with `sudo chmod 777 /var/lib/mpd/music`. Then find some music you'd like to copy on your Linux computer and use scp to copy it. For example: `scp -r Alt-J/ pi@192.168.157.28:/var/lib/mpd/music/`

Fix permissions

03 The files that we just copied will be owned by the Pi user, which isn't what we want. We're going to change the ownership of the music directory, and all subfiles/subdirectories, to the mpd user and the audio group:

```
sudo chown -R mpd:audo /var/lib/mpd/music
```

Configure the daemon

04 We want to edit /etc/mpd.conf. We need to use sudo to do it, so write `sudo nano /etc/mpd.conf` in the terminal. The first change is to make the daemon listen on all interfaces, so we can use MPD clients from other devices. Do this by changing the line:

```
bind_to_address    "localhost"
```

to...

```
bind_to_address    "any"
```

Configure a stream

05 At the moment, the only audio output is the 3.5mm one on the Pi. To set up a stream, scroll down the config file until you find the httpd stream output that is commented out. Uncomment the entry, and change the format line to produce stereo output instead of mono. Our entry was as follows:

```
audio_output {
        type        "httpd"
        name        "My HTTP
Stream"
        encoder     "vorbis"
        port        "8000"
        quality     "5.0"
 #bitrate           "128"
        format      "44100:16:2"
 }
```

Save the changes and restart the daemon with:

```
sudo /etc/init.d/mpd restart
```

"MPD can output audio to any sound card connected to the system, including iOS and Android"

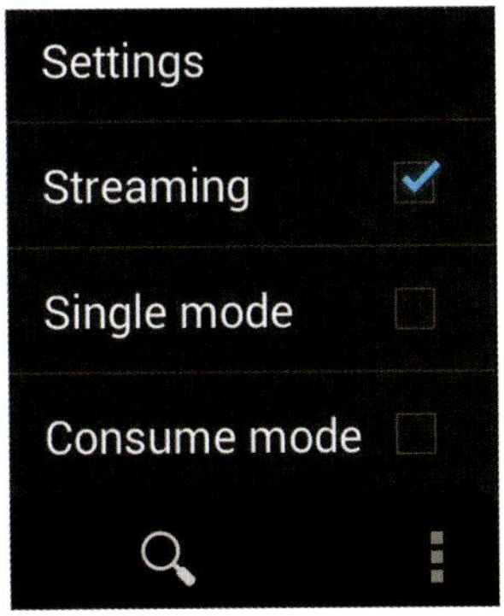

Set up a client

06 It's difficult to walk through setting up a client on each different platform, but the steps translate fairly easily. For Linux, we suggest Sonata, for Android we suggest MPDroid, and for iOS we suggest MPoD. We're going to set up MPDroid on Android, so go ahead and download that from the Play Store.

Connect to the server

07 Once in the MPDroid app, select WLAN-based connection and choose your access point. Then fill in the Host field with the IP address of your Pi and fill in the 'Streaming host' field with the same details. Everything else should be the default. Once you've done this, go to the Now Playing screen. We need to update the music library, as it has never been scanned before. To do this, press the Menu button,and go to Settings. Then select the Update option, with the caption 'Refresh MPD's Database'.

Playing music

08 Press the 'treble clef' button in the bottom-left corner. This will take you to the Artists section of the music library. To play music from an artist, all you need to do is long-press on the artist and select 'Add, replace and play'. If you have speakers or headphones connected to the Pi, you should hear music coming out of them. You may need to use the volume slider on the Now Playing screen to adjust the volume to suit.

To enable the stream (the real magic of our project) press the Menu button and tick the Stream option. After about ten seconds of buffering, the sound will be coming out of your Android device. Although this sounds like a long time for the music to buffer, once you have a playlist the device will play it seamlessly. You may be able to reduce this buffer time by looking at the improvements section in the next and final step...

Further improvements

09 This article has illustrated a very simple MPD setup. Further possible improvements include:

- Putting music on an external hard drive so that you have more storage space available;
- Tweaking the streaming settings to tax the Pi's CPU less (look at the 'encoder plugins' section of the user manual at **www.musicpd.org/doc/user**);
- Setting up a Samba share, to give access to the music files over the network which is compatible with all major operating systems.

What you'll need…

Latest Raspbian Image
www.raspberrypi.org/downloads

Pillow
https://github.com/python-imaging/Pillow

SimpleGUITk
https://github.com/dholm/simpleguitk/

Make a Pong clone with Python

We update the retro classic Pong for the Linux generation with a new library called SimpleGUITk

The Raspberry Pi is a fantastic way to start learning how to code. One area that can be very rewarding for amateur coders is game programming, allowing for a more interactive result and a greater sense of accomplishment. Game programming can also teach improvisation and advanced mathematics skills for code. We'll be using the fantastic SimpleGUITk module in Python, a very straightforward way of creating graphical interfaces based on Tkinter.

Below 'Tux for Two' is a great little Pong clone using the beloved Linux mascot, Tux, in the centre of the action

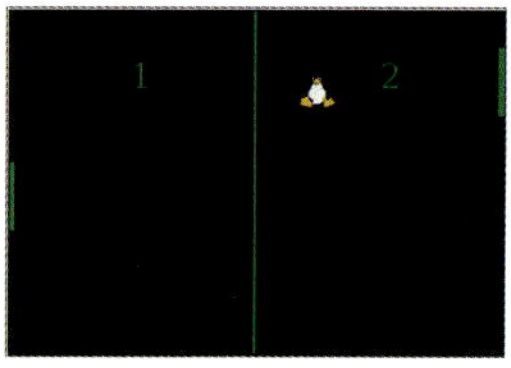

Python module preparation

01 Head to the websites we've listed in 'What you'll need' and download a zip of the source files from the GitHub pages. Update your Raspbian packages and then install the following:

```
$ sudo apt-get install python-dev python-setuptools tk8.5-dev
tcl8.5-dev
```

Install the modules

02 Open the terminal and use cd to move to the extracted Pillow folder. Once there, type:

```
$ sudo python setup.py install
```

Once that's complete, move to the **simpleguitk** folder and use the same command to install that as well.

Write your code

03 Launch IDLE 2, rather than IDLE 3, and open a new window. Use the code listing to create our game 'Tux for Two'. Be careful to follow along with the code to make sure you know what you're doing. This way, you can make your own changes to the game rules if you wish.

Set up the game

04 There's nothing too groundbreaking to start the code: Tux's and the paddles' initial positions are set, along with the initial speed and direction of Tux. These are also used when a point is won and the playing field is reset. The direction and speed is set to random for each spawn.

The SimpleGUI code

05 The important parts in the **draw** function are the **draw_line**, **draw_image** and **draw_text** functions. These are specifically from SimpleGUI, and allow you to easily put these objects on the screen with a position, size and colour. You need to tie them to an object, though – in this case, **canvas**. This tells the software that we want to put these items on the screen for people to see.

SimpleGUI setup code

06 The last parts are purely for the interface. We tell the code what to do when a key is depressed and then released, and give it a frame to work in. The frame is then told what functions handle the graphics, key functions etc. Finally, we give it **frame.start()** so it starts.

Full code listing

```
import simpleguitk as simplegui
import random

w, h = 600, 400
tux_r = 20
pad_w= 8
pad_h = 80

def tux_spawn(right):
    global tux_pos, tux_vel
    tux_pos = [0,0]
    tux_vel = [0,0]
    tux_pos[0] = w/2
    tux_pos[1] = h/2
    if right:
        tux_vel[0] = random.randrange(2, 4)
    else:
        tux_vel[0] = -random.randrange(2, 4)
    tux_vel[1] = -random.randrange(1, 3)

def start():
    global paddle1_pos, paddle2_pos, ↵
paddle1_vel, paddle2_vel
    global score1, score2
    tux_spawn(random.choice([True, False]))
    score1, score2 = 0,0
    paddle1_vel, paddle2_vel = 0,0
    paddle1_pos, paddle2_pos = h/2, h/2

def draw(canvas):
    global score1, score2, paddle1_pos, ↵
paddle2_pos, tux_pos, tux_vel
    if paddle1_pos > (h - (pad_h/2)):
        paddle1_pos = (h - (pad_h/2))
    elif paddle1_pos < (pad_h/2):
        paddle1_pos = (pad_h/2)
    else:
        paddle1_pos += paddle1_vel
    if paddle2_pos > (h - (pad_h/2)):
        paddle2_pos = (h - (pad_h/2))
    elif paddle2_pos < (pad_h/2):
        paddle2_pos = (pad_h/2)
    else:
        paddle2_pos += paddle2_vel
    canvas.draw_line([w / 2, 0],[w / 2, h], 4, ↵
"Green")
    canvas.draw_line([(pad_w/2), paddle1_ ↵
pos + (pad_h/2)], [(pad_w/2), paddle1_pos - ↵
(pad_h/2)], pad_w, "Green")
    canvas.draw_line([w - (pad_w/2), ↵
paddle2_pos + (pad_h/2)], [w - (pad_w/2), ↵
paddle2_pos - (pad_h/2)], pad_w, "Green")
    tux_pos[0] += tux_vel[0]
    tux_pos[1] += tux_vel[1]
    if tux_pos[1] <= tux_r or tux_pos[1] >= ↵
h - tux_r:
        tux_vel[1] = -tux_vel[1]*1.1
    if tux_pos[0] <= pad_w + tux_r:
        if (paddle1_pos+(pad_h/2)) >= ↵
tux_pos[1] >= (paddle1_pos-(pad_h/2)):
            tux_vel[0] = -tux_vel[0]*1.1
            tux_vel[1] *= 1.1
        else:
            score2 += 1
            tux_spawn(True)
    elif tux_pos[0] >= w - pad_w - tux_r:
        if (paddle2_pos+(pad_h/2)) >= ↵
tux_pos[1] >= (paddle2_pos-(pad_h/2)):
            tux_vel[0] = -tux_vel[0]
            tux_vel[1] *= 1.1
        else:
            score1 += 1
            tux_spawn(False)
    canvas.draw_image(tux, (265 / 2, 314 / 2), ↵
(265, 314), tux_pos, (45, 45))
    canvas.draw_text(str(score1), [150, 100], ↵
30, "Green")
    canvas.draw_text(str(score2), [450, 100], ↵
30, "Green")

def keydown(key):
    global paddle1_vel, paddle2_vel
    acc = 3
    if key == simplegui.KEY_MAP["w"]:
        paddle1_vel -= acc
    elif key == simplegui.KEY_MAP["s"]:
        paddle1_vel += acc
    elif key==simplegui.KEY_MAP["down"]:
        paddle2_vel += acc
    elif key==simplegui.KEY_MAP["up"]:
        paddle2_vel -= acc

def keyup(key):
    global paddle1_vel, paddle2_vel
    acc = 0
    if key == simplegui.KEY_MAP["w"]:
        paddle1_vel = acc
    elif key == simplegui.KEY_MAP["s"]:
        paddle1_vel = acc
    elif key==simplegui.KEY_MAP["down"]:
        paddle2_vel = acc
    elif key==simplegui.KEY_MAP["up"]:
        paddle2_vel = acc

frame = simplegui.create_frame("Tux for Two", ↵
w, h)
frame.set_draw_handler(draw)
frame.set_keydown_handler(keydown)
frame.set_keyup_handler(keyup)
tux = simplegui.load_image('http://upload. ↵
wikimedia.org/wikipedia/commons/a/af/Tux.png')

start()
frame.start()
```

What you'll need...

Latest Raspbian Image
www.raspberrypi.org/downloads

Breadboard

Connectors

Jumper wire

DSLR camera

Compatible shutter cable

Time-lapse camera trigger

Make shooting time-lapse video with your DSLR camera a cinch with our expert advice

You'd be forgiven for thinking that creating mesmerising time-lapse videos like those of Vincent Laforet (**www.laforetvisuals.com**) or John Eklund (**www.theartoftimelapse.com**) might be out of reach of the Average Joe. With the help of the Raspberry Pi and a sprinkling of Python code, though, that's no longer the case. In this guide we're going to trigger our DSLR camera to create pixel-perfect time-lapse imagery...

Set up the Raspberry Pi

01 For this tutorial we're assuming you're using a recent build of Raspbian. With the Raspberry Pi set up with a keyboard, mouse and monitor, open the terminal and type:

```
sudo apt-get update
```

Install the RPi.GPIO library

02 Next we want to make sure your development environment is set up. Follow these steps to make sure you're all set. In the terminal, type:

```
suda atp-get install python-dev
sudo apt-get install python-rpi.gpio
```

Set up the Pi Cobbler

03 For this tutorial we've used a cheap prototyping breadboard and an Adafruit Pi Cobbler to give us easy access to the Raspberry Pi's GPIO pins. As you can see from the picture, the Cobbler straddles the centre-point of the breadboard and a ribbon cable connects the two.

Full code listing

```
import RPi.GPIO as GPIO
import time

print '\nWelcome to the Complete Manual Time-lapse Tool.'
print "Just tell us how many shots you'd like to take and ↵
the interval between them.\n"
print "Try googling 'time-lapse interval calc' if you need ↵
help deciding.\n"


def main():
    shots = raw_input('How many shots would you like to ↵
take?\n ->')
    interval = raw_input('How frequently do you want to ↵
take them (in seconds)?\n ->')

    if shots.isdigit() and interval.isdigit():
        shots = int(shots)
        interval = int(interval)

        print "You'll be shooting for %d minutes.\n" % ↵
(shots * interval / 60)
        answer = raw_input('Are you ready to proceed?(yes/ ↵
no):')
        confirm = answer.lower() in ['yes', 'y']

        if confirm:
            GPIO.setmode(GPIO.BOARD)
            GPIO.setup(16, GPIO.OUT)
            taken = 1
            print
            print 'Starting a run of %d shots' % (shots)
```

```
            for i in range(0, shots):
                print
                print 'Shot %d of %d' % (taken, shots)
                taken +=1
                GPIO.output(16, GPIO.HIGH)
                time.sleep(0.5)
                GPIO.output(16, GPIO.LOW)
                time.sleep(interval)
            GPIO.cleanup()
        else:
            print "Let's try again (or press Ctrl + C to ↵
quit):\n"
            main()
    else:
        print "Oops - You can only enter numbers. Let's try ↵
again:\n"
        main()

    print
    print 'Thanks for using the Complete Manual Time- ↵
lapse Tool!\n'
    again = raw_input('Would you like to do another time- ↵
lapse? (yes/no):\n -> ')
    proceed = again.lower() in ['yes', 'y']

    if proceed:
        main()
    else:
        print '\nSee you next time!\n'
        quit()

if __name__ == '__main__':
    main()
```

Configure the breadboard

04 For the Raspberry Pi's GPIO to control the camera, we need to create a circuit between a pin on the GPIO (in this case pin 23 on the Cobbler – but it's actually physical pin 16) and the pin that connects to the 'head' or 'tip' of the camera cable that activates the shutter when connected. The base of the connector cable is always ground, so make sure you ground the 'GND' pin on the Cobbler and the middle pin on the audio jack. With the circuit complete, we can focus on the code.

The Time-lapse Photography Tool

05 We've created a small 55-line Python utility called The Linux User Time-lapse Photography Tool, which asks the user to input how many shots they'd like to take and the frequency they'd like them taken. It then takes that information and uses it in a For loop to activate the shutter using GPIO pin 16 . If you'd like to use the project 'in the field' we'd recommend using the Android app ConnectBot to SSH into your RasPi for input and feedback. Don't forget to start your script with `sudo python time_lapse_camera.py`

Creating a video

06 With your camera packed with images, we need to collect and output them as a video file. While it's possible on the Pi, copy them to an easily accessible folder on a separate Linux PC to make it much faster. We're going to use FFmpeg. With the terminal open in the folder where your images are stored, type: `ffmpeg -f image2 -i image%04d.jpg -vcodec libx264 -b 800k video.avi`. This assumes you have libx264 installed on your machine and the '`image%o4d.jpg`' assumes the file format and the number of digits it's dealing with (in this case: 'picture0001.jpg').

What you'll need...

Latest version of Raspbian
www.raspberrypi.org/downloads

picamera Python module
picamera.readthedocs.org

RasPi camera module
http://cpc.farnell.com

Pygame
www.pygame.org

Stop motion animation with the Camera board

Fancy yourself as the next Nick Park? Set up this DIY stop-motion studio and see what you can do

Did you know...

The LEGO Movie has inspired millions to try out stop-motion-animation. Don't miss out on the fun!

The Raspberry Pi camera module opens the door for your Pi projects to incorporate aspects of photography and movie making. We're combining both here to create a fully featured stop-motion animation application, Pi-Mation, which makes it incredibly easy to create impressive HD animations.

We've written this project with Python and it relies on two libraries that you will need to install. Picamera (**picamera.readthedocs.org**) is a pure Python interface to the Raspberry Pi camera module and is a must for all camera module owners. Pygame (**www.pygame.org**), on the other hand, ensures our images can be displayed on demand. The project in its current state is merely a proof-of-concept for a bigger stop motion animation application. It's not perfect either, but goes to prove that the Raspberry Pi in tandem with the Camera board and a bit of know-how can offer amazing results!

Keep an eye on **http://github.com/russb78/pi-mation** for updates on the project in the future...

Set up the camera module

01 First thing's first, you need to make sure your Raspberry Pi is up to date. In the terminal, type:

```
sudo apt-get update && sudo apt-get upgrade
```

Next we need to update the Pi's firmware and ensure camera module is activated. Bear in mind that this takes some time.

```
sudo rpi-update
sudo raspi-config
```

Full code listing

The first job is to import the libraries we'll be using with the project and set some key variables

```
import pygame, picamera, os, sys

pics_taken = 0
current_alpha, next_alpha = 128, 255
fps = 5
```

Next we initiate Pygame so we can use it in our project and set some key variables around it

```
pygame.init()
res = pygame.display.list_modes() # return the best resolution
# for your monitor
width, height = res[0]
print "Reported resolution is:", width, "x", height
start_pic = pygame.image.load(os.path.join('data', ↵ 'start_
screen.jpg'))
start_pic_fix = pygame.transform.scale(start_pic, (width,
height))
screen = pygame.display.set_mode([width, height])
pygame.display.toggle_fullscreen()
pygame.mouse.set_visible = False
```

Below Pi-Mation is available on GitHub via https://github.com/russb78/pi-mation

Next we use the picamera library to create our camera object and create our first function

We can preview our animation with the animate() function

We need to update the display so we can show the new images we've taken on screen

The functions here are vital to ensure Pi-mation can output videos and close cleanly

```
play_clock = pygame.time.Clock()
camera = picamera.PiCamera()
camera.resolution = (width, height)

def take_pic():
    global pics_taken, prev_pic
    pics_taken += 1
    camera.capture(os.path.join('pics', 'image_' + ↵ str(pics_
taken) + '.jpg'), use_video_port = True)
    prev_pic = pygame.image.load(os.path.join('pics', 'image_' +↵
str(pics_taken) + '.jpg'))

def delete_pic():
    global pics_taken, prev_pic
    if pics_taken >= 1:
        pics_taken -= 1
        prev_pic = pygame.image.load(os.path.join('pics', ↵
'image_' + str(pics_taken) + '.jpg'))

def animate():
    camera.stop_preview()
    for pic in range(1, pics_taken):
        anim = pygame.image.load(os.path.join('pics', 'image_' +↵
str(pic) + '.jpg'))
        screen.blit(anim, (0, 0))
        play_clock.tick(fps)
        pygame.display.flip()
    play_clock.tick(fps)
    camera.start_preview()

def update_display():
    screen.fill((0,0,0))
    if pics_taken > 0:
        screen.blit(prev_pic, (0, 0))
    play_clock.tick(30)
    pygame.display.flip()

def make_movie():
    camera.stop_preview()
    pygame.quit()
    print "\nQuitting Pi-Mation to transcode your video."
    os.system("avconv -r " + str(fps) + " -i " + str((os. ↵ path.
join('pics', 'image_%d.jpg'))) + " -vcodec libx264 video.mp4")
    sys.exit(0)

def change_alpha():
    global current_alpha, next_alpha
    camera.stop_preview()
    current_alpha, next_alpha = next_alpha, current_alpha
    return next_alpha

def quit_app():
    camera.close()
```

```
    pygame.quit()
    print "You've taken", pics_taken, " pictures. Don't ↵
forget to back them up!"
    sys.exit(0)

def intro_screen():
    intro = True
    while intro:
        for event in pygame.event.get():
            if event.type == pygame.KEYDOWN:
                if event.key == pygame.K_ESCAPE:
                    quit_app()
                elif event.key == pygame.K_F1:
                    camera.start_preview()
                    intro = False
        screen.blit(start_pic_fix, (0, 0))
        pygame.display.update()

def main():
    intro_screen()
    while True:
        for event in pygame.event.get():
            if event.type == pygame.KEYDOWN:
                if event.key == pygame.K_ESCAPE:
                    quit_app()
                elif event.key == pygame.K_SPACE:
                    take_pic()
                elif event.key == pygame.K_BACKSPACE:
                    delete_pic()
                elif event.key == pygame.K_RETURN:
                    make_movie()
                elif event.key == pygame.K_TAB:
                    camera.preview_alpha = change_alpha()
                    camera.start_preview()
                elif event.key == pygame.K_F1:
                    camera.stop_preview()
                    intro_screen()
                elif event.key == pygame.K_p:
                    if pics_taken > 1:
                        animate()
        update_display()

if __name__ == '__main__':
    main()
```

"The Raspberry Pi in tandem with the Camera board and a bit of know-how can offer amazing results!"

Install other dependencies

02 Next we'll make sure Pygame and picamera are installed:

```
sudo apt-get install python-setuptools
easy_install -user picamera
```

Finally, to install Pygame and the video apps, type:

```
sudo apt-get install python-pygame
sudo apt-get install libav-tools && sudo ↵
apt-get install omxplayer
```

Final setup

03 We're going to install Pi-Mation with Git, so let's make sure it's installed:

```
sudo apt-get install git
```

With a terminal open, navigate to your home directory (with cd ~) and type:

```
git clone https://github.com/ ↵
russb78/pi-mation.git
```

If you play with the code and break it, you can revert it back to its original state with:

```
git checkout ↵
pi-mation.py
```

Running and testing Pi-Mation

04 Now navigate into the pi-mation folder and run the application with:

```
python pi-mation.py
```

The controls are quite straightforward and displayed on screen when you first enter the application. You can press F1 at any time to return to the control screen. Have fun!

What you'll need...

A wireless internet connection

2 x momentary switches

4 x female-to-male leads (to connect your Pi to a breadboard)

2 x 220-ohm resistors

4 x male-to-male leads

Speakers connected to a 3.5mm headphone jack

Build a portable internet radio

Turn your Raspberry Pi into a portable Wi-Fi streaming radio

There are thousands of free radio stations on the internet, and with this project you can listen to all of them from one tiny little box. So let's build our streaming radio using a Raspberry Pi, a speaker and a few odds and ends...

Let's get set up

01 Firstly, we need to prepare our Pi. Using Raspbian, and a Pi connected to the internet, open a terminal and switch to the root user:

```
sudo su
```

And update your list of packages, then upgrade your Pi to the latest software:

```
apt-get update && apt-get
upgrade -y
```

Install some extra packages

02 We need to install the Python packages to access the GPIO. In a terminal, logged in as root, enter the following.

```
apt-get install python-rpi.
gpio
```

Now install MPlayer, which is what will be playing our audio.

```
apt-get install mplayer
```

Make the files executable and Install

03 To install the tools, we need to navigate to **PiAUISuite-master/Install**. We now need to make InstallAUISuite.sh executable for all users, so use:

```
chmod 777  InstallAUISuite.sh
```

Now that the file is executable, let's install:

```
sudo ./ InstallAUISuite.sh
```

Full code listing

We import the RPi GPIO library and set it to use BCM numbering system

Here we set up pins 23 and 24, which control the radio station selection

Here we say that if the button is pressed for 23, run the command below

Here we see the script kill any open MPlayer processes and then load the radio station

```
#!/usr/bin env python
import time import sleep
import os
import RPi.GPIO as GPIO
# I found loads of BBC Radio streams
# from http://bbcstreams.com/
GPIO.setmode(GPIO.BCM)
GPIO.setup(23 , GPIO.IN)
GPIO.setup(24 , GPIO.IN)
while True:
    if GPIO.input(23)==1:
        os.system('sudo killall mplayer')
        os.system('mplayer -playlist http://bbc.co.uk/ ↵
radio/listen/live/r1.asx &')
    if GPIO.input(24)==1:
        os.system('sudo killall mplayer')
        os.system('mplayer -playlist http://bbc.co.uk/ ↵
radio/listen/live/r6.asx &')
    sleep(0.1);
GPIO.cleanup()
```

Set up the software

04 Copy **radio.py** from **www.linuxuser.co.uk/tutorial-files** to your home directory. You can tweak it to suit your needs if you wish later no. Now open a terminal and switch to root, and edit your network interface config by doing the following:

```
nano /etc/network/interfaces
```

Wi-Fi configuration

05 We want the Pi to automatically connect to your router via Wi-Fi during boot. Edit your **/etc/network/interfaces** file to resemble this:

```
auto lo
iface lo inet loopback
iface eth0 inet dhcp
allow-hotplug wlan0
auto wlan0
iface wlan0 inet dhcp
wpa-ssid "ssid"
wpa-psk "password"
```

Replace the "ssid" and "password" with your own details, but keep the quotation marks.

Configure the radio to start at boot

06 In a terminal, as root, navigate to **/etc/init.d/** and then create a file called **radio** using nano.

```
nano radio
```

In that file, type in the following:

```
#! /bin/bash
modprobe snd_bcm2835
amixer cset numid=3 1
python /home/pi/radio.py
```

This loads the kernel module for the sound card Amixer sets the output to the 3.5mm headphone jack (that's what 1 means, HDMI is 2). Lastly it calls the Python script.

Make it executable

07 Save and exit radio in **/etc/init.d** by pressing Ctrl+X and then answer yes to the prompt. Now make radio executable by typing (as root):

```
chmod 755 radio
```

Then, as root, register radio to start on boot by typing in a terminal:

```
update-rc.d radio defaults
```

Raspi-config

08 In a terminal as root, use **raspi-config** to change the boot behaviour of your Pi. We don't want it to load the desktop, a terminal is all we need, as the project will not require a screen for future use. Once complete, reboot the Pi and watch as the output from boot whizzes across the screen.

First test

09 Once the Pi has finished loading, press one of the buttons on your breadboard. In a few seconds you should hear the audio come through the speakers that you attached to the headphone jack. That's it, you have a wireless internet radio. Why not add a mute function using amixer (**manpages.ubuntu.com/manpages/gutsy/man1/amixer.1.html**) and another momentary switch. Or even add an LCD screen (**www.rpiblog.com/2012/11/interfacing-16x2-lcd-with-raspberry-pi.html**) to show the station details.

What you'll need…

A portable hard drive

Raspbian
www.raspberrypi.org/downloads

PC with a desktop environment with Deluge
http://deluge-torrent.org

Build an always-on torrent box

Get the latest distros, packages and test builds faster with a low-power, mini torrent box

Torrenting your open source software has a number of advantages – it can be faster, alleviates bandwidth and allows you to share back with the community. Distros, packages and more are available via torrents, and the Raspberry Pi makes for a great tiny, low-wattage, always-on torrent box to better manage your files.

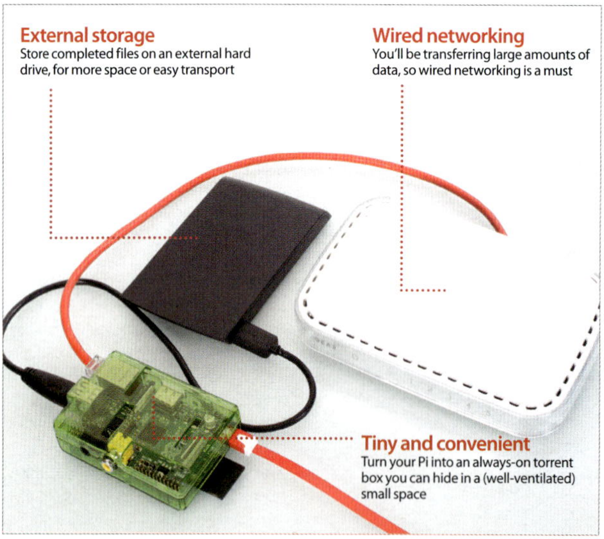

"The Raspberry Pi makes for a great tiny, low-wattage, always-on torrent box to better manage your files"

Install Raspbian

01 Raspbian works just fine for our torrent box. Install the image on an SD card and go through the basic setup process, making sure to enable SSH in the advanced options and to disable the desktop.

Remote access

02 Type ifconfig into your Pi's command line to find the IP address. At this point you can unplug the monitor and set it up remotely, but either way you can now access the Pi by typing:

```
$ ssh [user]@[IP address]
```

…and entering your password to log in.

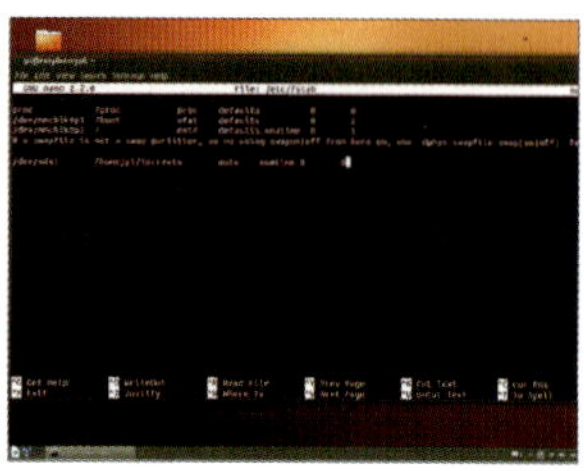

Mount hard drive

03 Unless you plan to reformat your portable drive, you'll need to install NTFS support onto your Pi. Type:

```
$ sudo apt-get install ntfs-3g
```

Add the hard drive to **/etc/fstab** (open it with `sudo nano /etc/fstab`) by adding the line:

```
/dev/[hard drive address]
[mount point] auto noatime 0 0
```

Use fdisk to find the name of the storage, and create a mount point such as /home/pi/torrents with mkdir. Reboot for it to mount.

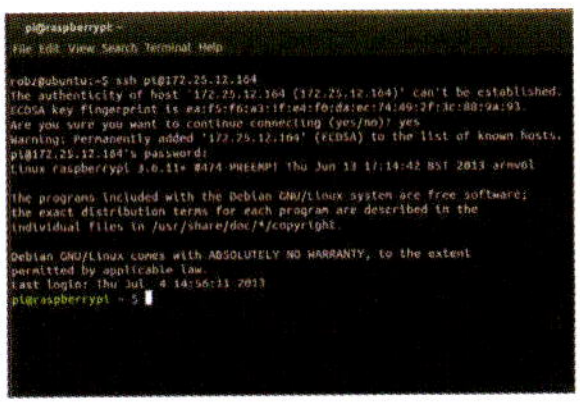

Install Deluge

04 We'll use Deluge for our torrents. Install it with:

```
$ sudo apt-get install deluged
deluge-console
```

Now start and then stop Deluge so it creates a config file we can edit with:

```
$ deluged
$ sudo pkill deluged
```

And finally, run the following to copy the config file in case we mess up:

$ cp ~/.config/deluge/auth ~/.config/deluge/auth.old

Basic configuration

05 Edit the file with:

```
$ nano ~/.config/deluge/
auth
```

And add to the bottom:

```
[user]:[password]:10
```

...to restrict access.

Now start it up with:

```
$ deluged
$ deluge-console
```

Remote connection

06 Now you're in the client, type the following three commands:

```
config -s allow_remote True
config allow_remote
exit
```

Restart the Deluge daemon with:

```
$ sudo pkill deluged &&
deluged
```

Now open the graphical client on your Linux PC.

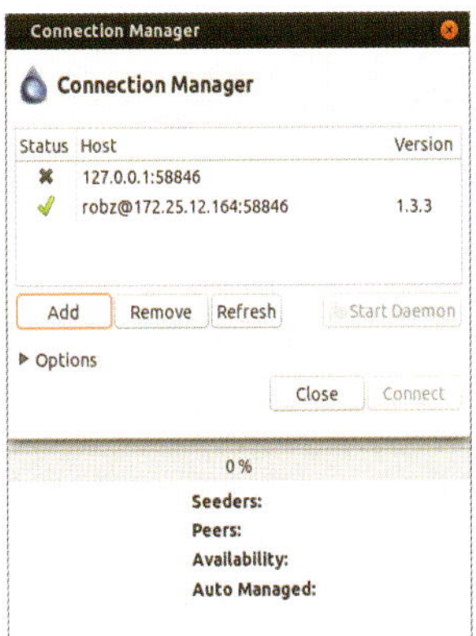

Remote interface

07 Go to Edit>Preferences> Interface, then disable Classic Mode and restart Deluge. Click Add on the Connection Manager, and enter the IP in Hostname and the user we set up earlier. Click Connect to see any torrents you have downloading or uploading.

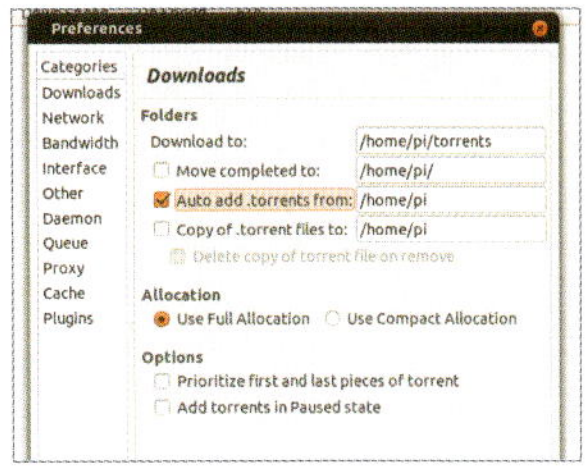

Download location

08 Go again to Edit then Preferences, and change to the Downloads tab if it's not on there already. Set the download location to the directory we mounted the hard drive to, and enable 'Auto add .torrents', setting it to any destination if you plan to dump torrents to the Pi.

Start on boot

09 An init script from Ubuntu can be used to have Deluge start on boot. Download it with:

```
$ sudo wget -O /etc/default/
deluge-daemon http://bit.
ly/13nKOSj
```

Open **/etc/default/deluge-daemon** with nano and change the username to the one we set up earlier. Save it, then download the full init script and update with:

```
$ sudo wget -O /etc/init.d/
deluge-daemon http://bit.
ly/13nKKlz
$ sudo chmod 755 /etc/init.d/
deluge-daemon
$ sudo update-rc.d deluge-
daemon defaults
```

What you'll need…

A router or switch

Smartphones & computers

Powered USB hub

The latest RasPBX image
www.raspberry-asterisk.org/downloads

Build a VoIP server

Use your Raspberry Pi as a voice over IP server, perfect for phone calls in the home or a small business

RasPBX is a project that brings Asterisk – industry-standard voice over IP software – to the Raspberry Pi. There are VoIP clients for many platforms, including hardware that converts VoIP to a conventional telephone line. Each client gets a phone number and can call other clients. You can also have conference calls, perfect for meetings over the phone. As an extension of this article, you could also share the VoIP server over the internet, allowing remote clients to connect.

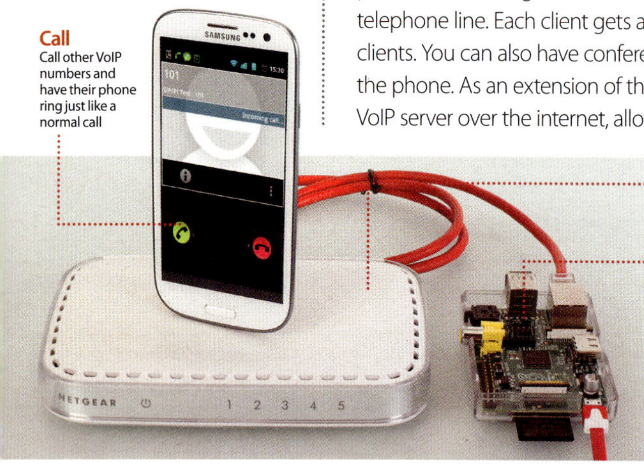

Call
Call other VoIP numbers and have their phone ring just like a normal call

Connect
We recommend using wired networking, especially if you want to 'set and forget' your VoIP server

Serve
The Raspberry Pi makes the perfect server for this kind of project

Initial setup

01 RasPBX is good to go as soon as the image is flashed to your SD card: there is a web interface for configuration, and SSH is included for remote login. As this will be a server, we'll log in with the user 'root' and password 'raspberry' and change the IP address to a static one so that we always know where it is on the network.

```
root@raspbx:~# ip addr show dev eth0 | grep inet
    inet 172.17.173.94/24 brd 172.17.173.255 scope global eth0
    inet6 fe80::ba27:ebff:fef3:9016/64 scope link
root@raspbx:~# ip route | grep default
default via 172.17.173.1 dev eth0
root@raspbx:~# cat /etc/resolv.conf
nameserver 127.0.0.1
nameserver 8.8.8.8
nameserver 8.8.8.4
```

Assign a static IP address

02 To set up the network configuration go:

```
iface eth0 inet static
  address 172.17.173.94
  netmask 255.255.255.0
  network 172.17.173.0
  broadcast 172.17.173.255
  gateway 172.17.173.1
```

Now that we have the network configuration, we can assign a static IP address. Open **/etc/network/interfaces** in an editor such as nano, and change the line:

```
iface eth0 inet dhcp
```

to a configuration similar to our expert's. We don't have to worry about DNS. Load your network config with:

```
sudo
/etc/init.d/networking restart
```

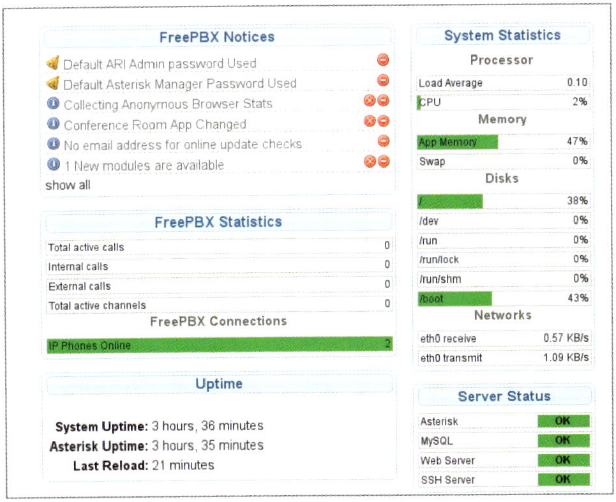

The web Interface

03 Type the static IP address of your Raspberry Pi into a web browser. You'll be taken to the FreePBX web interface for configuring Asterisk. Click the FreePBX Administration button and use the username 'admin', and password 'admin'. The User Control Panel allows users to listen to their voicemails.

Add extensions

04 Each device that will be connected needs its own extension. To add an extension, hover over the Applications tab, then select Extensions. Select Generic SIP Device as the device type and click Submit. The User Extension is the number to call to get to that device. The Display Name can either be the name of a person or just the same as the User Extension. The only other thing that you need to fill in is the secret, which is a passphrase that allows the device to connect. One of these will have been generated, but you can change it if you like. Scroll to the bottom and click Submit. Add as many extensions as you like.

Add a conference extension

05 Go to the Applications section and select Conferences. Choose a number and name for the conference, and a PIN number if you'd like users to require a PIN to join. Click Submit Changes once you're done.

Apply config

06 Changes such as adding extensions and conferences are not made until the Apply Config button is pressed, so be sure to do that before closing the web interface.

Trying it out

07 If you're using an Android phone, we recommend CSipSimple, which can be found on Google Play. We recommend Linphone for Linux clients. We'll use two Android phones as an example. When adding an account in CSipSimple, scroll down to the Generic wizards section and select Basic. Then fill in the information as shown in the image (below). Once you have two devices set up, try calling between the two.

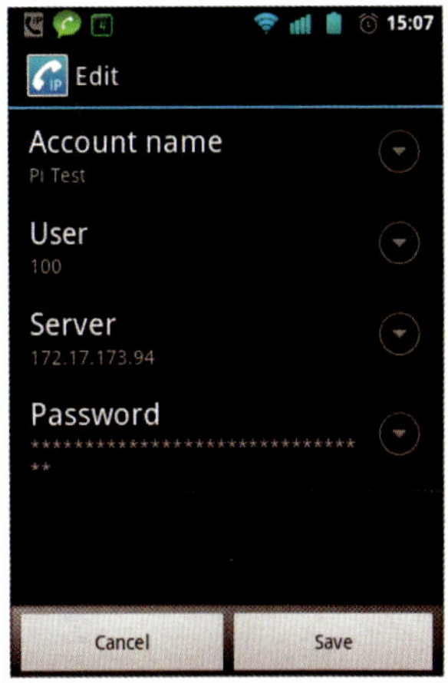

Trying a conference call

08 Call the conference number that you set up from one of the devices. You'll need to enter the PIN code you set followed by the # key. You'll be told that you are the only person in this conference, and will hear a notification whenever anyone else joins and leaves the conference.

"Each client gets a phone number and can call other clients. You can also have conference calls"

What you'll need...

Raspbian
www.raspberrypi.org/downloads

Wi-fi adapter

Create a portable wireless access point

With the help of a Wi-Fi adaptor, you can turn your Raspberry Pi into a wireless access point for other devices

Did you know...

Aside from XBMC setting up your Pi as a Wi-Fi access point is one of the most common projects to undertake.

The Raspberry Pi's portability makes it ideal for carrying around as an emergency wireless router and access point. Perfect if you're visiting a hotel without the service, or less tech-adept friends and family. Here's how to get it set up...

Install Raspbian

01 For this project, we recommend using Raspbian to power our access point. To do this install the image on an SD card and go through the basic setup process, making sure to enable SSH during installation. You can also turn off the desktop during setup as well if you don't plan to use it, though you might want to keep it for other projects.

Connect through SSH

02 Find the IP address of your Raspberry Pi by typing `ifconfig` into the command line, and make a note of it. Unplug your Raspberry Pi, plug in your wireless adaptor, and then plug the power back in. In a networked computer's terminal, type:

```
ssh [user]@[IP address]
```

Install DHCP

03 Install a DHCP server with:

```
sudo apt-get install hostapd isc-dhcp-server
```

Now we need to set it up. Edit the configuration file with:

```
sudo nano /etc/dhcp/dhcpd.conf
```

And start by putting a # in front of the two option domain-name entries, then remove the # in front of 'authoritative;' seven lines down

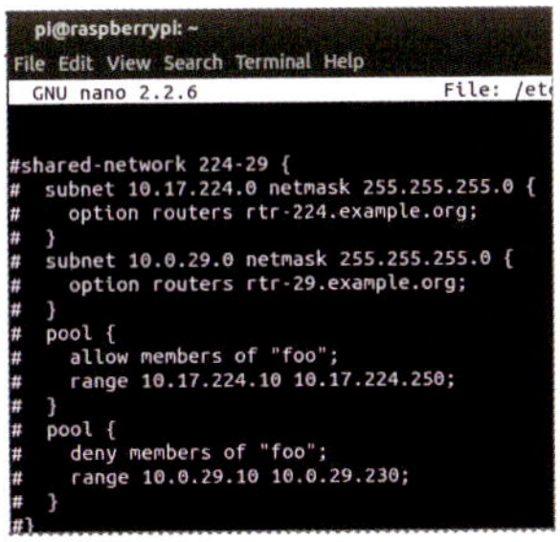

Server address

04 At the end of the configuration file, add these lines:

```
subnet 192.168.42.0 netmask
255.255.255.0 {
range 192.168.42.10
192.168.42.50;
option broadcast-address
192.168.42.255;
option routers 192.168.42.1;
default-lease-time 600;
max-lease-time 7200;
option domain-name "local";
option domain-name-servers
8.8.8.8, 8.8.4.4;
}
```

Disable Wi-Fi

05 Edit the server more with:

```
$ sudo nano /etc/
default/isc-dhcp-server
```

Set INTERFACES to 'wlan0' and save. Now open:

```
sudo nano /etc/network/
interfaces
```

Put a # in front of '`iface wlan0`' and the following lines with '`wpa roam`', '`iface default`' and any others affecting wlan0.

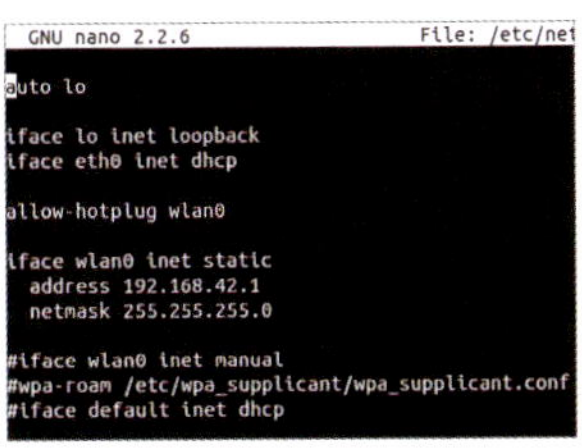

Enable access

06 After the line 'allow-hotplug wlan0', enter the following:

```
iface wlan0 inet static
    address 192.168.42.1
    netmask 255.255.255.0
```

Save and exit, then set wlan0's address with:

```
sudo ifconfig wlan0
192.168.42.1
```

Now create a new file to use to start creating the wireless network:

```
sudo nano /etc/hostapd/
hostapd.conf
```

Wireless networking

07 Create your wireless network with the following code:

```
interface=wlan0
driver=rtl871xdrv
ssid=[access point name]
hw_mode=g
channel=1
macaddr_acl=0
auth_algs=1
ignore_broadcast_ssid=0
wpa=2
wpa_passphrase=[password]
wpa_key_mgmt=WPA-PSK
wpa_pairwise=TKIP
rsn_pairwise=CCMP
```

Save and exit. Now edit **hostapd** to point it to this new file with:

```
sudo nano /etc/default/
hostapd
```

And then add:

```
/etc/hostapd/hostapd.conf to
DAEMON_CONF=""
```

Network addressing

08 Run:

```
sudo nano /etc/
sysctl.conf
```

And add `net.ipv4.ip_forward=1` to the bottom of the file.

Save this, and then finish by running:

```
sudo sh -c "echo 1 > /proc/
sys/net/ipv4/ip_forward"
```

Run the following three commands to make sure the internet is forwarded correctly:

```
sudo iptables -t nat
-A POSTROUTING -o eth0 -j
MASQUERADE
sudo iptables -A FORWARD
-i eth0 -o wlan0 -m state
--state RELATED,ESTABLISHED -j
ACCEPT
sudo iptables -A FORWARD -i
wlan0 -o eth0 -j ACCEPT
```

Finish up

09 So that this works after a reboot, type:

```
sudo sh -c "iptables-save >
/etc/iptables.ipv4.nat"
```

Then add `up iptables-restore < /etc/iptables.ipv4.nat` to the end of the **/etc/network/interfaces** file.

Finally, set it up as a daemon with:

```
sudo service hostapd start
sudo service isc-dhcp-server
start
sudo update-rc.d hostapd
enable
sudo update-rc.d isc-dhcp-
server enable
```

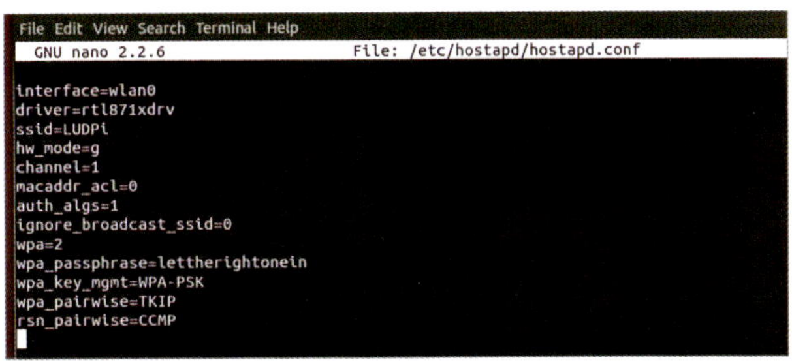

What you'll need...

A router or switch

A Linux-compatible webcam

Raspbian
www.raspberrypi.org/downloads

Powered USB hub

Did you know...

Most modern webcams are compatible with the Raspberry Pi, but check it supports Linux before you buy.

Build a security camera

Want to keep an eye on something from the comfort of your web browser? All you need is a Pi and a webcam!

This article will teach you how to use the MJPG-streamer software to stream video straight from a webcam to your web browser. You could record the stream, and also display multiple streams from multiple Raspberry Pis on one page. The streams can also be viewed from mobile devices and tablets.

Network investigation

01 The first job we need to do is investigate the network your Raspberry Pi is on, so we can assign it a static IP address. That way, we'll always know where it is on the network so we can access with ease.

```
pi@raspberrypi ~ $ ip addr show dev eth0 |
grep inet
    inet 172.17.173.94/24 brd 172.17.173.255
scope global eth0
pi@raspberrypi ~ $ ip route | grep default
default via 172.17.173.1 dev eth0
pi@raspberrypi ~ $ cat /etc/resolv.conf
nameserver 172.17.173.1
```

Assign a static IP address

02 Now that we have the network configuration, we can assign a static IP address. Open **/etc/network/interfaces** in an editor such as nano, and change the line:

```
iface eth0 inet dhcp
```

to a configuration similar to our expert's. Reboot to load the new configuration.

```
iface eth0 inet static
    address 172.17.173.94
    netmask 255.255.255.0
    network 172.17.173.0
    broadcast 172.17.173.255
```

Below It even works from mobile devices and tablets!

Installing the software

03 Log into the Raspbian system with the username 'pi' and the password 'raspberry'. The MJPG-streamer software isn't packaged for the Raspberry Pi, so we'll need to compile it ourselves. Update the package index with `sudo apt-get update`. We need to install Subversion, which we'll use to download source code. We'll also need libjpeg, and imagemagick, both of which are required by MJPG-streamer. Install these with:

```
sudo apt-get install subversion libjpeg8-dev imagemagick
```

Compile MJPG-streamer

04 Download and compile MJPG-streamer as shown below:

```
pi@raspberrypi ~ $ svn checkout svn://svn.code.sf.net/p/mjpg-streamer/code/mjpg-streamer-code
pi@raspberrypi ~ $ cd mjpg-streamer-code/mjpg-streamer
pi@raspberrypi ~/mjpg-streamer-code/mjpg-streamer $ make clean all
```

Testing it out

05 To start MJPG-streamer:

```
export LD_LIBRARY_PATH=.
./mjpg_streamer -i “input_uvc.so” -o “output_http.so -w ./www”
```

You have to export the library path variable to the current directory (.) so that the various input and output plug-ins can be used. Type your Raspberry Pi's IP address followed by :8080 into a browser and click the Stream tab. If the Stream tab doesn't work, try the example that uses JavaScript, as that should work on most browsers, including Android.

Start MJPG-streamer at boot

06 Edit the **/etc/rc.local** file (you'll need to use sudo) to include the following lines, ensuring that it still ends with exit 0:

```
export STREAMER_PATH=/home/pi/mjpg-streamer-code/mjpg-streamer
export LD_LIBRARY_PATH=$STREAMER_PATH
$STREAMER_PATH/mjpg_streamer -i “input_uvc.so” -o “output_http.so -w $STREAMER_PATH/www” &s
```

Reboot the Pi to check that it comes back up happily and starts the stream.

Recording the stream

07 You can easily download a motion JPEG stream and convert it to a more useful format using VLC:

```
cvlc http://172.17.173.94:8080/?action=stream --sout file/mp4:stream.mp4
```

Alternatively, you can just download the stream URL with wget like so:

```
wget http://172.17.173.94:8080/?action=stream
```

Multiple streams at once

08 Here is an example of how to put multiple streams on a single webpage. These streams could come from a number of different Raspberry Pis all over the house.

```
<html>
<h1>Streaming Example</h2>
<table border=”1”>
<tr>
<td><h2>Stream 1</h2></td>
<td><h2>Stream 2</h2></td>
</tr>
<tr>
<td><img src=”http://172.17.173.94:8080/?action=stream”/></td>
<td><img src=”http://172.17.173.94:8080/?action=stream”/></td>
</tr>
</table>
</html>
```

Extensions and improvements

09 This example setup is very basic and has a few flaws. There is no authentication or SSL encryption, which means the streams are insecure and shouldn't be shared over the internet. The HTTP module that comes with MJPG-streamer is quite simple, so you could get SSL by using a reverse proxy, such as Pound. You'd be able to do SSL for each Pi you had with a single Pound instance and access the different Pis by having something like 'stream1, stream2' in the URL.

> "Use the MJPG-streamer software to stream video straight from a webcam to your web browser"

What you'll need...

Raspbian
www.raspberrypi.org/downloads

Compatible Wi-Fi adaptor
www.adafruit.com/products/814

Build an Onion Pi and browse privately

Turn your Raspberry Pi into a highly secure and very portable router to keep safe and anonymous...

Elsewhere in this book we've shown you how to turn your Raspberry Pi into the ultimate portable wireless router, requiring very little power and giving you a wireless network wherever there's the most basic of internet connections. What if it's not enough to know you can search the web, though? What if you want to be wholly secure as you do it? Then it's time to upgrade the router with Tor to protect your privacy on the internet.

This 'Onion Pi', as dubbed by Adafruit, combines Raspbian and Tor to create and secure a wireless access point using just a Raspberry Pi. This will keep you anonymous online – a handy feature in a time of privacy concerns all around the web.

When the Pi is not connected to the internet, it should still function as a wireless router.

Did you know...

There is much interest in internet security today due to the actions of some government agencies.

It's all software
This isn't a hardware hack – a spare SD card can be used for the Tor router, and other SD cards can be used for different functions without any problems

Safety first
Using not much more than a Raspberry Pi, you can route one or more systems through a Tor-enabled access point, guaranteeing anonymity

Wi-Fi enabled
Connect everything over a wireless network – no need to directly connect to the Pi with a cable

Ethernet needed
Hook into the internet just about anywhere there's an internet connection – a relative's house, hotel rooms and more

Install Raspbian

01 Raspbian is the Raspberry Pi distro we'll be using for the Onion Pi. Download the zip file, extract the image and then apply it to an SD card using:

```
$ dd bs=4M if=[version number]-wheezy-raspbian.img of=/dev/[SD card location]
```

You can also use NOOBS to install Raspbian if you wish.

Set up Raspbian

02 Go through the initial Raspbian setup and make sure to turn on the SSH server, and to disable autoboot to desktop – this is unnecessary and will only use extra power. You can also tell it to fill up the rest of the card if there's room for it.

Pi IP

03 We'll be accessing your Raspberry Pi via SSH to set it up. To do this we need to know its IP address – you can find it by typing `ifconfig` into the command line. Make a note of it and turn off your Pi.

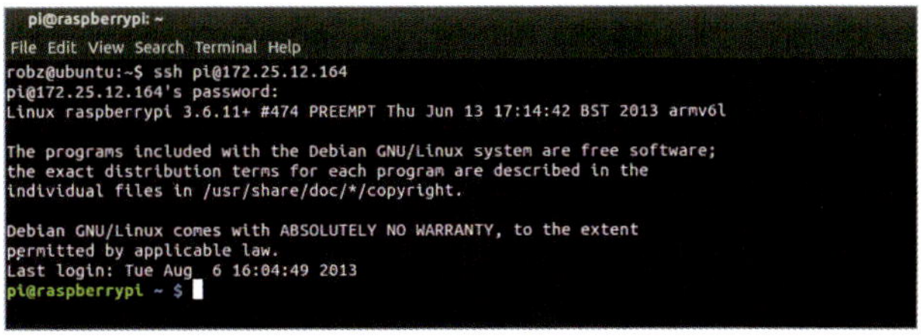

SSH connection

04 Plug your USB wireless adapter into the Pi and turn it back on. On another computer connected to the same network, open a terminal or type into the command line:

```
$ ssh [user]@[IP address]
```

Then enter the password for your Raspbian if it asks for it.

Install DHCP

05 To make life easier for any system connecting to the Pi access point, we need to install a DHCP server to it. We do this with:

```
$ sudo apt-get install hostapd isc-dhcp-server
```

DHCP will automatically assign IP addresses to network-attached devices, meaning you won't need static IPs.

Set up DHCP

06 Now we need to configure the DHCP server. Edit the configuration file with:

```
$ sudo nano /etc/dhcp/dhcpd.conf
```

And start by putting a # in front of the two option domain-name entries, then remove the # in front of authoritative, seven lines down.

Server address

07 At the end of the configuration file, add the following:

```
subnet 192.168.42.0 netmask 255.255.255.0 {
range 192.168.42.10 192.168.42.50;
option broadcast-address 192.168.42.255;
option routers 192.168.42.1;
default-lease-time 600;
max-lease-time 7200;
option domain-name "local";
option domain-name-servers 8.8.8.8, 8.8.4.4;
}
```

Save and exit.

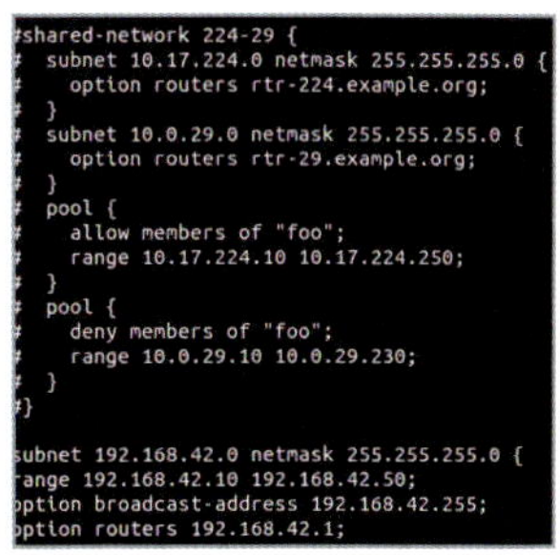

DHCP server

08 Edit the server configuration files so that it's set to work in conjunction with the wireless adaptor:

```
$ sudo nano /etc/default/isc-dhcp-server
```

Scroll to INTERFACES and change it to:

```
INTERFACES="wlan0"
```

Incoming Wi-Fi

09 We need to set up the Wi-Fi adaptor to be both static and accept incoming signals. First:

```
$ sudo nano /etc/network/interfaces
```

Put a # in front of iface wlan0 and following lines with wpa roam, iface default and any other affecting wlan0.

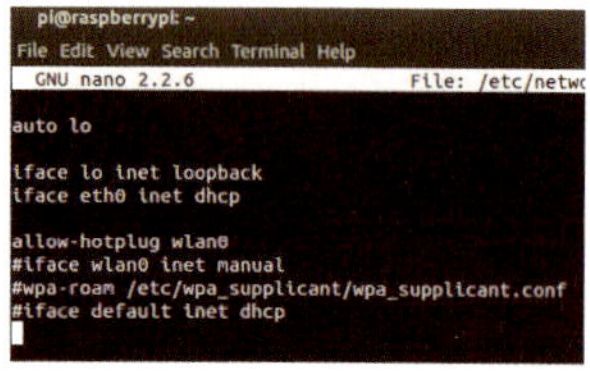

Static IP

10 Now give the wireless interface a static IP – after the line allow-hotplug wlan0, enter the following:

```
iface wlan0 inet static
        address 192.168.42.1
        netmask 255.255.255.0
```

Save and exit, and then set wlan0's address with:

```
$ sudo ifconfig wlan0
192.168.42.1
```

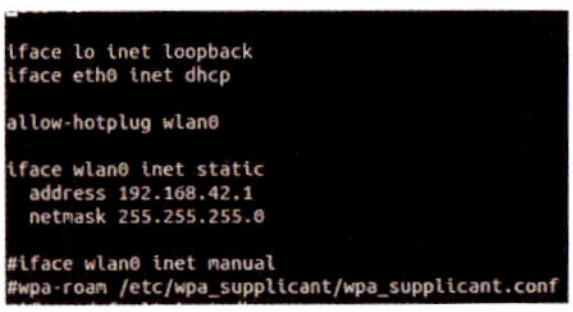

WLAN creation

11 We need to create a new file that holds all the information for our wireless network. We are going to make it password protected so that only the people we want to can access it. To create the file, start with:

```
$ sudo nano /etc/hostapd/
hostapd.conf
```

Once this is complete you can continue to the next step…

WLAN configuration

12 Assuming you've followed step 11 to open **hostapd.conf**. Write::

```
interface=wlan0
driver=rtl871xdrv
ssid=[access point name]
hw_mode=g
channel=1
macaddr_acl=0
auth_algs=1
ignore_broadcast_ssid=0
wpa=2
wpa_passphrase=[password]
wpa_key_mgmt=WPA-PSK
wpa_pairwise=TKIP
rsn_pairwise=CCMP
```

Hostapd

13 After saving and exiting, we need to edit hostapd to point it to this new file. Open it with:

```
$ sudo nano /etc/default/
hostapd
```

And then find the line #DAEMON_CONF="". Remove the #, and change it to:

```
DAEMON_CONF="/etc/hostapd/
hostapd.conf"
```

"The Onion Pi combines Raspbian and Tor. This will keep you anonymous online. A handy feature in a time of privacy concerns all around the web"

Network addressing

14 Setting up a NAT will allow multiple clients to connect. To do this, open a terminal window (if one isn't already open) and type the following:

```
$ sudo nano /etc/sysctl.conf
```

And add to the bottom of the file:

```
net.ipv4.ip_forward=1
```

Save this, and then finish by running:

```
$ sudo sh -c "echo 1 > /
proc/sys/net/ipv4/ip_forward"
```

IP tables

15 Run the following three commands to make sure the internet connection is forwarded correctly. Make sure you copy them carefully into the terminal.

```
sudo iptables -t nat -A
POSTROUTING -o eth0 -j
MASQUERADE
```

```
sudo iptables -A FORWARD
-i eth0 -o wlan0 -m state
--state RELATED,ESTABLISHED
-j ACCEPT
```

```
sudo iptables -A FORWARD -i
wlan0 -o eth0 -j ACCEPT
```

Apply configuration

16 So that this still continues to work even after the Raspberry Pi has been rebooted. Type:

```
$ sudo sh -c "iptables-save
> /etc/iptables.ipv4.nat"
```

Then add to the end of /etc/network/interfaces:

```
up iptables-restore < /etc/
iptables.ipv4.nat
```

Wi-Fi final

17 Finally, set it up as a daemon so it runs at boot with the following commands:

```
sudo service hostapd start
sudo service isc-dhcp-server start
sudo update-rc.d hostapd enable
sudo update-rc.d isc-dhcp-server enable
```

And the wireless access point part will be finished.

Install Tor

18 After a reboot, we now need to install Tor. Do this simply with:

```
$ sudo apt-get install tor
```

Once it's installed, you'll need to edit the Tor config file with:

```
$ sudo nano /etc/tor/torrc
```

Follow the next step to add all the necessary information to it.

Tor configure

19 Put this below the FAQ comment:

```
Log notice file /var/log/tor/notices.log
VirtualAddrNetwork 10.192.0.0/10
AutomapHostsSuffixes .onion,.exit
AutomapHostsOnResolve 1
TransPort 9040
TransListenAddress 192.168.42.1
DNSPort 53
DNSListenAddress 192.168.42.1
```

Table flush

20 We now need to flush the current IP tables so that we can get the routing to go through.

```
$ sudo iptables -F
$ sudo iptables -t nat -F
```

If you want to keep SSH open to connect remotely, you'll need to make an exception for that with:

```
$ sudo iptables -t nat -A PREROUTING -i wlan0 -p tcp --dport 22 -j REDIRECT --to-ports 22
```

Reroute

21 Route all DNS traffic first, using the following commands:

```
$ sudo iptables -t nat -A PREROUTING -i wlan0 -p udp --dport 53 -j REDIRECT --to-ports 53
```

And then route any TCP traffic with:

```
$ sudo iptables -t nat -A PREROUTING -i wlan0 -p tcp --syn -j REDIRECT --to-ports 9040
```

Check and save

22 You can check the table setup with the following terminal command. You'll need to save it if it works so read on.

```
$ sudo iptables -t nat -L
```

If you're happy with it, save it to the NAT file like before with:

```
$ sudo sh -c "iptables-save > /etc/iptables.ipv4.nat"
```

Logging

23 We should create a log file. This is important in case you need to debug later. To do this, use these three commands.

```
$ sudo touch /var/log/tor/notices.log
$ sudo chown debian-tor /var/log/tor/notices.log
$ sudo chmod 644 /var/log/tor/notices.log
```

You can also check it with:

```
$ ls -l /var/log/tor
```

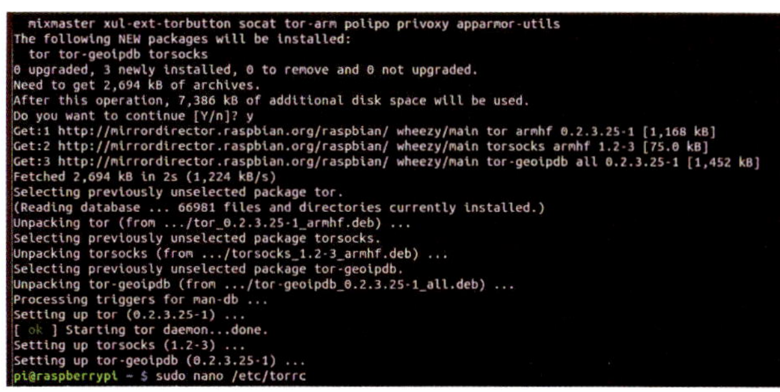

Secure the router

24 Finally, we can activate the Tor service so that we can start using the access point securely with:

```
$ sudo service tor start
```

You can check this if you wish with:

```
$ sudo service tor status
```

To make it turn on at boot, you simple add it to rc.d with:

```
$ sudo update-rc.d tor enable
```

What you'll need...

Raspbian
www.raspberrypi.org/downloads

Python
www.python.org/doc

Pygame
www.pygame.org/docs

Program a Space Invaders clone

Write your own RasPi shooter in 300 lines of Python

When you're learning to program in a new language or trying to master a new module, experimenting with a familiar and relatively simply project is a very useful exercise to help expand your understanding of the tools you're using. Our Space Invaders clone is one such example that lends itself perfectly to Python and the Pygame module – it's a simple game with almost universally understood rules and logic.

We've tried to use many features of Pygame, which is designed to make the creation of games and interactive applications easier. We've extensively used the Sprite class, which saves dozens of lines of extra code in making collision detection simple and updating the screen and its many actors a single-line command.

Have fun with the project and make sure you tweak and change things to make it your own!

Did you know...

Space Invaders was one of the biggest arcade hits in the world. It's a great first game since everyone knows how to play!

Right Pivaders is a Space Invaders clone we've made especially for the Pi

Full code listing

```
#!/usr/bin/env python2

import pygame, random

BLACK = (0, 0, 0)
BLUE = (0, 0, 255)
WHITE = (255, 255, 255)
RED = (255, 0, 0)
ALIEN_SIZE = (30, 40)
ALIEN_SPACER = 20
BARRIER_ROW = 10
BARRIER_COLUMN = 4
BULLET_SIZE  = (5, 10)
MISSILE_SIZE = (5, 5)
BLOCK_SIZE = (10, 10)
RES = (800, 600)

class Player(pygame.sprite.Sprite):
  def __init__(self):
    pygame.sprite.Sprite.__init__(self)
    self.size = (60, 55)
    self.rect = self.image.get_rect()
    self.rect.x = (RES[0] / 2) - (self.size ↵
[0] / 2)
    self.rect.y = 520
    self.travel = 7
    self.speed = 350
    self.time = pygame.time.get_ticks()

  def update(self):
    self.rect.x += GameState.vector * self. ↵
travel
    if self.rect.x < 0:
      self.rect.x = 0
    elif self.rect.x > RES[0] - self.size[0]:
      self.rect.x = RES[0] - self.size[0]

class Alien(pygame.sprite.Sprite):
  def __init__(self):
    pygame.sprite.Sprite.__init__(self)
    self.size = (ALIEN_SIZE)
    self.rect = self.image.get_rect()
    self.has_moved = [0, 0]
    self.vector = [1, 1]
    self.travel = [(ALIEN_SIZE[0] - 7), ↵
ALIEN_SPACER]
    self.speed = 700
    self.time = pygame.time.get_ticks()

  def update(self):
    if GameState.alien_time - self.time > ↵
self.speed:
      if self.has_moved[0] < 12:
        self.rect.x += self.vector[0] * self. ↵
travel[0]
        self.has_moved[0] +=1
      else:
        if not self.has_moved[1]:
          self.rect.y += self.vector[1] * ↵
self.travel[1]
        self.vector[0] *= -1
        self.has_moved = [0, 0]
        self.speed -= 20
        if self.speed <= 100:
          self.speed = 100
      self.time = GameState.alien_time

class Ammo(pygame.sprite.Sprite):
  def __init__(self, color, (width, height)):
    pygame.sprite.Sprite.__init__(self)
    self.image = pygame.Surface([width, ↵
height])
    self.image.fill(color)
    self.rect = self.image.get_rect()
    self.speed = 0
    self.vector = 0

  def update(self):
    self.rect.y += self.vector * self.speed
    if self.rect.y < 0 or self.rect.y > RES[1]:
      self.kill()

class Block(pygame.sprite.Sprite):
  def __init__(self, color, (width, height)):
    pygame.sprite.Sprite.__init__(self)
    self.image = pygame.Surface([width, ↵
height])
    self.image.fill(color)
    self.rect = self.image.get_rect()
class GameState:
  pass

class Game(object):
  def __init__(self):
    pygame.init()
    pygame.font.init()
    self.clock = pygame.time.Clock()
    self.game_font = pygame.font.Font(
    'data/Orbitracer.ttf', 28)
    self.intro_font = pygame.font.Font(
    'data/Orbitracer.ttf', 72)
    self.screen = pygame.display.set_ ↵
mode([RES[0], RES[1]])
    self.time = pygame.time.get_ticks()
    self.refresh_rate = 20
    self.rounds_won = 0
    self.level_up = 50
    self.score = 0
    self.lives = 2
    self.player_group = pygame.sprite.Group()
    self.alien_group = pygame.sprite.Group()
    self.bullet_group = pygame.sprite.Group()
    self.missile_group = pygame.sprite.Group()
    self.barrier_group = pygame.sprite.Group()
```

Setting up dependencies

01 If you're looking to get a better understanding of programming games with Python and Pygame, we strongly recommend you copy the Pivaders code in this tutorial into your own program. It's great practice and gives you a chance to tweak elements of the game to suit you, be it a different ship image, changing the difficulty or the ways the alien waves behave. If you just want to play the game, that's easily achieved too, though. Either way, the game's only dependency is Pygame, which (if it isn't already) can be installed from the terminal by typing:

```
sudo apt-get install python-pygame
```

Installation

02 For Pivaders we've used Git, a brilliant form of version control used to safely store the game files and retain historical versions of your code. Git should already be installed on your Pi; if not, you can acquire it by typing:

```
sudo apt-get install git
```

As well as acting as caretaker for your code, Git enables you to clone copies of other people's projects so you can work on them, or just use them. To clone Pivaders, go to your home folder in the terminal (`cd ~`), make a directory for the project (mkdir pivaders), enter the directory (cd pivaders) and type:

```
git pull https://github.com/russb78/pivaders.git
```

Testing Pivaders

03 With Pygame installed and the project cloned to your machine (you can also find the .zip on this issue's cover DVD – simply unpack it and copy it to your home directory to use it), you can take it for a quick test drive to make sure everything's set up properly. All you need to do is type python pivaders.py from within the pivaders directory in the terminal to get started. You can start the game with the space bar, shoot with the same button and simply use the left and right arrows on your keyboard to move your ship left and right.

Creating your own clone

04 Once you've racked up a good high score (anything over 2,000 points is respectable) and got to know our simple implementation, you'll get more from following along with and exploring the code and our brief explanations of what's going on. For those who want to make their own project, create a new project folder and use either IDLE or Leafpad (or perhaps install Geany) to create and save a .py file of your own.

Global variables & tuples

05 Once we've imported the modules we need for the project, there's quite a long list of variables in block capitals. The capitals denote that these variables are constants (or global variables). These are important numbers that never change – they represent things referred to regularly in the code, like colours, block sizes and resolution. You'll also notice that colours and sizes hold multiple numbers in braces – these are tuples. You could use square brackets (to make them lists), but we use tuples here since they're immutable, which means you can't reassign individual items within them. Perfect for constants, which aren't designed to change anyway.

Classes – part 1

06 A class is essentially a blueprint for an object you'd like to make. In the case of our player, it contains all the required info, from which you can make multiple copies (we create a player instance in the make_player() method halfway through the project). The great thing about the classes in Pivaders is that they inherit lots of capabilities and shortcuts from Pygame's Sprite class, as denoted by the pygame.sprite. Sprite found within the braces of the first line of the class. You can read the docs to learn more about the Sprite class via **www.pygame.org/docs/ref/sprite.html**.

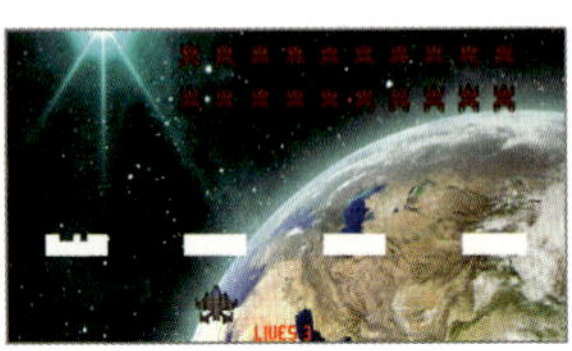

"We've tried to use many features of Pygame, which is designed to make the creation of games and interactive applications easier"

```
    self.all_sprite_list = pygame.sprite. ↵
Group()
    self.intro_screen = pygame.image.load(
    'data/start_screen.jpg').convert()
    self.background = pygame.image.load(
    'data/Space-Background.jpg').convert()
    pygame.display.set_caption('Pivaders - ↵
ESC to exit')
    pygame.mouse.set_visible(False)
    Player.image = pygame.image.load(
    'data/ship.png').convert()
    Player.image.set_colorkey(BLACK)
    Alien.image = pygame.image.load(
    'data/Spaceship16.png').convert()
    Alien.image.set_colorkey(WHITE)
    GameState.end_game = False
    GameState.start_screen = True
    GameState.vector = 0
    GameState.shoot_bullet = False

  def control(self):
    for event in pygame.event.get():
      if event.type == pygame.QUIT:
        GameState.start_screen = False
        GameState.end_game = True
      if event.type == pygame.KEYDOWN \
      and event.key == pygame.K_ESCAPE:
        if GameState.start_screen:
          GameState.start_screen = False
          GameState.end_game = True
          self.kill_all()
        else:
          GameState.start_screen = True
    self.keys = pygame.key.get_pressed()
    if self.keys[pygame.K_LEFT]:
      GameState.vector = -1
    elif self.keys[pygame.K_RIGHT]:
      GameState.vector = 1
    else:
      GameState.vector = 0
    if self.keys[pygame.K_SPACE]:
      if GameState.start_screen:
        GameState.start_screen = False
        self.lives = 2
        self.score = 0
        self.make_player()
        self.make_defenses()
        self.alien_wave(0)
      else:
        GameState.shoot_bullet = True

  def splash_screen(self):
    while GameState.start_screen:
      self.kill_all()
      self.screen.blit(self.intro_screen, ↵
[0, 0])
      self.screen.blit(self.intro_font.render(
      "PIVADERS", 1, WHITE), (265, 120))
```

```
      self.screen.blit(self.game_font.render(
      "PRESS SPACE TO PLAY", 1, WHITE), ↵
(274, 191))
      pygame.display.flip()
      self.control()

  def make_player(self):
    self.player = Player()
    self.player_group.add(self.player)
    self.all_sprite_list.add(self.player)

  def refresh_screen(self):
    self.all_sprite_list.draw(self.screen)
    self.refresh_scores()
    pygame.display.flip()
    self.screen.blit(self.background, [0, 0])
    self.clock.tick(self.refresh_rate)

  def refresh_scores(self):
    self.screen.blit(self.game_font.render(
    "SCORE " + str(self.score), 1, WHITE), ↵
(10, 8))
    self.screen.blit(self.game_font.render(
    "LIVES " + str(self.lives + 1), 1, RED), ↵
(355, 575))

  def alien_wave(self, speed):
    for column in range(BARRIER_COLUMN):
      for row in range(BARRIER_ROW):
        alien = Alien()
        alien.rect.y = 65 + (column * (
        ALIEN_SIZE[1] + ALIEN_SPACER))
        alien.rect.x = ALIEN_SPACER + (
        row * (ALIEN_SIZE[0] + ALIEN_SPACER))
        self.alien_group.add(alien)
        self.all_sprite_list.add(alien)
        alien.speed -= speed

  def make_bullet(self):
    if GameState.game_time - self.player. ↵
time > self.player.speed:
      bullet = Ammo(BLUE, BULLET_SIZE)
      bullet.vector = -1
      bullet.speed = 26
      bullet.rect.x = self.player.rect.x + 28
      bullet.rect.y = self.player.rect.y
      self.bullet_group.add(bullet)
      self.all_sprite_list.add(bullet)
      self.player.time = GameState.game_time
    GameState.shoot_bullet = False

  def make_missile(self):
    if len(self.alien_group):
      shoot = random.random()
      if shoot <= 0.05:
        shooter = random.choice([
        alien for alien in self.alien_group])
        missile = Ammo(RED, MISSILE_SIZE)
```

Classes – part 2

07 In Pivader's classes, besides creating the required attributes for the object, you'll also notice all the classes have an update() method apart from the Block class (a method is a function within a class). The update() method is called in every loop through the main game and simply asks the iteration of the class we've created to move. In the case of a bullet from the Ammo class, we're asking it to move down the screen. If it goes off either end, we destroy it.

Ammo

08 What's most interesting about classes, though, is that you can use one class to create lots of different things. You could, for example, have a pet class. From that class you could create a cat (that meows) and a dog (that barks). They're different in many ways, but they're both furry and have four legs, so can be created from the same parent class. We've done exactly that with our Ammo class, using it to create both the player bullets and the alien missiles. They're different colours and they shoot in opposite directions, but they're fundamentally one and the same.

The game

09 Our final class is called Game. This is where all the main functionality of the game itself comes in, but remember, so far this is still just a list of ingredients – nothing can actually happen until a 'Game' object is created (right at the bottom of the code). The Game class is where the central mass of the game resides, so we initialise Pygame, set the imagery for our protagonist and extraterrestrial antagonist and create some GameState attributes that we use to control key aspects of external classes, like changing the player's vector (direction).

The main loop

10 There are a lot of methods (class functions) in the Game class, and each is designed to control a particular aspect of either setting up the game or the gameplay itself. The logic that dictates what happens within any one round of the game is contained in the main_loop() method right at the bottom of the pivaders.py script and is the key to unlocking exactly what variables and functions you need for your game.

Main loop key logic – part 1

11 Firstly the game checks that the end_game attribute is false – if it's true, the entire loop in main_loop() is skipped and we go straight to pygame.quit(), exiting the game. This flag is set to true only if the player closes the game window or presses the Esc key when on the start_screen. Assuming end_game and start_screen are false, the main loop can start proper, with the control() method, which checks to see if the location of the player needs to change. Next we attempt to make an enemy missile and we use the random module to limit the number of missiles that can be created. Next we call the update() method for each and every actor on the screen using a simple for loop. This makes sure everyone's up to date and moved before we check collisions in calc_collisions().

Main loop key logic – part 2

12 Once collisions have been calculated, we need to see if the game is still meant to continue. We do so with is_dead() and defenses_breached() – if either of these methods returns true, we know we need to return to the start screen. On the other hand, we also need to check to see if we've killed all the aliens, from within win_round(). Assuming we're not dead, but the aliens are, we know we can call the next_round() method, which creates a fresh batch of aliens and increases their speed around the screen. Finally, we refresh the screen so everything that's been moved, shot or killed can be updated or removed from the screen. Remember, the main loop happens 20 times a second – so the fact we don't call for the screen to update right at the end of the loop is of no consequence.

```
            missile.vector = 1
            missile.rect.x = shooter.rect.x + 15
            missile.rect.y = shooter.rect.y + 40
            missile.speed = 10
            self.missile_group.add(missile)
            self.all_sprite_list.add(missile)

    def make_barrier(self, columns, rows, spacer):
        for column in range(columns):
            for row in range(rows):
                barrier = Block(WHITE, (BLOCK_SIZE))
                barrier.rect.x = 55 + (200 * spacer) ↵
+ (row * 10)
                barrier.rect.y = 450 + (column * 10)
                self.barrier_group.add(barrier)
                self.all_sprite_list.add(barrier)

    def make_defenses(self):
        for spacing, spacing in ↵
enumerate(xrange(4)):
            self.make_barrier(3, 9, spacing)

    def kill_all(self):
        for items in [self.bullet_group, self. ↵
player_group,
        self.alien_group, self.missile_group, ↵
self.barrier_group]:
            for i in items:
                i.kill()

    def is_dead(self):
        if self.lives < 0:
            self.screen.blit(self.game_font.render(
            "The war is lost! You scored: " + str(
            self.score), 1, RED), (250, 15))
            self.rounds_won = 0
            self.refresh_screen()
            pygame.time.delay(3000)
            return True

    def win_round(self):
        if len(self.alien_group) < 1:
            self.rounds_won += 1
            self.screen.blit(self.game_font.render(
            "You won round " + str(self.rounds_won) +
            "  but the battle rages on", 1, RED), ↵
(200, 15))
            self.refresh_screen()
            pygame.time.delay(3000)
            return True

    def defenses_breached(self):
        for alien in self.alien_group:
            if alien.rect.y > 410:
                self.screen.blit(self.game_font.render(
                "The aliens have breached Earth ↵
defenses!",
                1, RED), (180, 15))
                self.refresh_screen()
                pygame.time.delay(3000)
                return True

    def calc_collisions(self):
        pygame.sprite.groupcollide(
        self.missile_group, self.barrier_group, ↵
True, True)
        pygame.sprite.groupcollide(
        self.bullet_group, self.barrier_group, ↵
True, True)
        if pygame.sprite.groupcollide(
        self.bullet_group, self.alien_group, ↵
True, True):
            self.score += 10
        if pygame.sprite.groupcollide(
        self.player_group, self.missile_group, ↵
False, True):
            self.lives -= 1

    def next_round(self):
        for actor in [self.missile_group,
        self.barrier_group, self.bullet_group]:
            for i in actor:
                i.kill()
        self.alien_wave(self.level_up)
        self.make_defenses()
        self.level_up += 50

    def main_loop(self):
        while not GameState.end_game:
            while not GameState.start_screen:
                GameState.game_time = pygame.time. ↵
get_ticks()
                GameState.alien_time = pygame.time. ↵
get_ticks()
                self.control()
                self.make_missile()
                for actor in [self.player_group, ↵
self.bullet_group,
                self.alien_group, self.missile_group]:
                    for i in actor:
                        i.update()
                if GameState.shoot_bullet:
                    self.make_bullet()
                self.calc_collisions()
                if self.is_dead() or self.defenses_ ↵
breached():
                    GameState.start_screen = True
                if self.win_round():
                    self.next_round()
                self.refresh_screen()
            self.splash_screen()
        pygame.quit()

if __name__ == '__main__':
    pv = Game()
    pv.main_loop()
```

What you'll need...

Raspbian
www.raspberrypi.org/downloads

Python
www.python.org/doc

Pygame
www.pygame.org/docs

Art assets
opengameart.org

Pivaders Pt 2: graphics & sound

This time we'll expand our Space Invaders clone to include immersive animation and sound

We had great fun creating our basic Space Invaders clone, Pivaders, in the previous guide. Pygame's ability to group, manage and detect collisions thanks to the Sprite class really made a great difference to our project, not just in terms of code length, but in simplicity too. If you missed the first part of the project, you can find the v0.1 code listing on GitHub via **git.io/cBVTBg**, while you can find version v0.2 of the code, including all the images, music and sound effects we've used at **git.io/8QsK-w**.

To help keep our project code manageable and straightforward (as your projects grow keeping your code easy to follow becomes increasingly harder) we integrated a few animation methods into our Game class and opted to use a sprite sheet. Not only does it make it very easy to draw to the screen, but it also keeps the asset count under control and keeps performance levels up, which is especially important for the Raspberry Pi. We hope you have fun using our techniques to add animation and sound to your projects!

Did you know...

Space Invaders is one of the most cloned games in the world! It makes a great first project for game programmers.

Setting up dependencies

01 You'll get much more from the exercise if you download the code (**git.io/8QsK-w**) and use it for reference as you create your own animations and sound effects. Regardless of whether you just want to simply preview and play or walk-through the code to get a better understanding of basic game creation, you're still going to need to satisfy some basic dependencies. The two key requirements here are Pygame and Git, both of which are installed by default on up-to-date Raspbian installations. That's easy!

Downloading pivaders

02 Git is a superb version control solution that helps programmers safely store their code and associated files. Not only does it help you retain a full history of changes, it means you can 'clone' entire projects to use and work on from places like **github.com**. To clone the version of the project we created for this tutorial, go to your home folder from the command line (cd ~) and type:

```
git pull  https://github.com/russb78/pivaders.git
```

This creates a folder called pivaders.

Navigating the project

03 Within pivaders sits a licence, readme and a second pivaders folder. This contains the main game file, pivaders.py, which launches the application. Within the data folder you'll find subfolders for both graphics and sound assets, as well as the font we've used for the title screen and scores. To take pivaders for a test-drive, simply enter the pivaders subdirectory (cd pivaders/pivaders) and type:

```
python pivaders.py
```

Use the arrow keys to steer left and right and the space bar to shoot. You can quit with the Escape key.

Code listing (starting from line 87)

```
class Game(object):
    def __init__(self):
        pygame.init()
        pygame.font.init()
        self.clock = pygame.time.Clock()
        self.game_font = pygame.font.Font(
        'data/Orbitracer.ttf', 28)
        self.intro_font = pygame.font.Font(
        'data/Orbitracer.ttf', 72)
        self.screen = pygame.display.set_mode([RES[0], RES[1]])
        self.time = pygame.time.get_ticks()
        self.refresh_rate = 20; self.rounds_won = 0
        self.level_up = 50; self.score = 0
        self.lives = 2
        self.player_group = pygame.sprite.Group()
        self.alien_group = pygame.sprite.Group()
        self.bullet_group = pygame.sprite.Group()
        self.missile_group = pygame.sprite.Group()
        self.barrier_group = pygame.sprite.Group()
        self.all_sprite_list = pygame.sprite.Group()
        self.intro_screen = pygame.image.load(
        'data/graphics/start_screen.jpg').convert()
        self.background = pygame.image.load(
        'data/graphics/Space-Background.jpg').convert()
        pygame.display.set_caption('Pivaders - ESC to exit')
        pygame.mouse.set_visible(False)
        Alien.image = pygame.image.load(
        'data/graphics/Spaceship16.png').convert()
        Alien.image.set_colorkey(WHITE)
        self.ani_pos = 5 # 11 images of ship
        self.ship_sheet = pygame.image.load(
        'data/graphics/ship_sheet_final.png').convert_alpha()
        Player.image = self.ship_sheet.subsurface(
                    self.ani_pos*64, 0, 64, 61)
        self.animate_right = False
        self.animate_left = False
        self.explosion_sheet = pygame.image.load(
        'data/graphics/explosion_new1.png').convert_alpha()
        self.explosion_image = self.explosion_sheet.subsurface(
0, 0, 79, 96)
        self.alien_explosion_sheet = pygame.image.load(
        'data/graphics/alien_explosion.png')
        self.alien_explode_graphics = self.alien_explosion_sheet.↵
subsurface(0, 0, 94, 96)
        self.explode = False
        self.explode_pos = 0; self.alien_explode = False
        self.alien_explode_pos = 0
        pygame.mixer.music.load('data/sound/10_Arpanauts.ogg')
        pygame.mixer.music.play(-1)
        pygame.mixer.music.set_volume(0.7)
        self.bullet_fx = pygame.mixer.Sound(
        'data/sound/medetix__pc-bitcrushed-lazer-beam.ogg')
        self.explosion_fx = pygame.mixer.Sound(
        'data/sound/timgormly__8-bit-explosion.ogg')
        self.explosion_fx.set_volume(0.5)
        self.explodey_alien = []
```

Animation & sound

04 Compared with the game from last month's tutorial, you'll see it's now a much more dynamic project. The ship now leans into the turns as you change direction and corrects itself when stationary. When you shoot an alien ship, it explodes with several frames of animation and should you take fire, a smaller explosion occurs on your ship. Music, lasers and explosion sound effects also accompany the animations as they happen.

Finding images to animate

05 Before we can program anything, it's wise to have assets set up correctly. We've opted to use sprite sheets; these can be found online or created with GIMP with a little practice. They're a mosaic made up of individual 'frames' of equally sized and spaced images representing each frame. We found ours at **opengameart.org**.

Tweaking assets

06 While many of the assets you'll find online can be used as is, you may want to import them into an image-editing application like GIMP to configure them to suit your needs. We started with the central ship sprite and centred it into a new window. We set the size and width of the frame and then copy-pasted the other frames either side of it. We ended up with 11 frames of exactly the same size and width in a single document. Pixel-perfect precision on size and width is key, so we can just multiply it to find the next frame.

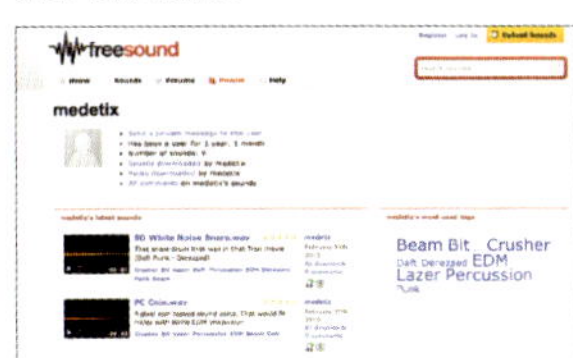

Loading the sprite sheet

07 Since we're inheriting from the Sprite class to create our Player class, we can easily alter how the player looks on screen by changing Player.image. First, we need to load our ship sprite sheet with pygame.image.load(). Since we made our sheet with a transparent background, we can append .convert_alpha() to the end of the line so the ship frames render correctly (without any background). We then use subsurface to set the initial Player.image to the middle ship sprite on the sheet. This is set by self.ani_pos, which has an initial value of 5. Changing this value will alter the ship image drawn to the screen: '0' would draw it leaning fully left, '11' fully to the right.

Animation flags

08 Slightly further down the list in the initialising code for the Game class, we also set two flags for our player animation: self.animate_left and self.animate_right. As you'll see in the Control method of our Game class, we use these to 'flag' when we want animations to happen with True and False. It also allows us to 'automatically' animate the player sprite back to its natural resting state (otherwise the ship will continue to look as if it's flying left when it has stopped).

The animation method

09 We use flags again in the code for the player: animate_player(). Here we use nested if statements to control the animation and physically set the player image. It states that if the animate_right flag is True and if the current animation position is different to what we want, we incrementally increase the ani_pos variable and set the player's image. The Else statement then animates the ship sprite back to its resting state and the same logic is then applied in the opposite direction.

```
        GameState.end_game = False
        GameState.start_screen = True
        GameState.vector = 0
        GameState.shoot_bullet = False

    def control(self):
        for event in pygame.event.get():
            if event.type == pygame.QUIT:
                GameState.start_screen = False
                GameState.end_game = True
            if event.type == pygame.KEYDOWN \
            and event.key == pygame.K_ESCAPE:
                if GameState.start_screen:
                    GameState.start_screen = False
                    GameState.end_game = True
                    self.kill_all()
                else:
                    GameState.start_screen = True
        self.keys = pygame.key.get_pressed()
        if self.keys[pygame.K_LEFT]:
            GameState.vector = -1
            self.animate_left = True
            self.animate_right = False
        elif self.keys[pygame.K_RIGHT]:
            GameState.vector = 1
            self.animate_right = True
            self.animate_left = False
        else:
            GameState.vector = 0
            self.animate_right = False
            self.animate_left = False

        if self.keys[pygame.K_SPACE]:
            if GameState.start_screen:
                GameState.start_screen = False
                self.lives = 2
                self.score = 0
                self.make_player()
                self.make_defenses()
                self.alien_wave(0)
            else:
                GameState.shoot_bullet = True
                self.bullet_fx.play()

    def animate_player(self):
        if self.animate_right:
            if self.ani_pos < 10:
                Player.image = self.ship_sheet.subsurface(
                    self.ani_pos*64, 0, 64, 61)
                self.ani_pos += 1
        else:
            if self.ani_pos > 5:
                self.ani_pos -= 1
                Player.image = self.ship_sheet.subsurface(
                    self.ani_pos*64, 0, 64, 61)

        if self.animate_left:
            if self.ani_pos > 0:
                self.ani_pos -= 1
```

```
                Player.image = self.ship_sheet.subsurface(
                    self.ani_pos*64, 0, 64, 61)
        else:
            if self.ani_pos < 5:
                Player.image = self.ship_sheet.subsurface(
                    self.ani_pos*64, 0, 64, 61)
                self.ani_pos += 1

    def player_explosion(self):
        if self.explode:
            if self.explode_pos < 8:
                self.explosion_image = self.explosion_sheet. ↵
subsurface(0, self.explode_pos*96, 79, 96)
                self.explode_pos += 1
                self.screen.blit(self.explosion_image, [self.player.
↵rect.x -10, self.player.rect.y - 30])
            else:
                self.explode = False
                self.explode_pos = 0

    def alien_explosion(self):
        if self.alien_explode:
            if self.alien_explode_pos < 9:
                self.alien_explode_graphics = self.alien_
explosion_ ↵sheet.subsurface(0, self.alien_explode_pos*96, 94,
96)
                self.alien_explode_pos += 1
                self.screen.blit(self.alien_explode_graphics, ↵
[int(self. explodey_alien[0]) - 50 , int(self.explodey_alien[1]) -
60])
            else:
                self.alien_explode = False
                self.alien_explode_pos = 0
                self.explodey_alien = []

    def splash_screen(self):
        while GameState.start_screen:
            self.kill_all()
            self.screen.blit(self.intro_screen, [0, 0])
            self.screen.blit(self.intro_font.render(
            "PIVADERS", 1, WHITE), (265, 120))
            self.screen.blit(self.game_font.render(
            "PRESS SPACE TO PLAY", 1, WHITE), (274, 191))
            pygame.display.flip()
            self.control()
            self.clock.tick(self.refresh_rate / 2)

    def make_player(self):
        self.player = Player()
Find the rest of the code at github.com/russb78/pivaders
```

"Sprite sheets make it easy to draw to the screen, but it also keeps the asset count down and performance levels up"

Animating explosions

10 The player_explosion() and alien_explosion() methods that come after the player animation block in the Game class are similar but simpler executions of the same thing. As we only need to run through the same predefined set of frames (this time vertically), we only need to see if the self.explode and self.alien_explode flags are True before we increment the variables that change the image.

Adding music

11 Pygame makes it easy to add a musical score to a project. Just obtain a suitable piece of music in your preferred format (we found ours via freemusicarchive.org) and load it using the Mixer Pygame class. As it's already been initialised via pygame.init(), we can go ahead and load the music. The music.play(-1) requests that the music should start with the app and continue to loop until it quits. If we replaced -1 with 5, the music would loop five times before ending. Learn more about the Mixer class via **www.pygame.org/docs/ref/mixer.html.**

Using sound effects

12 Loading and using sounds is similar to how we do so for images in Pygame. First we load the sound effect using a simple assignment. For the laser beam, the initialisation looks like this:

```
self.bullet_fx = pygame.
mixer.Sound('location/of/file')
```

Then we simply trigger the sound effect at the appropriate time. In the case of the laser, we want it to play whenever we press the space bar to shoot, so we place it in the Game class's Control method, straight after we raise the shoot_bullet flag. You can get different sounds from **www.freesound.org**.

What you'll need…

- A toy RC car with two channels (steering and drive)
- Adafruit PWM I2C servo driver
- Female-to-female jumper cables
- 5V battery power bank

Estimated cost: £60 / $100

Components from
www.modmypi.com

Build a Raspberry Pi-powered car

Make use of cutting-edge web technologies to take control of a remote controlled car with a smartphone or tablet…

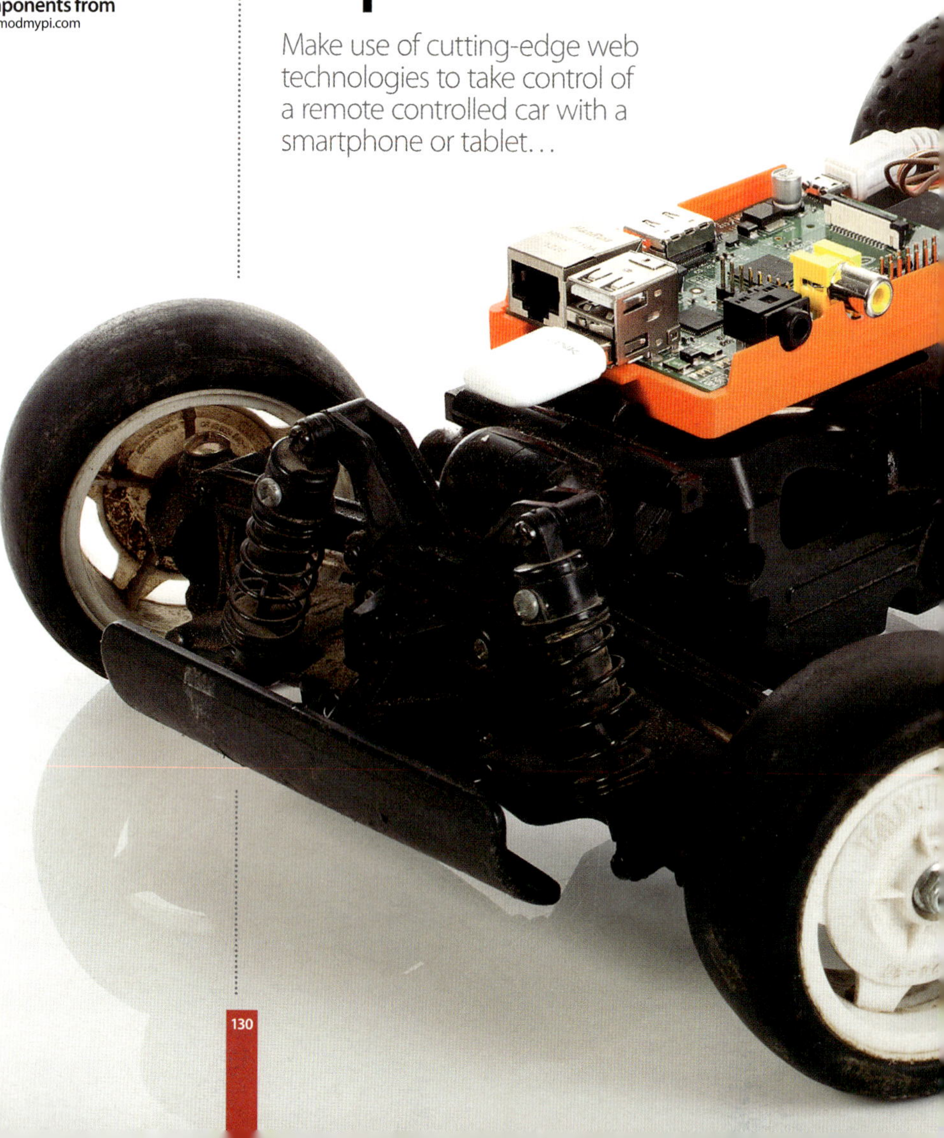

Did you know…

You can make this project work with just about any remote controlled car. Follow the guide for more details.

Web technologies are moving forward at a huge pace, cloud technologies are bringing mass computing to individuals, and hardware has reached a perfect moment in time where sensors, displays and wireless technology have all evolved into efficient and affordable devices. We truly are at a point where nearly anyone can take an idea from nothing to a working product in a week and at very little cost. Just like this project, which is fun, quick and easy to build on and a fantastic way to learn. We're going to grab an old remote-control car, rip off its radio receiver and replace it with the Raspberry Pi, hook it up on the network, fire up a bleeding-edge web server and then get your smartphone or tablet to control it by tilting the device. By the end of this, not only will you have a fun toy, you will have learnt about the basic technologies that are starting to power the world's newest and biggest economy for the foreseeable future. Welcome to tomorrow!

Raspberry Pi-controlled car build process

To help our toy car come to life using the latest web technologies and our credit card-sized computer, we're going to need to make some pretty significant changes to its workings. Fortunately, the most complex aspects of the build can be accomplished with a couple of affordable purchases, namely a servo controller board to take care of the steering and throttle, and a 5V battery pack to keep the Raspberry Pi running smoothly.

Identify and remove old radio

01 This project is effectively replacing the car's normal transmitter and receiver. Notice the three sockets on the original receiver: one goes to the motor controller and one to the steering servo. Some remote-control cars also have separate battery for the electronics, but those (especially with an electronic speed controller with BEC) get their 5V power supply directly from the speed controller, saving on components. If you don't have a speed controller with 5V BEC, you'll need to get a 5V supply elsewhere. Many shops sell 5V battery power supplies – often as mobile phone emergency top-ups. **www.modmypi.com** sells a suitable 5V battery power bank for under £20 and you should get a couple of hours of use from your Raspberry Pi.

Attach the servo cables to the new controller

02 We soldered our 16-channel I2C servo controller board from **www.modmypi.com** as per its instructions and simply plugged channel 0 (steering) and channel 1 (motor) headers onto it. There are six cables in total: the bottom two are ground, the middle two are the power and the top two are the PWM (pulse-width modulation) signals. This is a good time to think of places to mount the extra components and the best fixing method seems to be sticky-back Velcro.

Connect the I2C bus to the Raspberry Pi

03 We're using the Raspberry Pi's I2C bus to control the servo interface board, which only needs four cables – they all go between the Raspberry Pi and the servo controller board as pictured. Visit **http://bit.ly/N3nq4J** for a tutorial on how to set up I2C on the Raspberry Pi.

From top to bottom we need to use the 1. GND, 2. SCL, 3. SDA and 4. VCC, which map directly to the same ports on the Raspberry Pi. Essentially this is power, ground and two communication channels.

Hooking it up to the Raspberry Pi

04 On a Rev 1 Raspberry Pi, the cables look the same. Though the Rev boards have different labelling, the physical pins are in the same place. Bottom left (closest to the RasPi power connector) is the 3.3V power; next to that is the SDA header, which is the data channel. Next to that in the bottom right is the SCL channel, which controls the clock of the I2C devices. And finally – on the top-right port – is the Ground. We recommend printing a labelled image of the GPIO pins.

Overview of the main components

05 You should now have the servo board in the middle with the steering servo and speed controller on one side and the Raspberry Pi on the other. The motor is connected to the other end of the speed controller (that end should have much thicker wires); the speed controller also has two thick wires going to the main car's battery – in this case a 7.2V NiCad. We now have two very separate power systems with the high current motors on one side and the low current electronics on the other. Let's make sure it stays that way!

Find everything a home

06 We can now put it together. Use plenty of sticky-back Velcro, tie wraps or elastic bands to keep everything secure and find spaces in the car's body to hide the wires where possible. While it is possible to stick or screw the Raspberry Pi directly to the car, we recommend to use at least the bottom half of a case for added protection and ease of access. Insert your SD card, network cable or Wi-Fi dongle and power supply. Sit back and admire your hacking skills!

Control your Raspberry Pi-powered car

Control a toy car with a smartphone and the latest web technologies

What you'll need…

A RasPi car, ready to go

An internet connection

A reasonably modern smartphone/tablet

Pi car source code
github.com/shaunuk/picar

Did you know…

Our code will send instructions to our car over twenty times per second. It will be very responsive to drive!

Now we have our fantastic Raspberry Pi-powered car all wired and charged, it's time to make it come alive. We're using the best web technologies that the JavaScript programming language offers, to harness the natural movement of your hand and wirelessly drive the vehicle. Each little movement will trigger an event that calculates what the car should do and then sends it over a socket connection.

Download and install the software

01 To get the I2C connectivity working, you can follow the steps from pages 64-65. Next we'll need to find a home for our new project code – how about /var/www/picar? Type `sudo mkdir /var/www/picar` in the terminal to make the directory and then change into that directory: `cd /var/www/picar`

Now, to download the project using Git, type `sudo git clone http://github.com/shaunuk/picar`. If you haven't got Git, install it with `sudo apt-get install git`.

This will download the custom software for driving the car, but we still need the web server and some other bits before we can start burning rubber…

Below All you need to finish off your project is access to a smartphone or tablet

Download and install Node.js

02 Next we're using Node.js and its package tool, the Node package manager (npm). Type `sudo wget http://nodejs.org/dist/v0.10.21/node-v0.10.21-linux-arm-pi.tar.gz`. This will download a fairly recent version of Node.js – the version Raspbian has in its repositories is way too old and just doesn't work with the new technologies we're about to use. Extract the node package by typing:

```
sudo tar -xvzf node-v0.10.21-linux-arm-pi.tar.gz
```

Configure Node.js

03 To make it easy to run from everywhere, we will create symbolic links for Node and npm binaries. Type `sudo ln -s /var/www/node-v0.10.21-linux-arm-pi/bin/node /bin/node` and then `sudo ln -s /var/www/node-v0.10.21-linux-arm-pi/bin/npm /bin/npm`. Then, to get the extra modules, type `npm install socket.io node-static socket.io adafruit-i2c-pwm-driver sleep optimist`

Below You need to adjust some of the variables to control your particular remote controlled car set-up

Get to know the project

04 Now we have everything, you should see three files: the server (app.js), the client (socket.html) and the jQuery JavaScript library for the client. The server not only drives the servos, but it is a web server and sends the socket.html file and jQuery to the browser when requested – it's a really neat and simple setup and just right for what we're trying to achieve.

Test the servos

05 Our handy little program (app.js) has a special mode just for testing. We use two keywords here: beta for servo 0 (steering) and gamma for servo 1 (motor control). Type node app.js beta=300. You should see the front wheels turn. Now the numbers need experimenting with. On our example, 340 was left, 400 was centre and 470 was right. Do the same for the motor by typing node app.js gamma=400 and take note of the various limits of your car.

"We're using the best web technologies that the JavaScript programming language has to offer"

Configure sensible defaults

06 Now you know what your car is capable of, we can set the defaults in app.js and socket.html. Edit app.js and find the section that says 'function emergencyStop'. Adjust the two numbers to your car's rest values. Then open socket.html and adjust the predefined values under 'Define your variables here'.

Going for a spin

07 We're almost ready to try it out, but you need to know the IP address of your Pi car, so type ifconfig at the terminal. Then fire up the app by typing node app.js. Now grab the nearest smartphone or tablet, making sure it's on the same network as your Pi. Open the web browser and go to **http://[your IP address]:8080/socket.html**. You should get an alert message saying 'ready' and as soon as you hit OK, the gyro data from your phone will be sent to the car and you're off!

Full code listing

socket.html

```
<html>
<head>
<script src="jquery-2.0.3.min.js"
language="javascript"></script>
<script src="/socket.io/socket.io.js"></
script>
<meta name="viewport" content="user-
scalable=no, initial-scale=1.0, maximum-
scale=1.0;" />
<script>
//------ Define your variables here
var socket = io.connect(window.location.
hostname+':8080');
var centerbeta = 400; //where's the middle?
var minbeta = '340'; //right limit
var maxbeta = '470'; //left limit
var multbeta = 3; //factor to multiply the
// raw gyro figure
var centergamma = 330;
var ajustmentgamma = 70; //what do we do to
the angle to get to 0?
var mingamma = 250; //backwards limit
var maxgamma = 400; //forward limit
var multgamma = 1; //factor to multiply the
//raw gyro figure by to get the desired
//rate of acceleration
window.lastbeta='0';
window.lastgamma='0';
$(function(){
  window.gyro = 'ready';
  alert('Ready -- Lets race !');
});
window.ondeviceorientation = function(event)
{
  beta = centerbeta+(Math.round(↵
event.beta*-1)*multbeta);
  if (beta >= maxbeta) {
    beta=maxbeta;
  }
  if (beta <= minbeta) {
    beta=minbeta;
```

```
  }
gamma = event.gamma;
  gamma = ((Math.round(event. ↵
gamma)+ajustmentgamma)* multgamma)+ ↵
centergamma;
//stop sending the same command more than
once
send = 'N';
if (window.lastbeta != beta) { send = 'Y' }
if (window.lastgamma != gamma) { send = 'Y'
}
window.lastbeta=beta;
window.lastgamma=gamma;
if (window.gyro == 'ready' && send=='Y')  {
//don't send another command until ready...
  window.gyro = 'notready';
    socket.emit('fromclient', { beta: beta
↵ gamma: gamma } );
    window.gyro = 'ready'; }}
```

app.js

```
//declare required modules
var app = require('http').
createServer(handler)
  , io = require('socket.io').listen(app)
  , fs = require('fs')
  , static = require('node-static')
  , sys = require('sys')
  , PwmDriver = require('adafruit-i2c-pwm-
driver')
  , sleep = require('sleep')
  , argv = require('optimist').argv;
  app.listen(8080);
//set the address and device name of the ↵
breakout board
pwm = new PwmDriver(0x40,'/dev/i2c-0');
//set pulse widths
setServoPulse = function(channel, pulse) {
  var pulseLength;
  pulseLength = 1000000;
  pulseLength /= 60;
  print("%d us per period" % pulseLength);
  pulseLength /= 4096;
  print("%d us per bit" % pulseLength);
  pulse *= 1000;
  pulse /= pulseLength;
  return pwm.setPWM(channel, 0, pulse);
};
//set pulse frequency
pwm.setPWMFreq(60);
//Make a web server on port 8080
var file = new(static.Server)();
function handler(request, response) {
  console.log('serving file',request.url)
  file.serve(request, response);
};
console.log('Pi Car we server listening ↵
on port 8080 visit http://ipaddress:8080/ ↵
socket.html');

lastAction = "";
function emergencyStop(){
 //center front wheels
  pwm.setPWM(0, 0, 400);
 //stop motor
  pwm.setPWM(1, 0, 330);
  console.log('###EMERGENCY STOP - signal ↵
lost or shutting down');
}

if (argv.beta) {
  console.log("\nPerforming one off servo ↵
position move to: "+argv.beta);
  pwm.setPWM(0, 0, argv.beta);
//using direct i2c pwm module
  pwm.stop();
  return process.exit();
}
if (argv.gamma) {
  console.log("\nPerforming one off servo ↵
position move to: "+argv.gamma);
  pwm.setPWM(1, 0, argv.gamma); //using
direct i2c pwm module
  pwm.stop();
  return process.exit();
}
//fire up a web socket server
io.sockets.on('connection', function (socket)
{
  socket.on('fromclient', function (data) {
  console.log("Beta: "+data.beta+" Gamma:
"+data.gamma);
  //exec("echo 'sa "+data+"' > /dev/
// ttyAMA0", puts);
//using http://electronics.chroma.se/rpisb.php
  //exec("picar.py 0 "+data.beta, puts);
 //using python adafruit module
  pwm.setPWM(0, 0, data.beta);
//using direct i2c pwm module
  pwm.setPWM(1, 0, data.gamma);
//using direct i2c pwm module
  clearInterval(lastAction);
//stop emergency stop timer
  lastAction = setInterval(emergencySt ↵
op,1000);
//set emergency stop timer
  });
});
process.on('SIGINT', function() {
  emergencyStop();
  console.log("\nGracefully shutting down
from SIGINT ↵ (Ctrl-C)");
  pwm.stop();
  return process.exit();
});
```

What you'll need…

Raspbian
www.raspberrypi.org/downloads

Python
www.python.org/doc

Program a quadcopter

How do you push the limits of the Pi? You give it wings. Andy Baker shows us how it's done…

The Raspberry Pi is a fantastic project board. Since we love a challenge, we set out looking for something that would really push the limits of our hacking and coding skills. We chose a quadcopter.

This article uses the Python code available online as a guide through what's needed to build a quadcopter, metaphorically bolting it together so that by the end, you don't just understand the code but also the interaction with the real-world to enable you to build your own quadcopter with confidence. You can find Andy's code on his blog.

Did you know…

Andy Baker, the writer of this article, keeps a blog at **blog.pistuffing.co.uk** that gives great insight into his project.

Right Put your Raspberry Pi in the sky with our expert coding guide!

Sensor viewpoint diagram

How sensors in the quadcopter's point of view are converted to the Earth (horizontal/vertical) viewpoint to provide horizontal motion

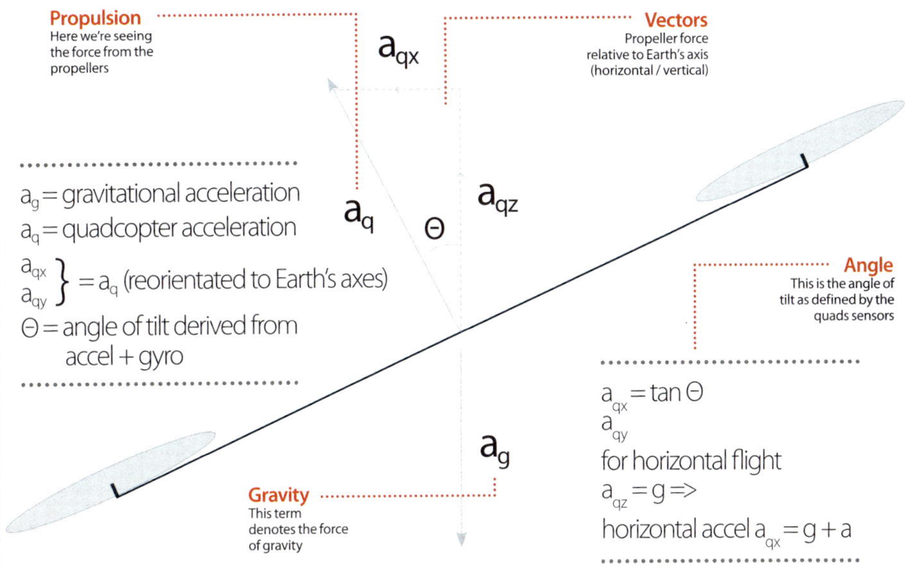

Interpreter

01 The command interpreter converts a series of commands either from a radio control or programmed into the code itself. The commands combine the direction and speed compared to the horizon that the user want the quadcopter to follow. The code converts these commands into a series of targets for vertical speed, horizontal speed and yaw speed – any command from a pair of joysticks can be broken down into a set of these targets.

Inputs

02 The inputs to the quadcopter come from a series of electronic sensors providing information about its movement in the air. The main two are an accelerometer which measures acceleration force (including gravity) in the three axes of the quadwcopter, and a gyroscope which measures the angular speed with which the quadcopter is pitching (nose/tail up and down), rolling (left/right side up and down), and yawing (spinning clockwise and anticlockwise around the central axis of the quadcopter itself).

Axes

03 The accelerometer is relative to the orientation of quadcopter axes, but the command targets are relative to the Earth's axes – the horizon and gravity. To convert the sensor output between the quadcopter axes and the Earth axes requires the use of a bit of mathematics, specifically trigonometry. You also need knowledge of the tilt angles in pitch and roll axes of the quadcopter with respect to the Earth. It's pretty complicated stuff, but the diagrams on these pages should help you understand the logic.

Above Kits are available as ready-to-fly (RTF) if you just want the joy of flight, but where's the challenge in that? We started with an almost-ready-to-fly (ARF) kit – the DJI Flame Wheel F450 – all the hardware, but none of the control electronics or software. Many enthusiasts have created DIY quadcopters using Arduino microcontrollers, so we knew a DIY build was possible, but very few, if any, have successfully used the Raspberry Pi

Did you know…

You can buy Ready To Fly (RTF) quadcopter kits from a lot of online retails. Prices start from £150 / $200, but rise quickly!

Angles

04 Both the accelerometer and gyro can provide this angle information, but both have flaws. The accelerometer output can be used to calculate the angle by using the Euler algorithm. However, the accelerometer output is plagued by noise from the motors/propellers, meaning a single reading can be hugely inaccurate; on the plus side, the average reading remains accurate over time.

In contrast, the gyro output does not suffer from the noise, but since it is the angular speed being measured, it needs to be integrated over time to find the absolute angle of the quadcopter in comparison to the horizon. Rounding errors in the integration lead to ever increasing errors over time, ultimately curtailing the maximum length of a flight.

Filter

05 Although independently they are both flawed, they can be merged mathematically such that each compensates for the flaws in the other, resulting in a noise-free, long-term accurate reading. There are many versions of these mathematical noise/drift filters. The best common one is by Kalman; the one we've chosen is slightly less accurate, but easier to understand and therefore to code: the complementary filter.

Now with an accurate angle in hand, it's possible to convert accelerometer sensor data to inputs relative to the Earth's axes and work out how fast the quadcopter is moving up, down, left, right and forwards and backwards compared to the targets that have been set.

PIDs

06 So we now have a target for what we want the quadcopter to do, and an input for what it's doing, and some motors to close the gap between the two; all we need now is a way to join these together. A direct mathematical algorithm is nigh on impossible – accurate weight of the quadcopter, power per rotation of each blade, weight imbalance etc would need to be incorporated into the equation. And yet none of these factors is stable: during flights (and crashes!), blades get damaged, batteries move in the frame, grass/mud/moisture changes the weight of the 'copter, humidity and altitude would need to be accounted for. Hopefully it's clear this approach simply won't fly.

Instead, an estimation method is used with feedback from the sensors to fine-tune that estimate. Because the estimation/feedback code loop spins at over 100 times a second, this approach can react to 'errors' very quickly indeed, and yet it knows nothing about all the factors which it is compensating for – that's all handled blindly by the feedback; this is the PID algorithm. It takes the target, subtracts the feedback input, resulting in the error. The error is then processed via a Proportional, Integral and a Differential algorithm to produce the output.

Blender

07 The outputs are applied to each ESC in turn: the vertical speed output is applied equally to all blades; the pitch rate output is split 50/50 subtracting from the front blades and adding to the back, producing the pitch. Roll is handled similarly. Yaw too is handled in a similar way, but applied to diagonal blades which spin in the same direction.

These ESC-specific outputs are then converted to a PWM signal to feed to the hardware ESCs with the updated propeller/motor speeds.

Understanding quadcopters...

Although this article focuses on software, a very basic background in the hardware from the kit is necessary to provide context.

A quadcopter has four propellers (hence the name) pointing upwards to the sky, each attached to its own brushless DC motor at one of the four corners of (usually) a square frame. Two motors spin clockwise, two anticlockwise, to minimise angular momentum of the quadcopter in flight.

Each motor is driven independently by an electronic speed controller (ESC). The motors themselves have three sets of coils (phases), and the ESCs convert a pulse-width-modulation (PWM) control signal from software/hardware to the three phase high-current output to drive the motors at a speed determined by the control signal. The power for the ESCs and everything else on the system comes from a Lithium Polymer battery (LiPo) rated at 12V, 3300mA with peak surge current of 100A – herein lies the power!

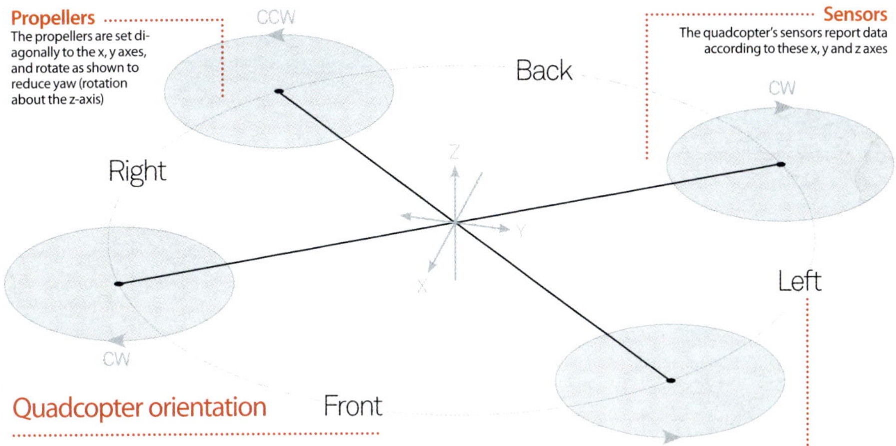

Propellers
The propellers are set diagonally to the x, y axes, and rotate as shown to reduce yaw (rotation about the z-axis)

Sensors
The quadcopter's sensors report data according to these x, y and z axes

Quadcopter orientation

The orientation of the quadcopter compared to the direction of travel, the rotation of the propellers and the axes used in the code

Orientation
The overall orientation of the quadcopter depicting front, back, left and right in relation to the sensor and propeller layouts

Code and reality

08 In this code, there are nine PIDs in total. In the horizontal plane, for both the X and Y axes, the horizontal speed PID converts the user-defined desired speed to required horizontal acceleration/ angle of tilt; the angles PID then converts this desired tilt angle to desired tilt rate which the rotation speed PID converts to changes in motors speeds fed to the front/back or left/right motors for pitch/roll respectively.

In the vertical direction, a single PID converts the desired rate of ascent/descent to the acceleration output applied to each plate equally.

Finally, prevention of yaw (like a spinning top) uses two PIDs – one to set the desired angle of yaw, set to 0, and one to set the yaw rotation speed. The output of these is fed to the diagonally opposing motors which spin in the same direction. The most critical of the nine are pitch/roll/yaw stability. These ensure that whatever other requirements enforced by other PIDs and external factors, the quadcopter is stable in achieving those other targets; without this stability, the rest of the PIDs cannot work. Pitch is controlled by relative speed differences between the front and back propellers; roll by left and right differences, and yaw by clockwise/anticlockwise differences from the corresponding PIDs' outputs. The net outputs of all three PIDs are then applied to the appropriate combination of motors' PWM channels to set the individual pulse widths.

With stability assured, some level of take-off, hover and landing can be achieved using the vertical speed PID. Placing the quadcopter on a horizontal surface, set the target to 0.5 m/s and off she zooms into the air, while the stability PID ensures that the horizontal attitude on take-off is maintained throughout the short flight, hover and landing.

Up to this stage, the PIDs are independent. But what about for horizontal movement target, and suppression of drifting in the wind?

This is where things get event more complicated. Taking the drift suppression first, a quadcopter in a headwind will drift backwards due to the force applied by the wind. To compensate for this, it must tilt nose down at some angle so that some of the propellers' thrust is applied horizontally to counteract the wind. In doing so, some of the power keeping the 'copter hovering at a fixed height is now battling the wind; unless the overall power is increased, the 'copter will start descending.

Horizontal movement is more complex still. The target is to move forwards at say 1 metre per second. Initially the requirement is similar to the headwind compensation – nose down plus increased power will apply a forward force leading to forward acceleration. But once that horizontal speed is attained, the quadcopter needs to level off to stop the acceleration, but at the same time, friction in the air will slow the movement. So there's a dynamic tilting fore/aft to maintain this stable forward velocity.

Both wind-drift suppression and controlled horizontal movement use something called nested PIDs; the X and Y axes horizontal speed PIDs' outputs are used as the pitch and roll angle PIDs targets; their output feeds the pitch and roll rate PIDs to ensure stability while meeting those angular targets. The sensor feedback ensures that as the desired horizontal speed is approached, the horizontal speed PID errors shrink, reducing the targets for the angular pitch PID, thus bringing the quadcopters nose back up to horizontal again.

Hopefully it now becomes clearer why accurate angle tracking is critical: in the nose-down, headwind example, the input to the vertical speed PID from the sensors is reduced by the cosine of the measured angle of 'copter tilt with respect to the horizon.

Similarly, X and Y axis speed PID sensor inputs need compensating by pitch and roll angles when comparing target speeds against accelerometer readings. Don't forget to check the diagrams in the article for clear, graphical representations of many of the themes we're covering.

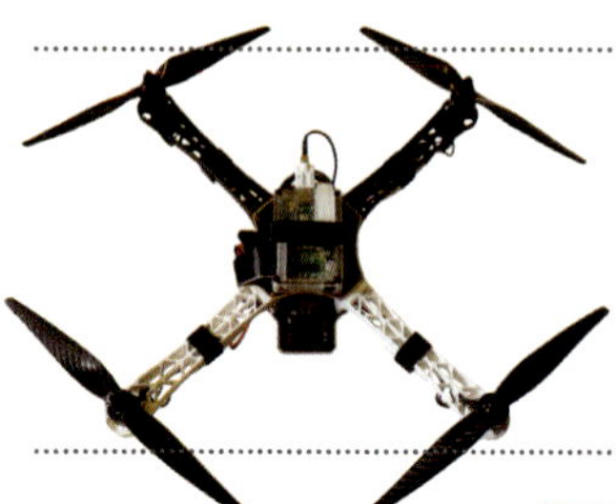

"Taking the drift suppression first, a quadcopter in a headwind will drift backwards due to the force applied by the wind"

Experimentation and tuning

09 While the code accurately reflects everything we've described here, there's one critical set of steps which can only be found through live testing; these are the PID gains. For each PID running, there is an independent Proportional, Integral and Differential gain that can only be found with estimation/experimentation. The results for every quadcopter will be different. Luckily there is a relatively safe way to proceed.

First, find the PWM take-off speed: this is done by sitting your quadcopter on the ground and slowly increasing the PWM value until she starts looking light-footed – for your expert, this was about the 1590us pulse width (or 1000us + 590us, as shown in the code).

Next, sorting out the stability PIDs – assuming your quadcopter is square and its balance is roughly central, then the result of pitch tuning also applies to yaw tuning. For pitch tuning, disable two diagonally opposed motors and rest these on a surface – the quadcopter sits horizontal in between. Power up the dangling motors' PWM to just under take-off speed (1550us pulse width in our expert's case). Does the quad rock manically, wobble in some pretence of control, self-right when nudged, or do nothing? Tweak the P gain accordingly. Once P gain is good, add a touch of I gain – this will ensure return to 0 as well as stability. D gain is optional, but adds firmness and crisp response. Tapping a D-gain stable quad is like knocking on a table – it doesn't move.

Vertical speed PID can be guesstimated. 1590us is taking off; desired take-off speed is 0.5m/s so a P gain of 100 is okay. No I or D gain needed. With that a real take-off, hover and landing are safe, which is good as these are the only way to tune the directional PIDs. Just be cautious here – excessive gains lead to quadcopters slamming into walls or performing somersaults in mid-air before powering themselves into the ground. Best executed outside in a large open field/garden/park where the ground is soft after overnight rain!

There isn't a shortcut to this, so just accept there will be crashes and damage and enjoy the carnage as best you can!

Assuming all the above has gone to plan, then you have a quadcopter that takes off, hovers and lands even in breezy conditions. Next step is to add a remote control, but we'll save that for another day!